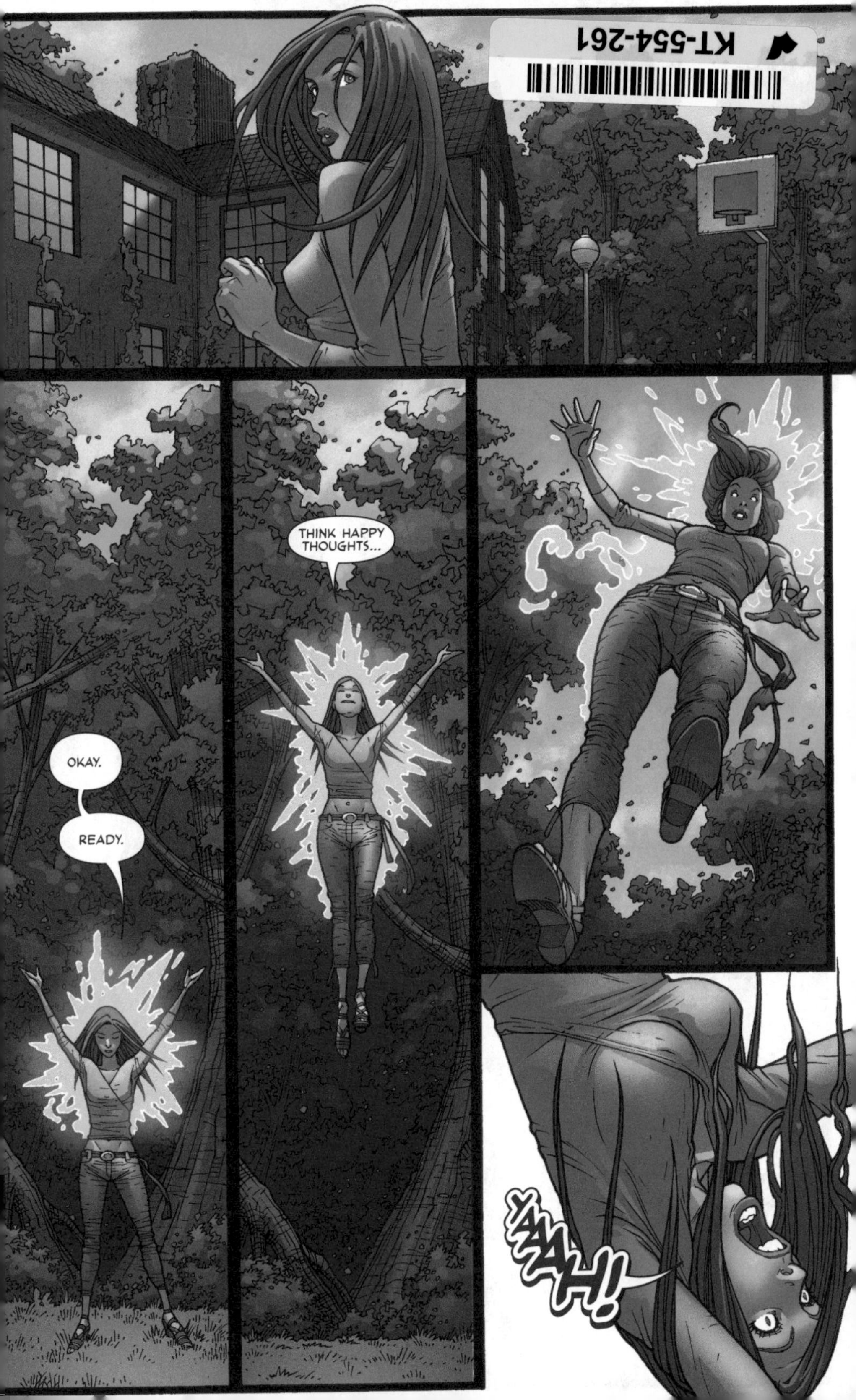
OKAY.
READY.
THINK HAPPY THOUGHTS...
YAAAH!

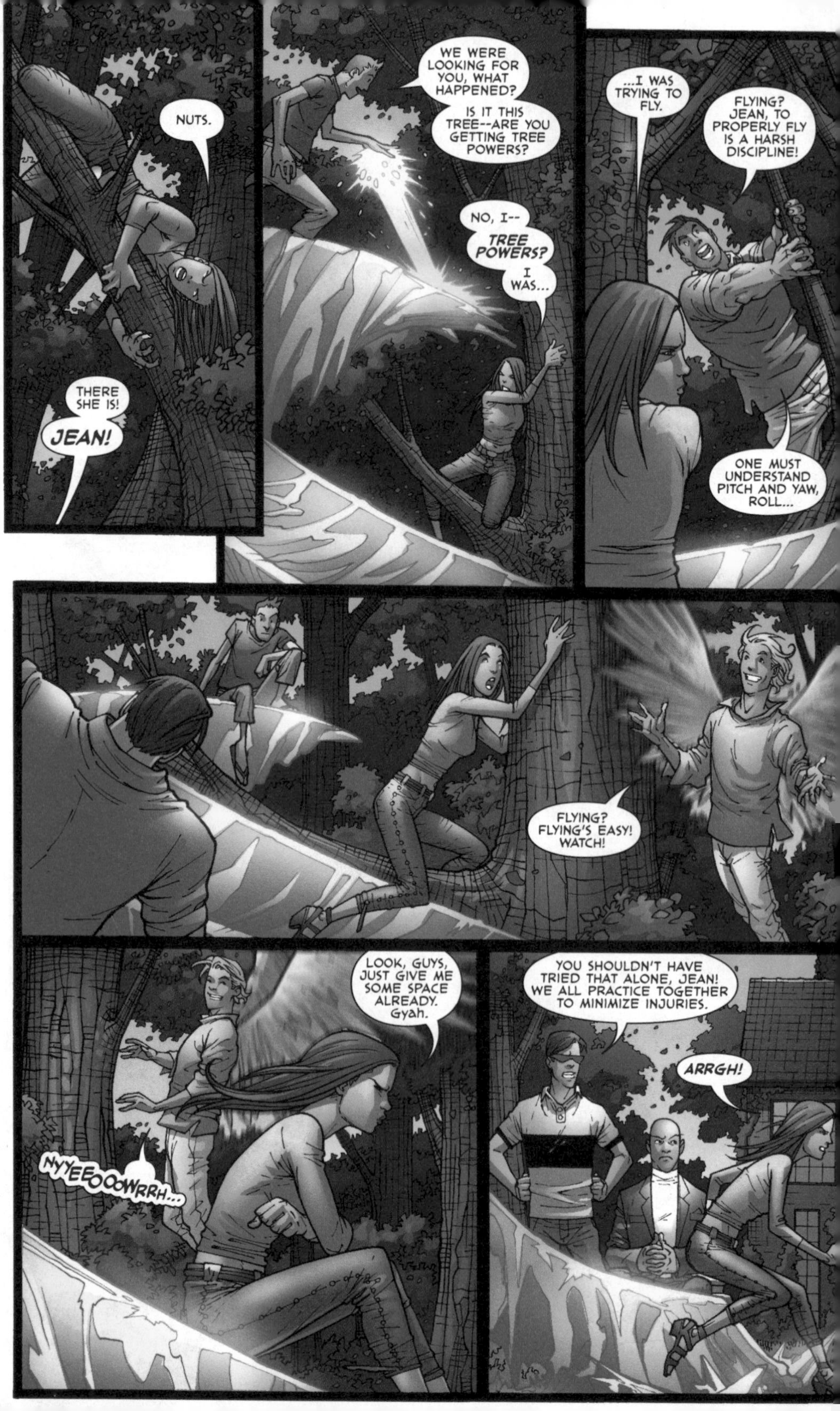
NUTS.
THERE SHE IS!
JEAN!
WE WERE LOOKING FOR YOU, WHAT HAPPENED?
IS IT THIS TREE--ARE YOU GETTING TREE POWERS?
NO, I--
TREE POWERS?
I WAS...
...I WAS TRYING TO FLY.
FLYING? JEAN, TO PROPERLY FLY IS A HARSH DISCIPLINE!
ONE MUST UNDERSTAND PITCH AND YAW, ROLL...
FLYING? FLYING'S EASY! WATCH!
LOOK, GUYS, JUST GIVE ME SOME SPACE ALREADY. Gyah.
NYYEEOOOWRRH...
YOU SHOULDN'T HAVE TRIED THAT ALONE, JEAN! WE ALL PRACTICE TOGETHER TO MINIMIZE INJURIES.
ARRGH!

**X-MEN**

...ASS

...N (Issue #10)

...MITA JR.,

...#3, #5, #9,

...CHSTEIN
...UCK

...ST

Publisher: **DAN BUCKLEY**
Executive Producer: **ALAN FINE**

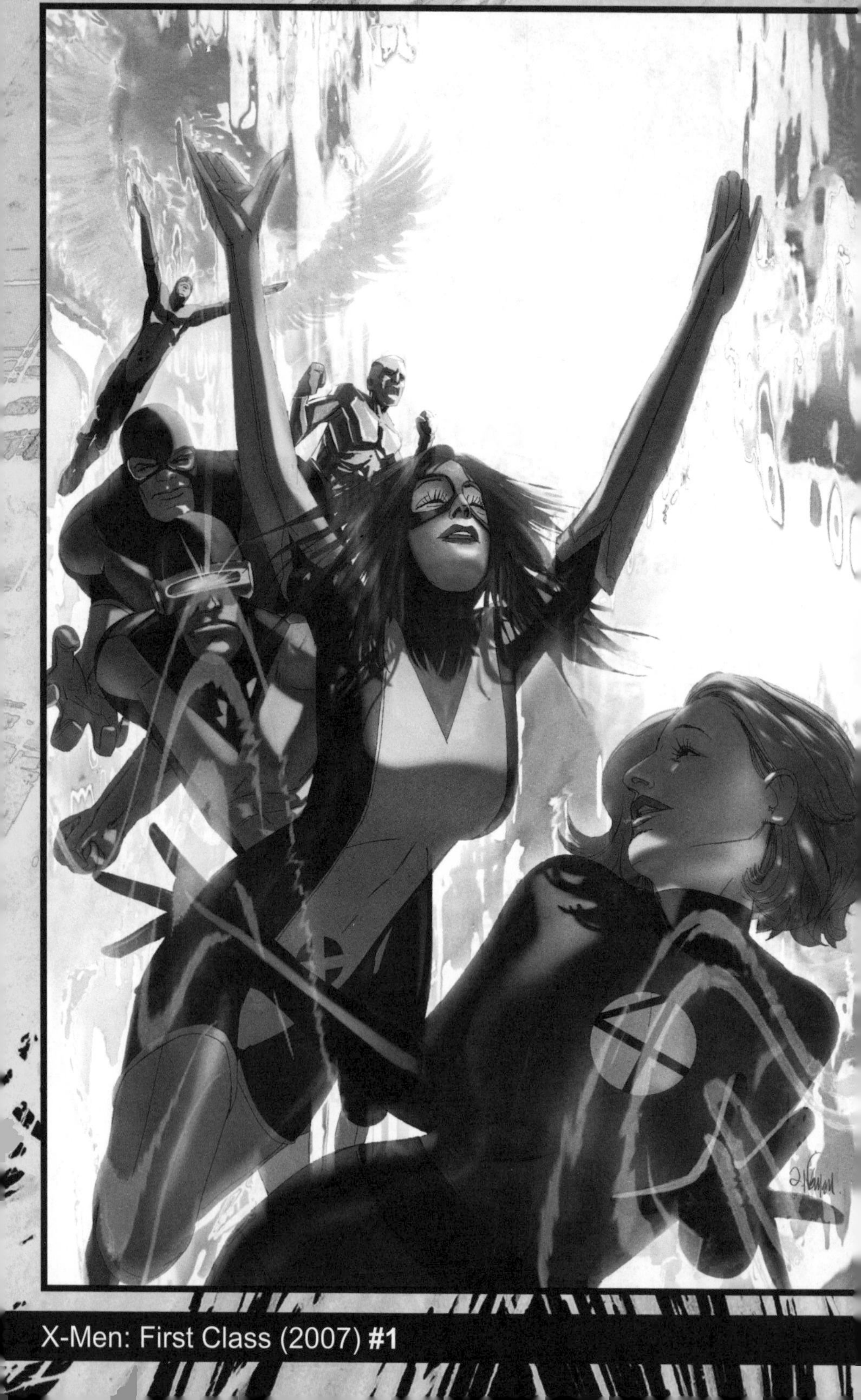

X-Men: First Class (2007) **#1**

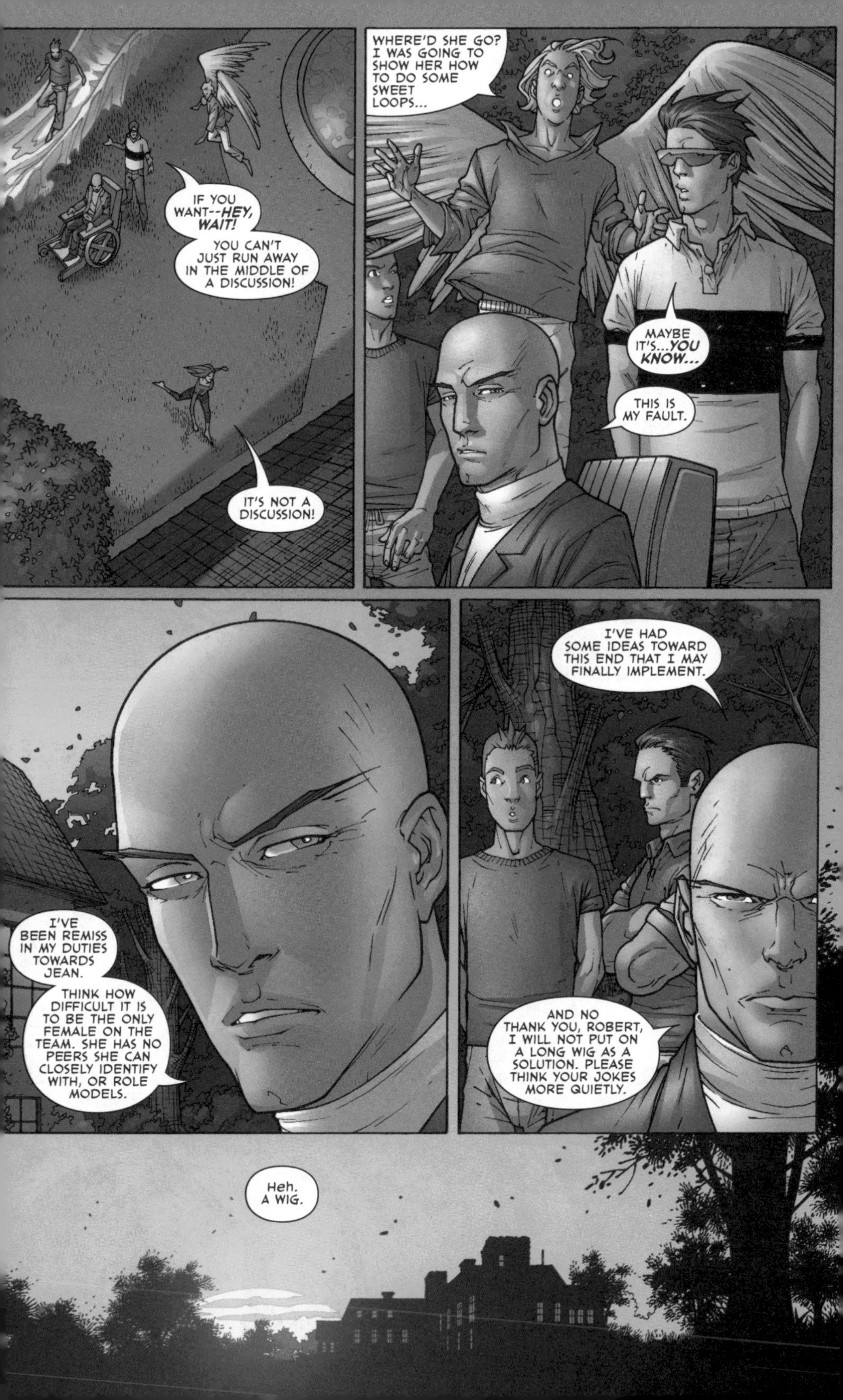
IF YOU WANT--HEY, WAIT!
YOU CAN'T JUST RUN AWAY IN THE MIDDLE OF A DISCUSSION!
IT'S NOT A DISCUSSION!
WHERE'D SHE GO? I WAS GOING TO SHOW HER HOW TO DO SOME SWEET LOOPS...
MAYBE IT'S...YOU KNOW...
THIS IS MY FAULT.
I'VE BEEN REMISS IN MY DUTIES TOWARDS JEAN.
THINK HOW DIFFICULT IT IS TO BE THE ONLY FEMALE ON THE TEAM. SHE HAS NO PEERS SHE CAN CLOSELY IDENTIFY WITH, OR ROLE MODELS.
I'VE HAD SOME IDEAS TOWARD THIS END THAT I MAY FINALLY IMPLEMENT.
AND NO THANK YOU, ROBERT, I WILL NOT PUT ON A LONG WIG AS A SOLUTION. PLEASE THINK YOUR JOKES MORE QUIETLY.
Heh. A WIG.

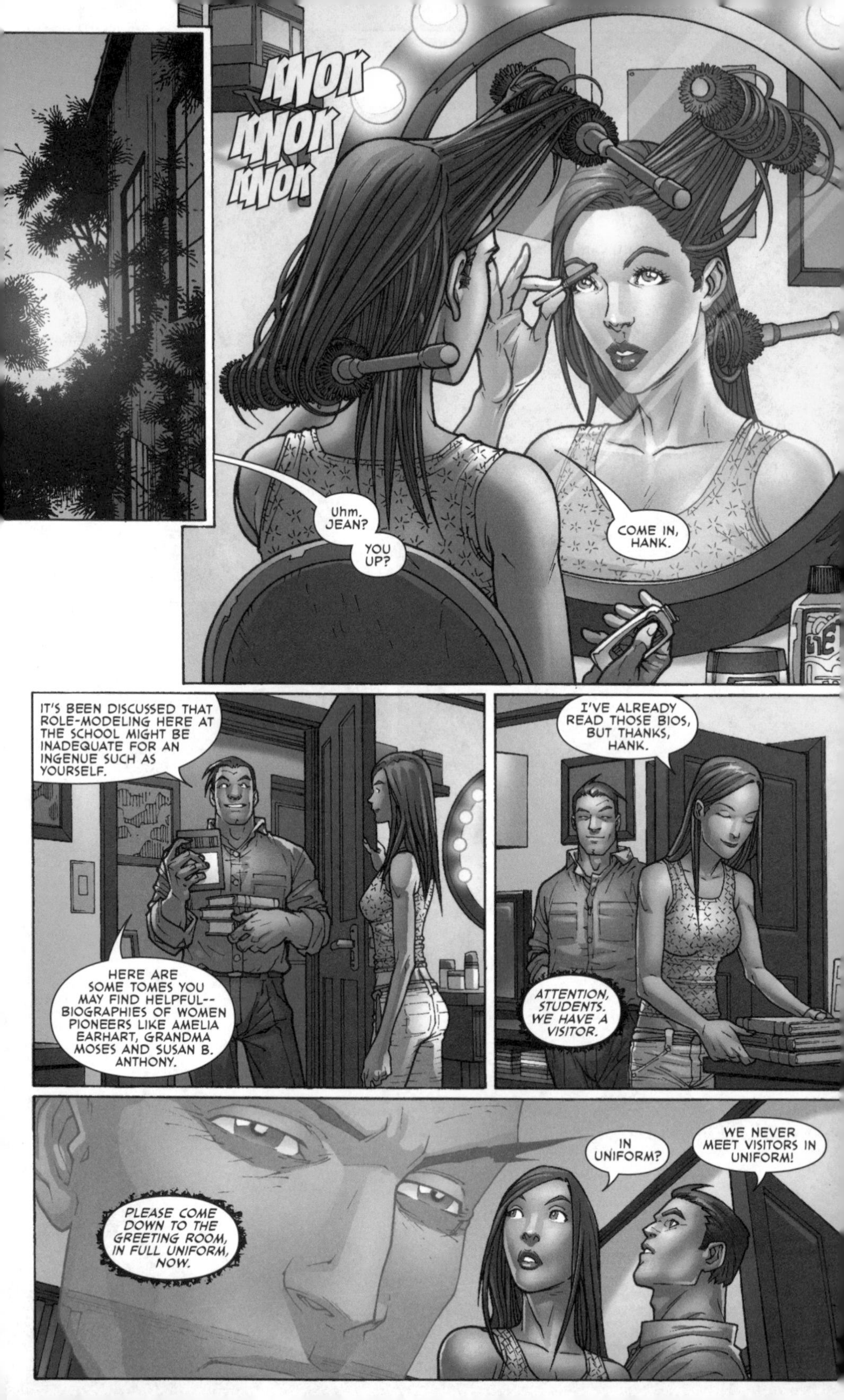
KNOK KNOK KNOK
Uhm. JEAN?
YOU UP?
COME IN, HANK.
IT'S BEEN DISCUSSED THAT ROLE-MODELING HERE AT THE SCHOOL MIGHT BE INADEQUATE FOR AN INGENUE SUCH AS YOURSELF.
HERE ARE SOME TOMES YOU MAY FIND HELPFUL-- BIOGRAPHIES OF WOMEN PIONEERS LIKE AMELIA EARHART, GRANDMA MOSES AND SUSAN B. ANTHONY.
I'VE ALREADY READ THOSE BIOS, BUT THANKS, HANK.
ATTENTION, STUDENTS. WE HAVE A VISITOR.
PLEASE COME DOWN TO THE GREETING ROOM, IN FULL UNIFORM, NOW.
IN UNIFORM?
WE NEVER MEET VISITORS IN UNIFORM!

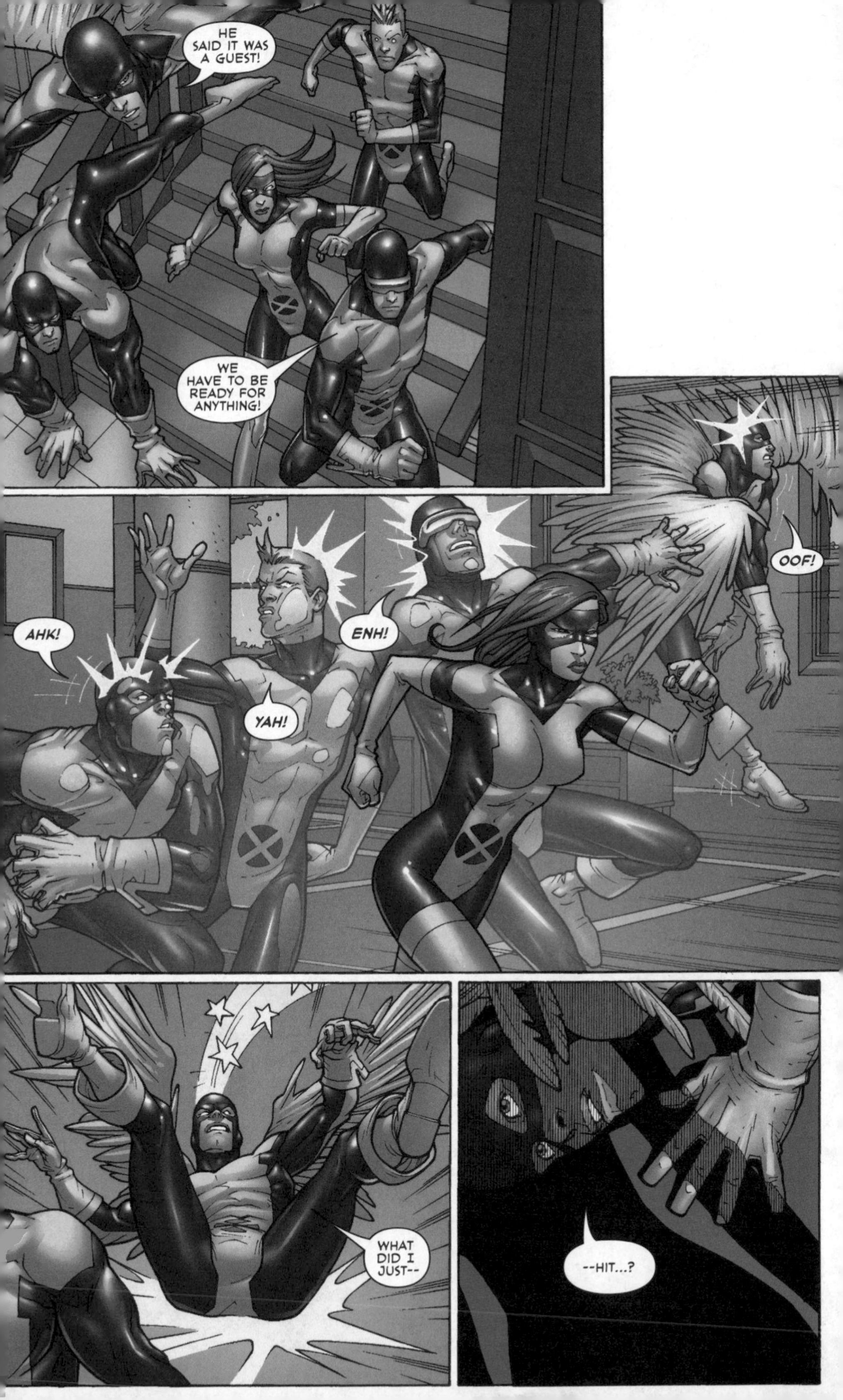
HE SAID IT WAS A GUEST!
WE HAVE TO BE READY FOR ANYTHING!
OOF!
ENH!
AHK!
YAH!
WHAT DID I JUST--
--HIT...?

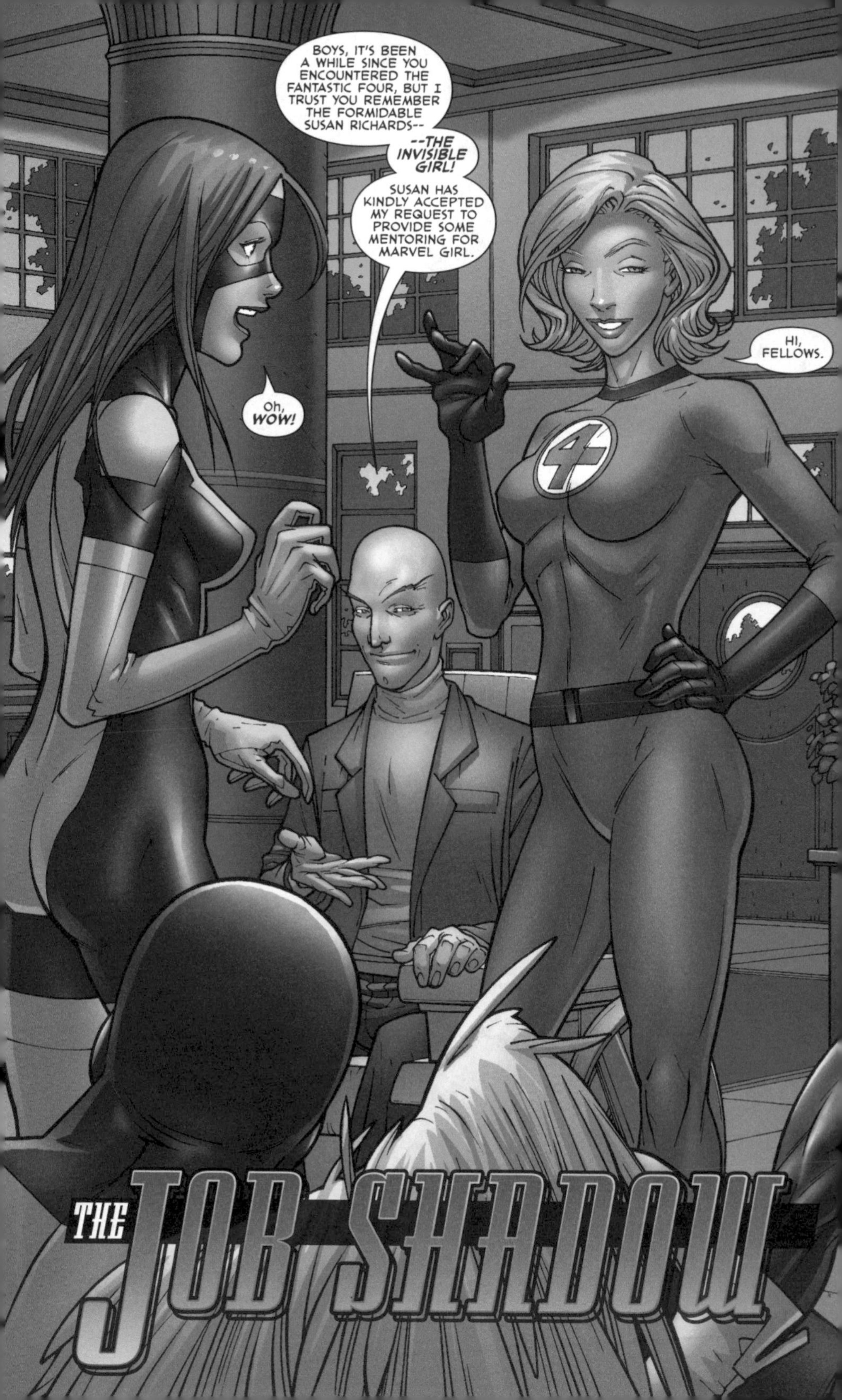
BOYS, IT'S BEEN A WHILE SINCE YOU ENCOUNTERED THE FANTASTIC FOUR, BUT I TRUST YOU REMEMBER THE FORMIDABLE SUSAN RICHARDS--
--THE INVISIBLE GIRL!
SUSAN HAS KINDLY ACCEPTED MY REQUEST TO PROVIDE SOME MENTORING FOR MARVEL GIRL.
HI, FELLOWS.
Oh, WOW!
THE JOB SHADOW

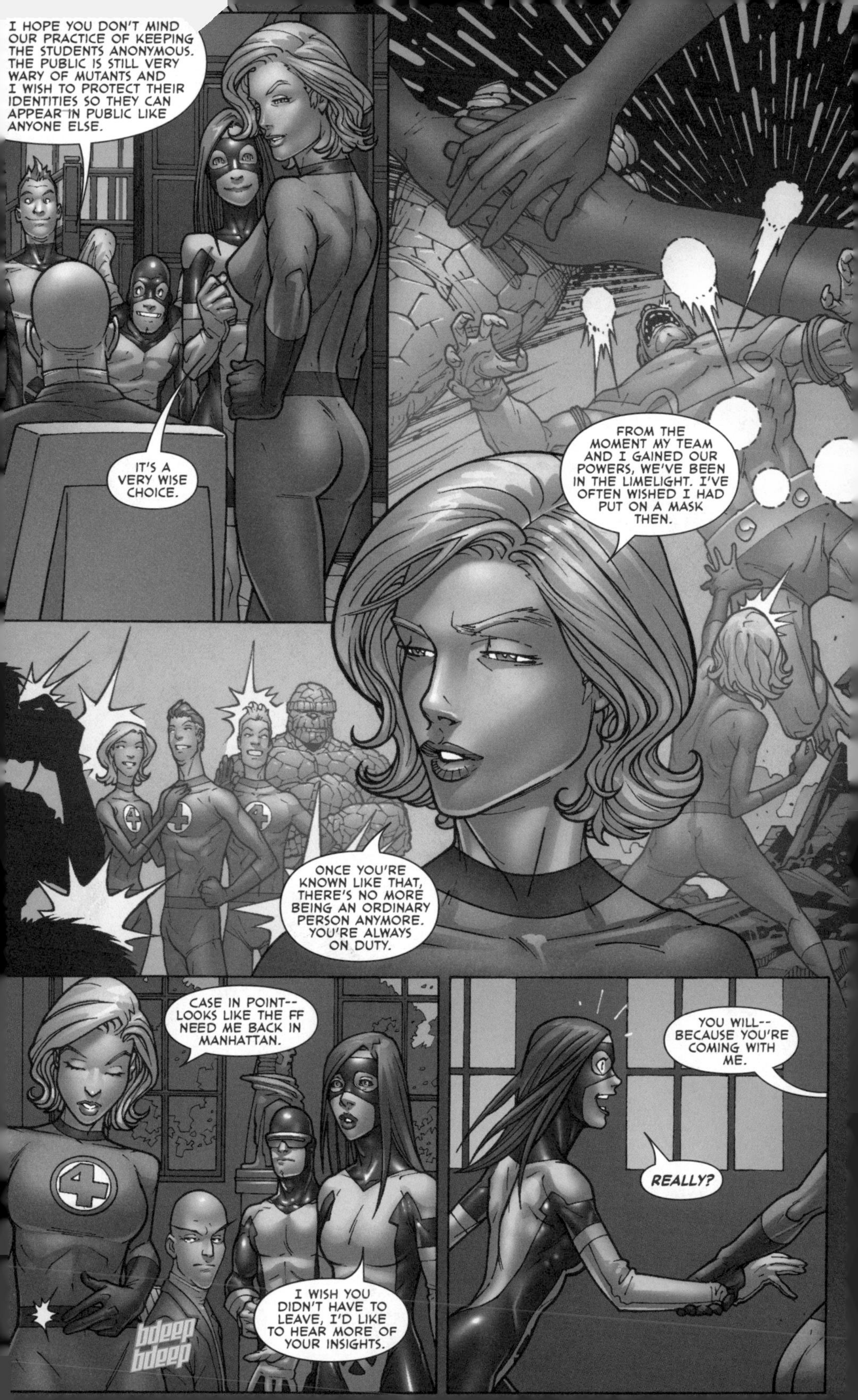
I HOPE YOU DON'T MIND OUR PRACTICE OF KEEPING THE STUDENTS ANONYMOUS. THE PUBLIC IS STILL VERY WARY OF MUTANTS AND I WISH TO PROTECT THEIR IDENTITIES SO THEY CAN APPEAR IN PUBLIC LIKE ANYONE ELSE.
IT'S A VERY WISE CHOICE.
FROM THE MOMENT MY TEAM AND I GAINED OUR POWERS, WE'VE BEEN IN THE LIMELIGHT. I'VE OFTEN WISHED I HAD PUT ON A MASK THEN.
ONCE YOU'RE KNOWN LIKE THAT, THERE'S NO MORE BEING AN ORDINARY PERSON ANYMORE. YOU'RE ALWAYS ON DUTY.
CASE IN POINT-- LOOKS LIKE THE FF NEED ME BACK IN MANHATTAN.
I WISH YOU DIDN'T HAVE TO LEAVE, I'D LIKE TO HEAR MORE OF YOUR INSIGHTS.
YOU WILL-- BECAUSE YOU'RE COMING WITH ME.
REALLY?

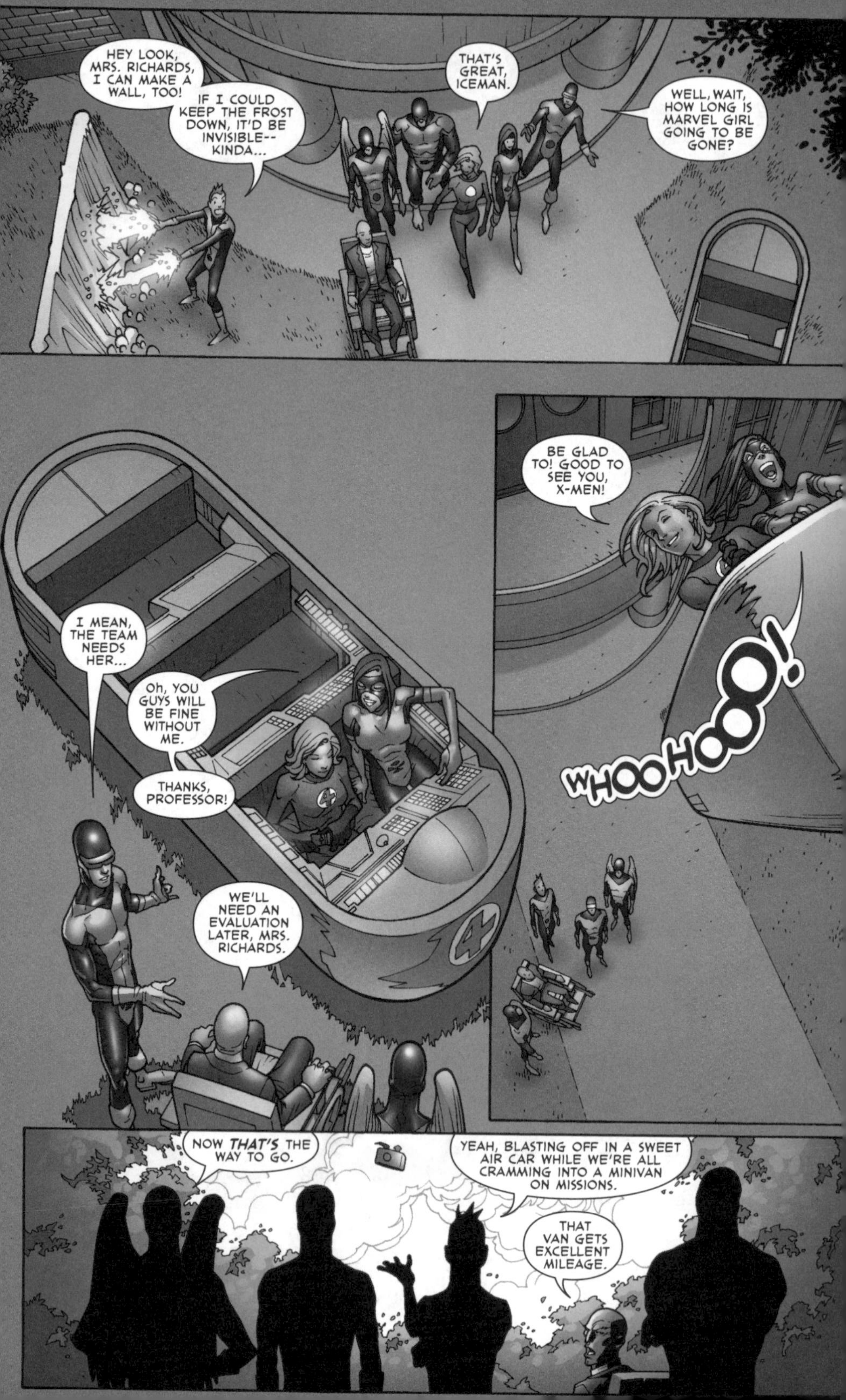
HEY LOOK, MRS. RICHARDS, I CAN MAKE A WALL, TOO!
IF I COULD KEEP THE FROST DOWN, IT'D BE INVISIBLE--KINDA...
THAT'S GREAT, ICEMAN.
WELL, WAIT, HOW LONG IS MARVEL GIRL GOING TO BE GONE?
I MEAN, THE TEAM NEEDS HER...
Oh, YOU GUYS WILL BE FINE WITHOUT ME.
THANKS, PROFESSOR!
WE'LL NEED AN EVALUATION LATER, MRS. RICHARDS.
BE GLAD TO! GOOD TO SEE YOU, X-MEN!
WHOOHOOO!
NOW THAT'S THE WAY TO GO.
YEAH, BLASTING OFF IN A SWEET AIR CAR WHILE WE'RE ALL CRAMMING INTO A MINIVAN ON MISSIONS.
THAT VAN GETS EXCELLENT MILEAGE.

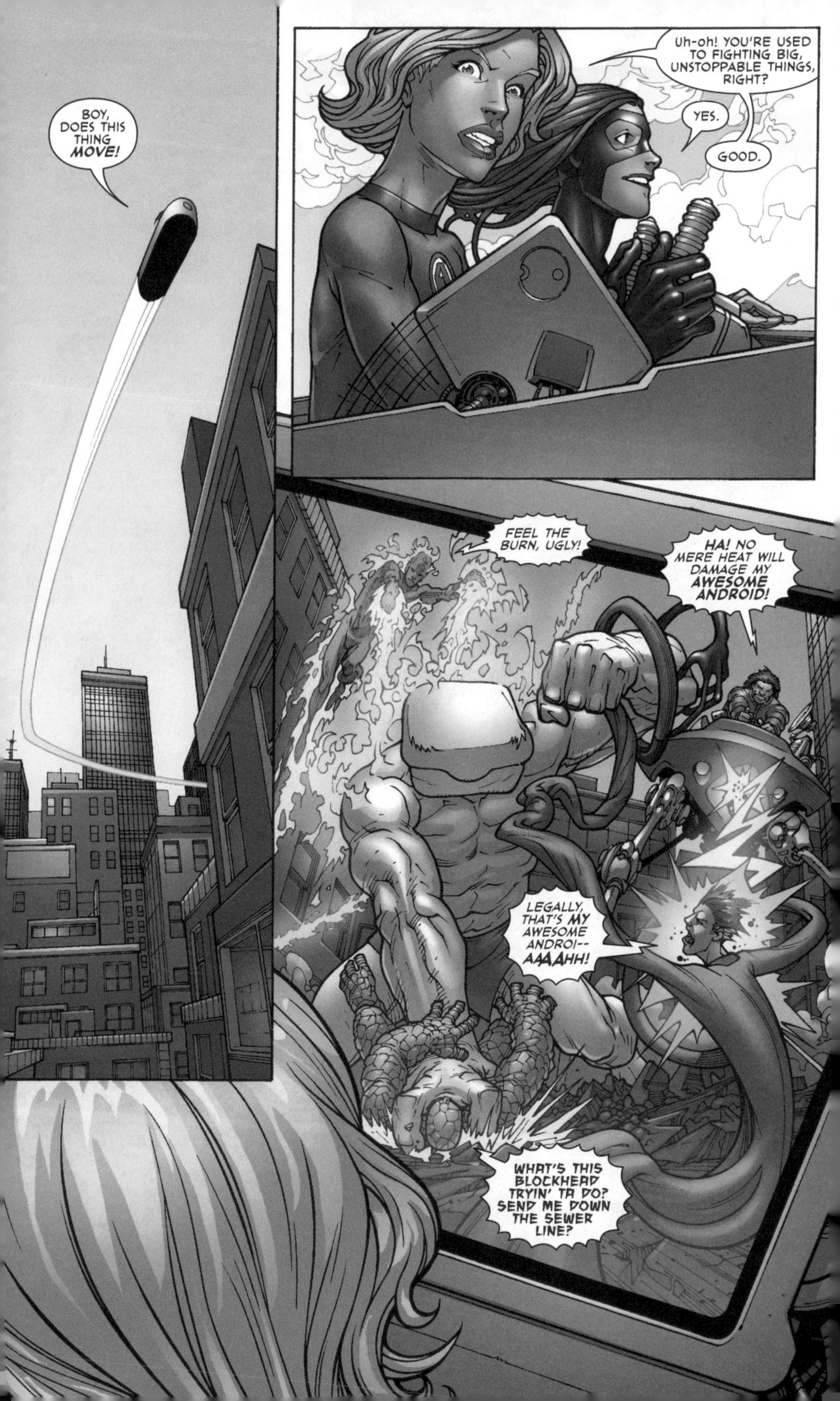
BOY, DOES THIS THING MOVE!
Uh-oh! YOU'RE USED TO FIGHTING BIG, UNSTOPPABLE THINGS, RIGHT?
YES.
GOOD.
FEEL THE BURN, UGLY!
HA! NO MERE HEAT WILL DAMAGE MY AWESOME ANDROID!
LEGALLY, THAT'S MY AWESOME ANDROI-- AAAAHH!
WHAT'S THIS BLOCKHEAD TRYIN' TA DO? SEND ME DOWN THE SEWER LINE?

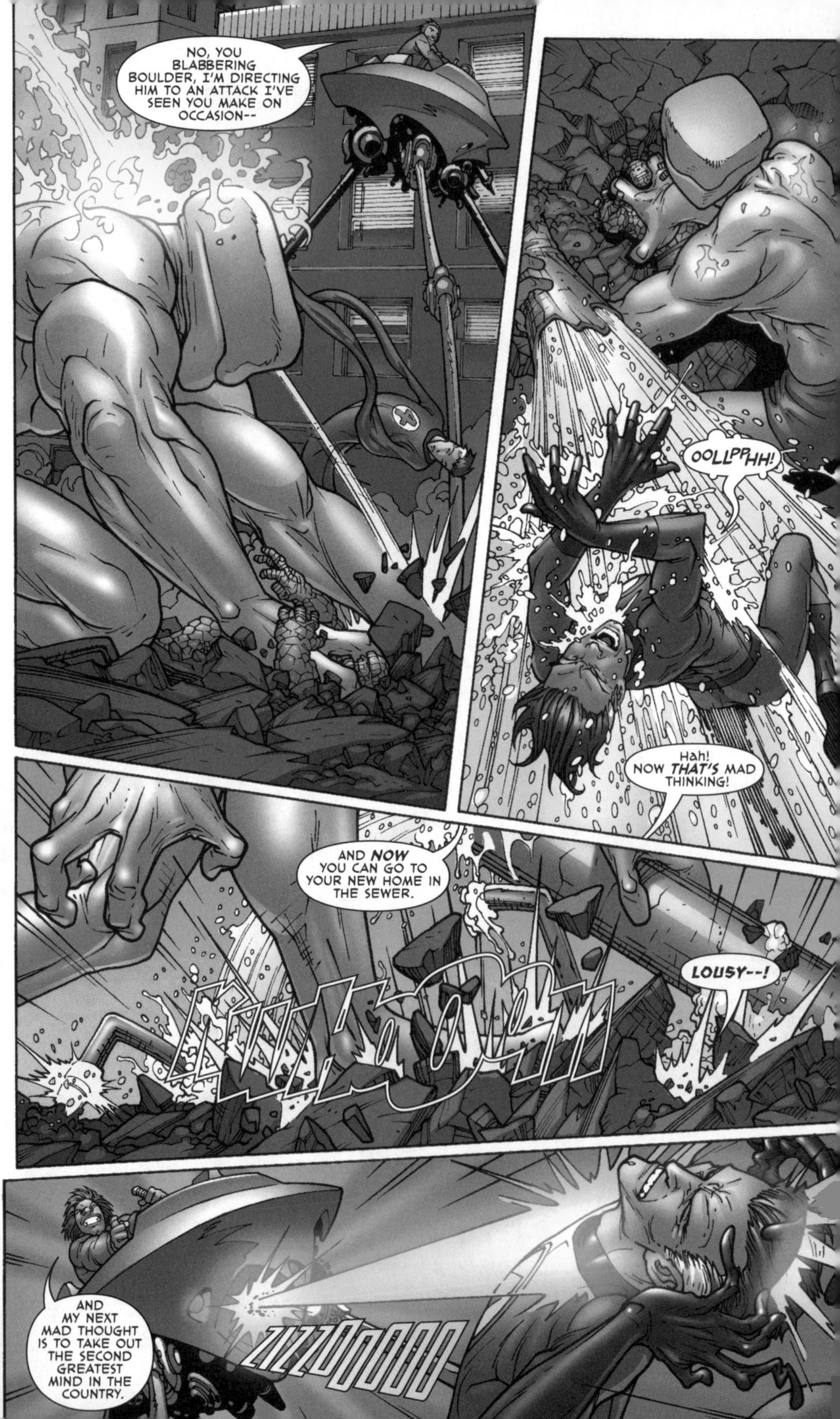
NO, YOU BLABBERING BOULDER, I'M DIRECTING HIM TO AN ATTACK I'VE SEEN YOU MAKE ON OCCASION--
OOLLPPHH!
Hah! NOW THAT'S MAD THINKING!
AND NOW YOU CAN GO TO YOUR NEW HOME IN THE SEWER.
LOUSY--!
AND MY NEXT MAD THOUGHT IS TO TAKE OUT THE SECOND GREATEST MIND IN THE COUNTRY.

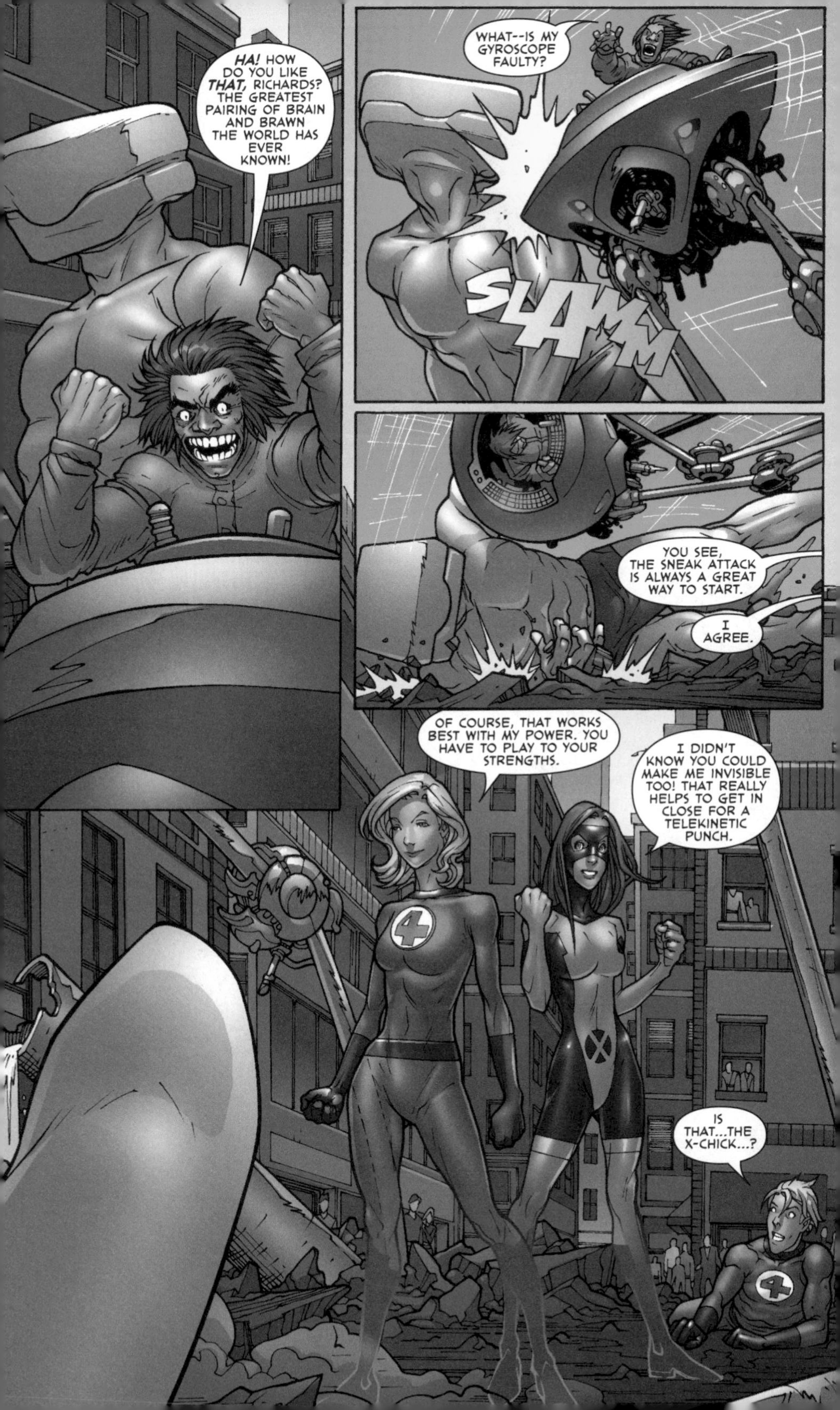
HA! HOW DO YOU LIKE THAT, RICHARDS? THE GREATEST PAIRING OF BRAIN AND BRAWN THE WORLD HAS EVER KNOWN!
WHAT--IS MY GYROSCOPE FAULTY?
SLAMM
YOU SEE, THE SNEAK ATTACK IS ALWAYS A GREAT WAY TO START.
I AGREE.
OF COURSE, THAT WORKS BEST WITH MY POWER. YOU HAVE TO PLAY TO YOUR STRENGTHS.
I DIDN'T KNOW YOU COULD MAKE ME INVISIBLE TOO! THAT REALLY HELPS TO GET IN CLOSE FOR A TELEKINETIC PUNCH.
IS THAT...THE X-CHICK...?

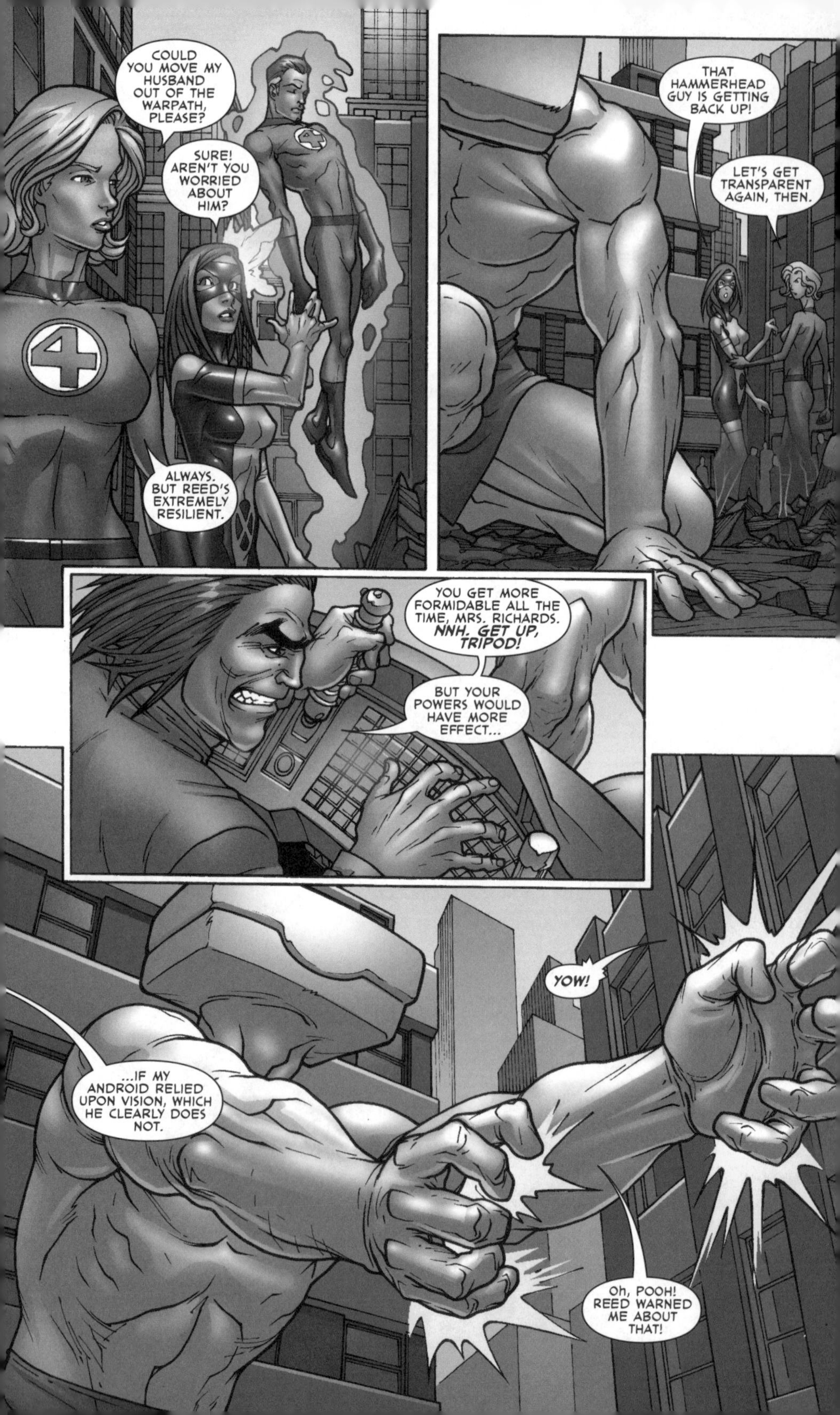
COULD YOU MOVE MY HUSBAND OUT OF THE WARPATH, PLEASE?
SURE! AREN'T YOU WORRIED ABOUT HIM?
ALWAYS. BUT REED'S EXTREMELY RESILIENT.
THAT HAMMERHEAD GUY IS GETTING BACK UP!
LET'S GET TRANSPARENT AGAIN, THEN.
YOU GET MORE FORMIDABLE ALL THE TIME, MRS. RICHARDS. NNH. GET UP, TRIPOD!
BUT YOUR POWERS WOULD HAVE MORE EFFECT...
...IF MY ANDROID RELIED UPON VISION, WHICH HE CLEARLY DOES NOT.
YOW!
Oh, POOH! REED WARNED ME ABOUT THAT!

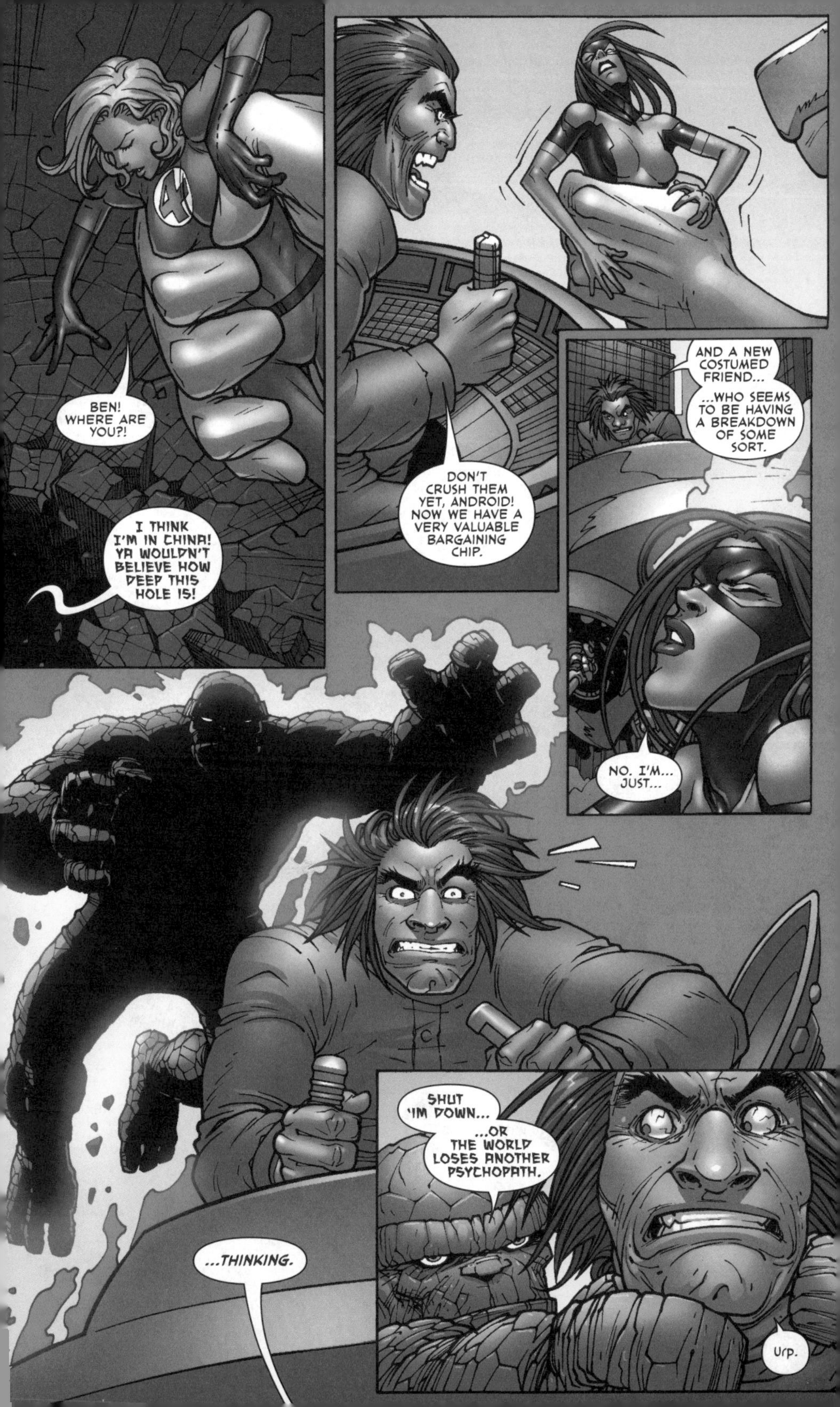
BEN! WHERE ARE YOU?!
I THINK I'M IN CHINA! YA WOULDN'T BELIEVE HOW DEEP THIS HOLE IS!
DON'T CRUSH THEM YET, ANDROID! NOW WE HAVE A VERY VALUABLE BARGAINING CHIP.
AND A NEW COSTUMED FRIEND...
...WHO SEEMS TO BE HAVING A BREAKDOWN OF SOME SORT.
NO. I'M... JUST...
...THINKING.
SHUT 'IM DOWN...
...OR THE WORLD LOSES ANOTHER PSYCHOPATH.
Urp.

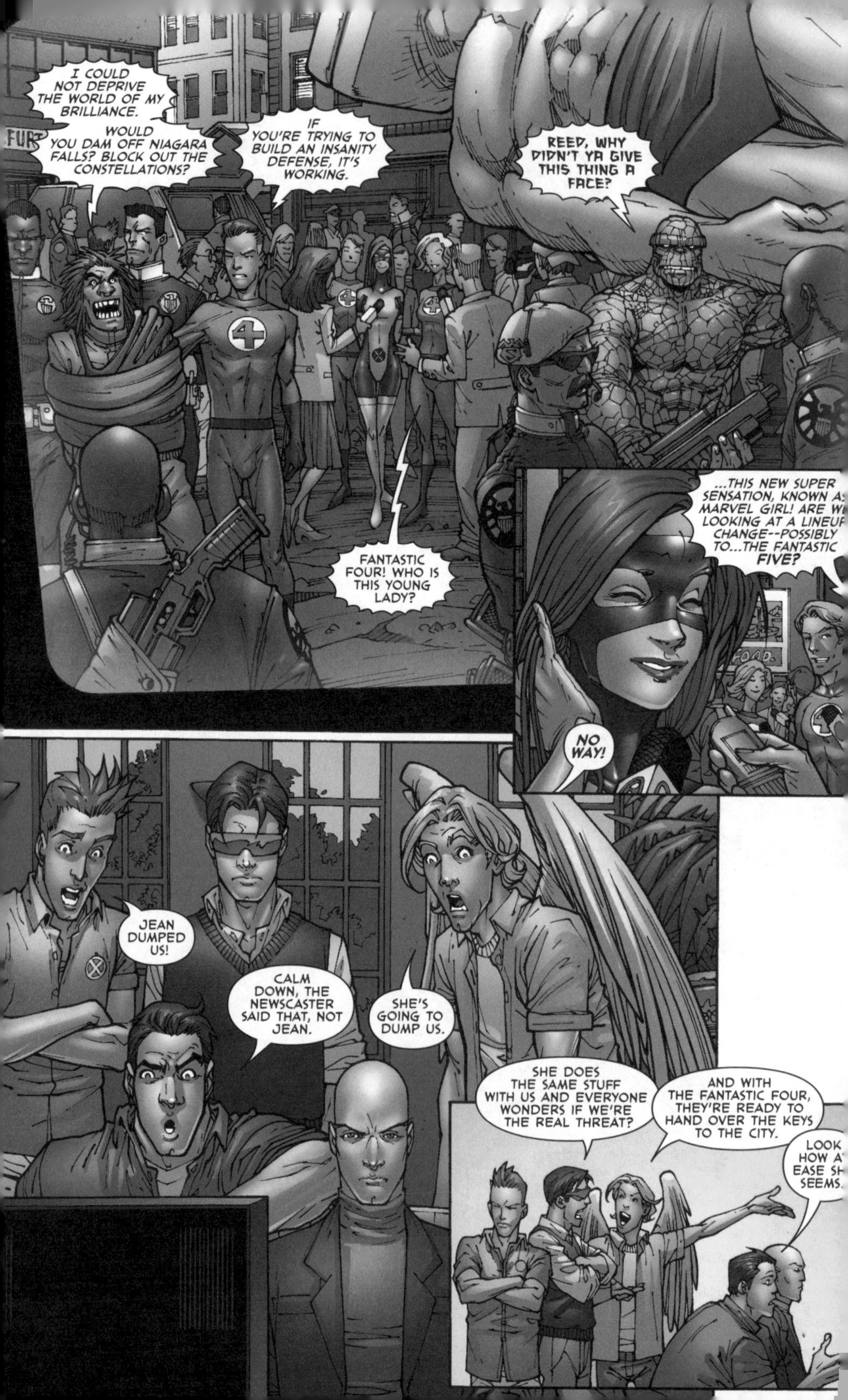
I COULD NOT DEPRIVE THE WORLD OF MY BRILLIANCE.
WOULD YOU DAM OFF NIAGARA FALLS? BLOCK OUT THE CONSTELLATIONS?
IF YOU'RE TRYING TO BUILD AN INSANITY DEFENSE, IT'S WORKING.
REED, WHY DIDN'T YA GIVE THIS THING A FACE?
FANTASTIC FOUR! WHO IS THIS YOUNG LADY?
...THIS NEW SUPER SENSATION, KNOWN AS MARVEL GIRL! ARE WE LOOKING AT A LINEUP CHANGE--POSSIBLY TO...THE FANTASTIC FIVE?
NO WAY!
JEAN DUMPED US!
CALM DOWN, THE NEWSCASTER SAID THAT, NOT JEAN.
SHE'S GOING TO DUMP US.
SHE DOES THE SAME STUFF WITH US AND EVERYONE WONDERS IF WE'RE THE REAL THREAT?
AND WITH THE FANTASTIC FOUR, THEY'RE READY TO HAND OVER THE KEYS TO THE CITY.
LOOK HOW AT EASE SHE SEEMS.

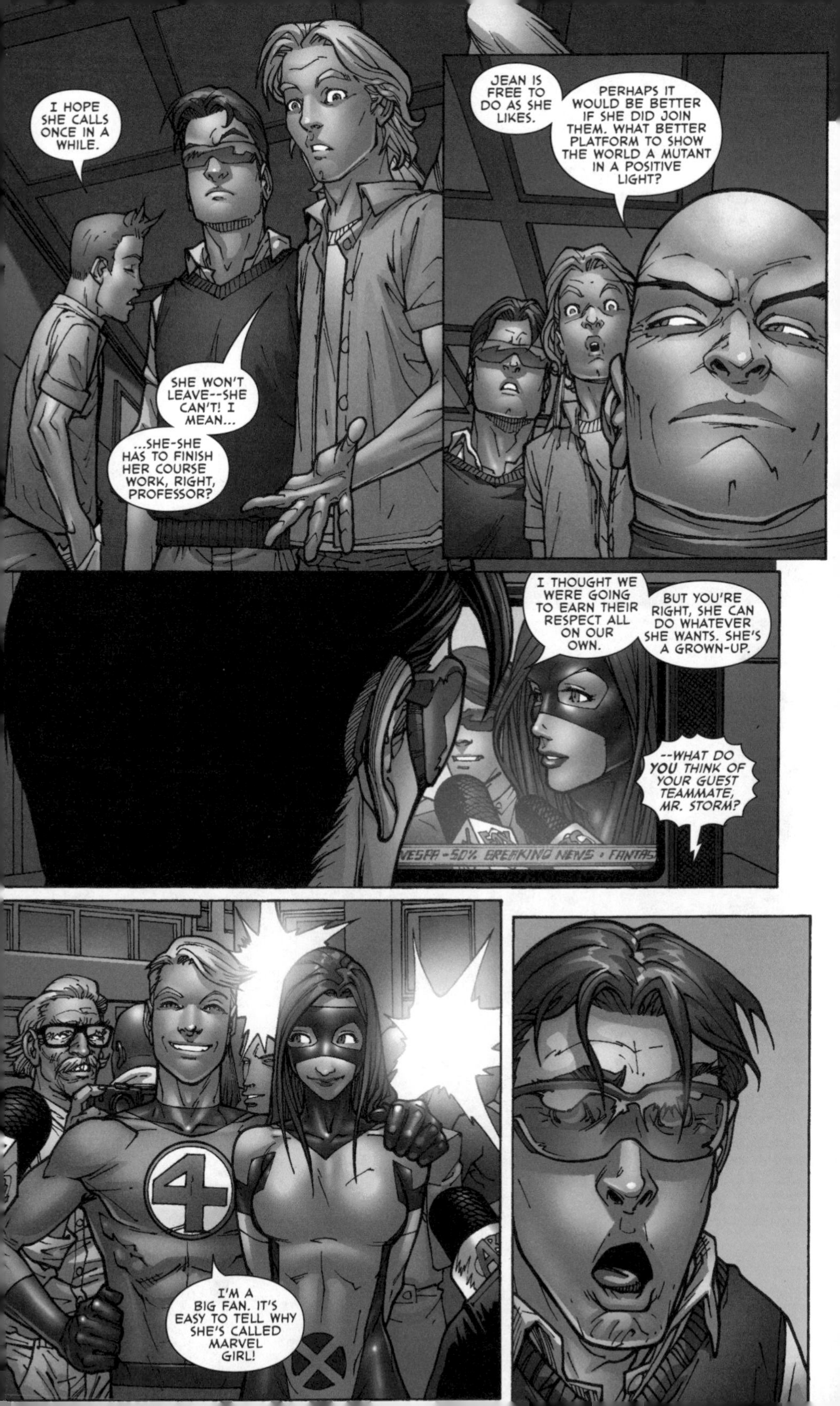

I HOPE SHE CALLS ONCE IN A WHILE.
SHE WON'T LEAVE--SHE CAN'T! I MEAN...
...SHE-SHE HAS TO FINISH HER COURSE WORK, RIGHT, PROFESSOR?
JEAN IS FREE TO DO AS SHE LIKES.
PERHAPS IT WOULD BE BETTER IF SHE DID JOIN THEM. WHAT BETTER PLATFORM TO SHOW THE WORLD A MUTANT IN A POSITIVE LIGHT?
I THOUGHT WE WERE GOING TO EARN THEIR RESPECT ALL ON OUR OWN.
BUT YOU'RE RIGHT, SHE CAN DO WHATEVER SHE WANTS. SHE'S A GROWN-UP.
--WHAT DO *YOU* THINK OF YOUR GUEST TEAMMATE, MR. STORM?
VESPA -50% BREAKING NEWS • FANTAS
I'M A BIG FAN. IT'S EASY TO TELL WHY SHE'S CALLED MARVEL GIRL!

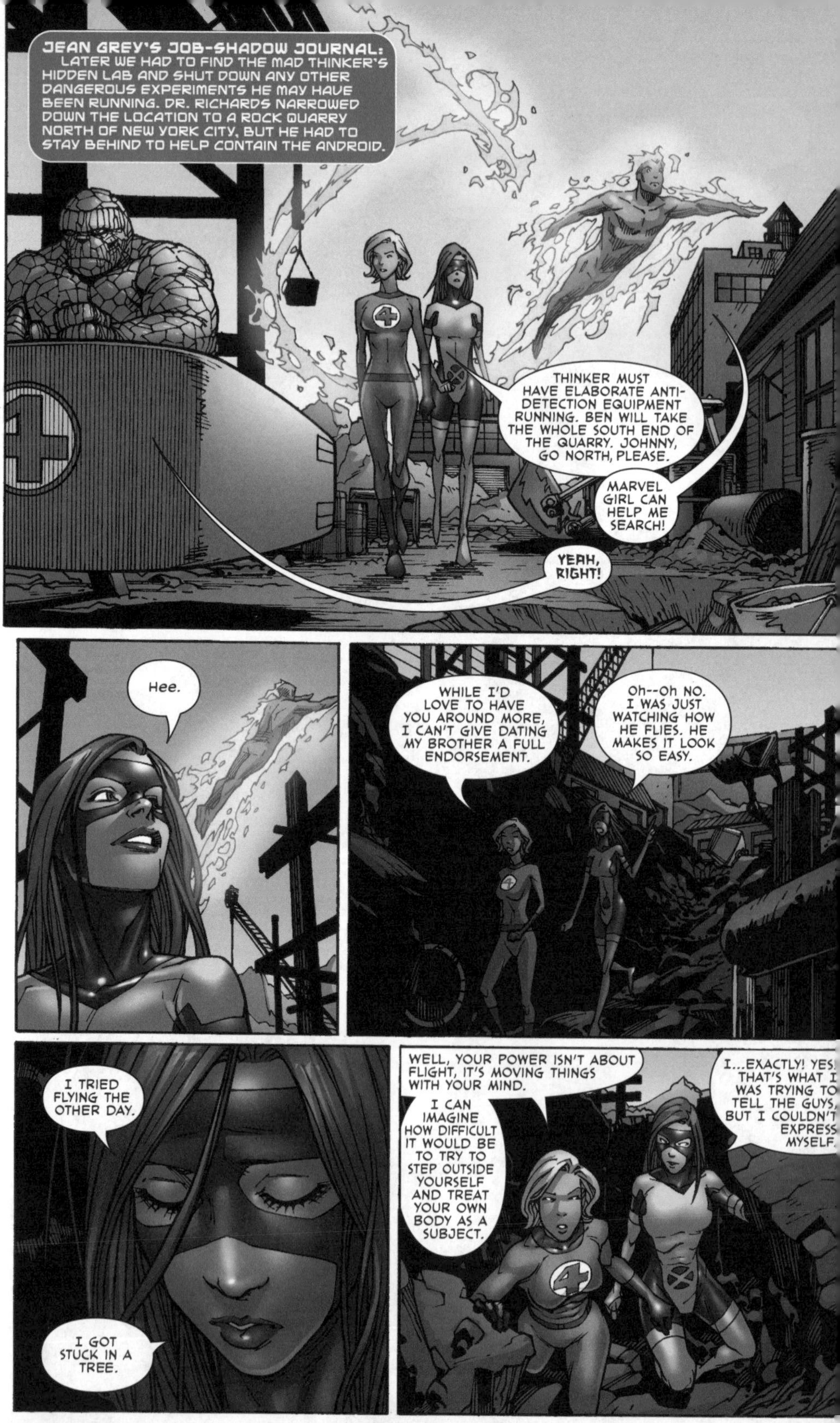
JEAN GREY'S JOB-SHADOW JOURNAL:
LATER WE HAD TO FIND THE MAD THINKER'S HIDDEN LAB AND SHUT DOWN ANY OTHER DANGEROUS EXPERIMENTS HE MAY HAVE BEEN RUNNING. DR. RICHARDS NARROWED DOWN THE LOCATION TO A ROCK QUARRY NORTH OF NEW YORK CITY, BUT HE HAD TO STAY BEHIND TO HELP CONTAIN THE ANDROID.
THINKER MUST HAVE ELABORATE ANTI-DETECTION EQUIPMENT RUNNING. BEN WILL TAKE THE WHOLE SOUTH END OF THE QUARRY. JOHNNY, GO NORTH, PLEASE.
MARVEL GIRL CAN HELP ME SEARCH!
YEAH, RIGHT!
Hee.
WHILE I'D LOVE TO HAVE YOU AROUND MORE, I CAN'T GIVE DATING MY BROTHER A FULL ENDORSEMENT.
Oh--Oh NO. I WAS JUST WATCHING HOW HE FLIES. HE MAKES IT LOOK SO EASY.
I TRIED FLYING THE OTHER DAY.
I GOT STUCK IN A TREE.
WELL, YOUR POWER ISN'T ABOUT FLIGHT, IT'S MOVING THINGS WITH YOUR MIND.
I CAN IMAGINE HOW DIFFICULT IT WOULD BE TO TRY TO STEP OUTSIDE YOURSELF AND TREAT YOUR OWN BODY AS A SUBJECT.
I...EXACTLY! YES! THAT'S WHAT I WAS TRYING TO TELL THE GUYS, BUT I COULDN'T EXPRESS MYSELF.

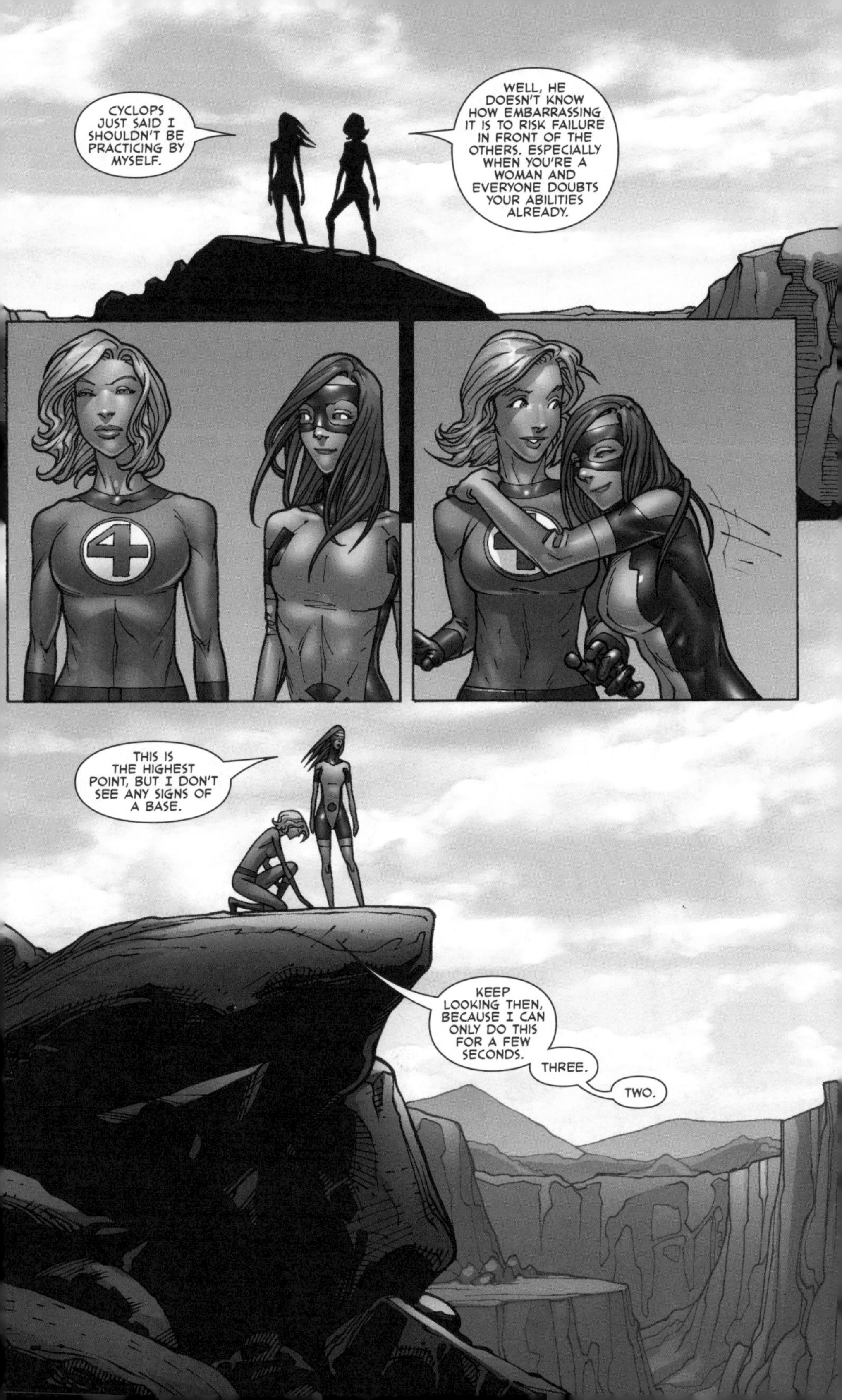
CYCLOPS JUST SAID I SHOULDN'T BE PRACTICING BY MYSELF.
WELL, HE DOESN'T KNOW HOW EMBARRASSING IT IS TO RISK FAILURE IN FRONT OF THE OTHERS. ESPECIALLY WHEN YOU'RE A WOMAN AND EVERYONE DOUBTS YOUR ABILITIES ALREADY.
THIS IS THE HIGHEST POINT, BUT I DON'T SEE ANY SIGNS OF A BASE.
KEEP LOOKING THEN, BECAUSE I CAN ONLY DO THIS FOR A FEW SECONDS.
THREE.
TWO.

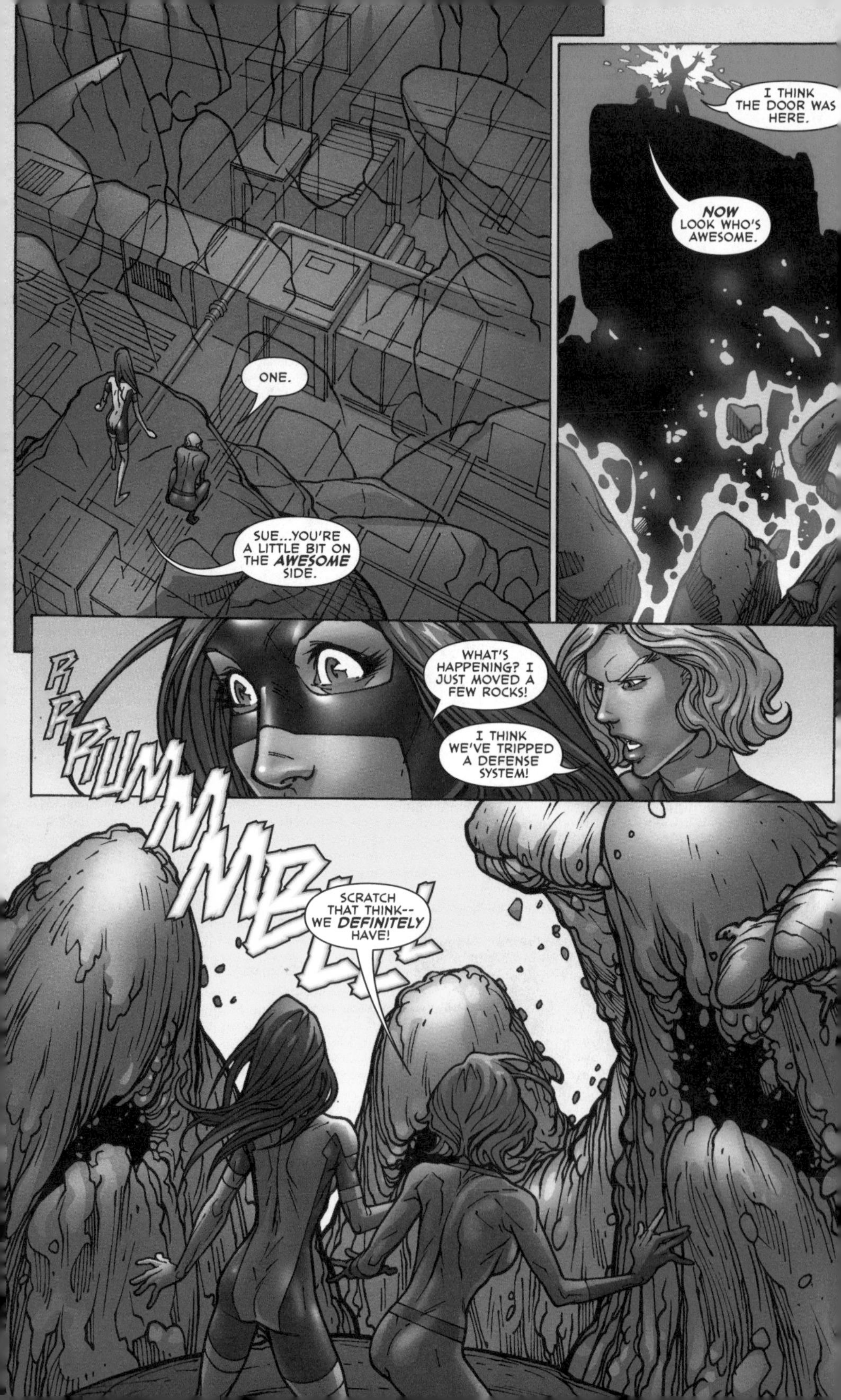

ONE.
SUE...YOU'RE A LITTLE BIT ON THE AWESOME SIDE.
I THINK THE DOOR WAS HERE.
NOW LOOK WHO'S AWESOME.
RRRUMMMBLLL
WHAT'S HAPPENING? I JUST MOVED A FEW ROCKS!
I THINK WE'VE TRIPPED A DEFENSE SYSTEM!
SCRATCH THAT THINK-- WE DEFINITELY HAVE!

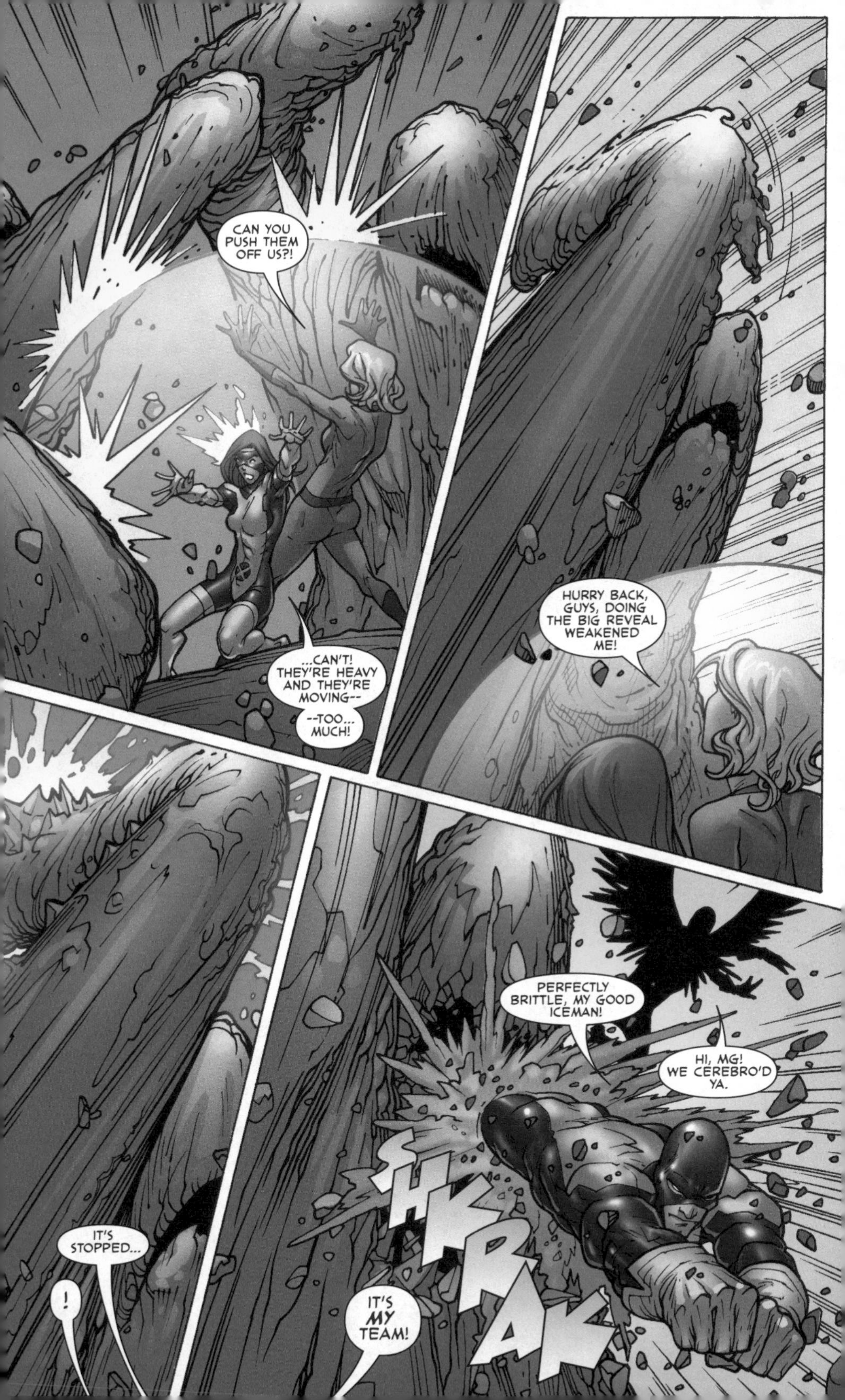
CAN YOU PUSH THEM OFF US?!
...CAN'T! THEY'RE HEAVY AND THEY'RE MOVING--
--TOO... MUCH!
HURRY BACK, GUYS, DOING THE BIG REVEAL WEAKENED ME!
IT'S STOPPED...
!
IT'S MY TEAM!
SHKRAK
PERFECTLY BRITTLE, MY GOOD ICEMAN!
HI, MG! WE CEREBRO'D YA.

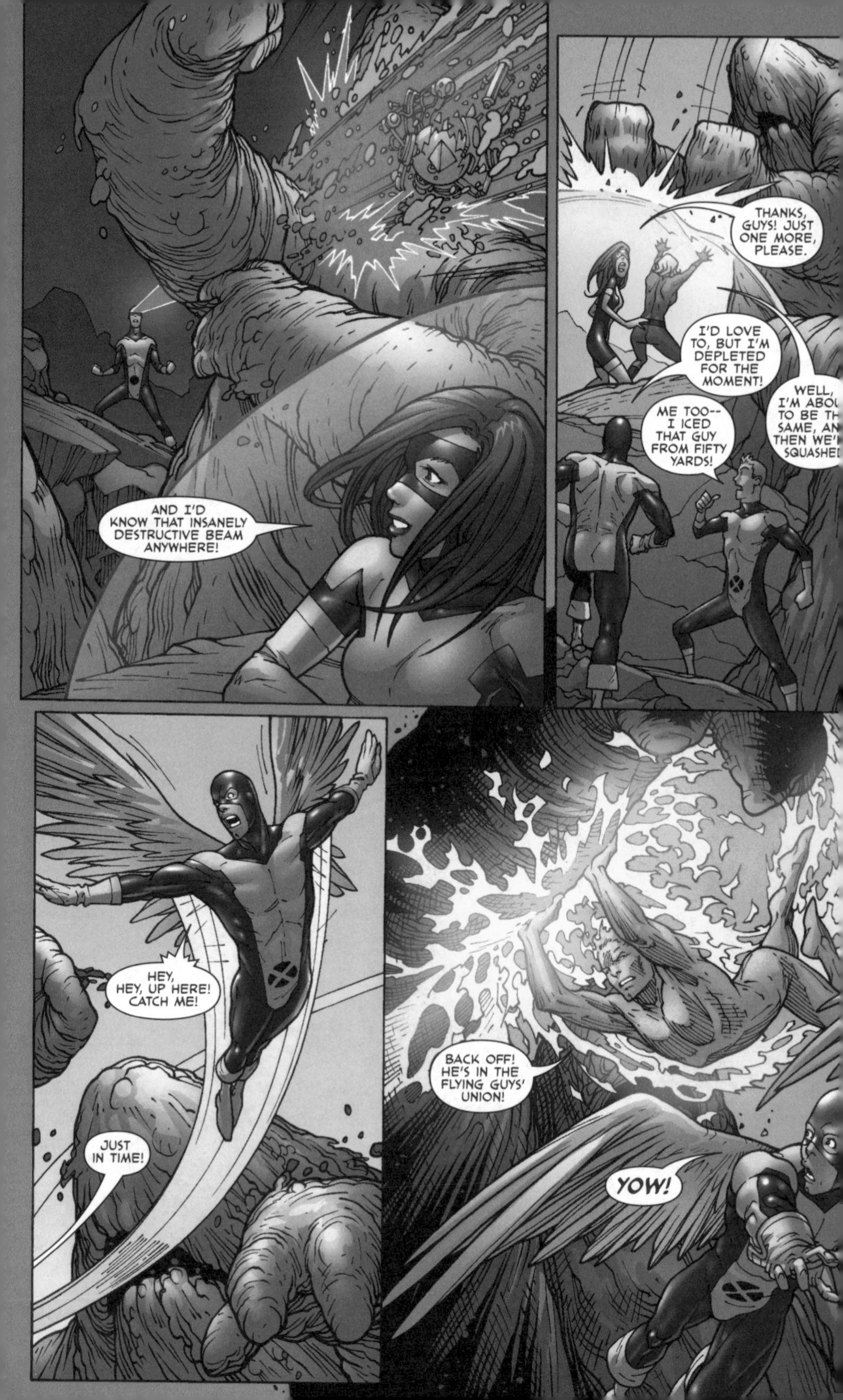

AND I'D KNOW THAT INSANELY DESTRUCTIVE BEAM ANYWHERE!
THANKS, GUYS! JUST ONE MORE, PLEASE.
I'D LOVE TO, BUT I'M DEPLETED FOR THE MOMENT!
ME TOO-- I ICED THAT GUY FROM FIFTY YARDS!
HEY, HEY, UP HERE! CATCH ME!
JUST IN TIME!
BACK OFF! HE'S IN THE FLYING GUYS' UNION!
YOW!

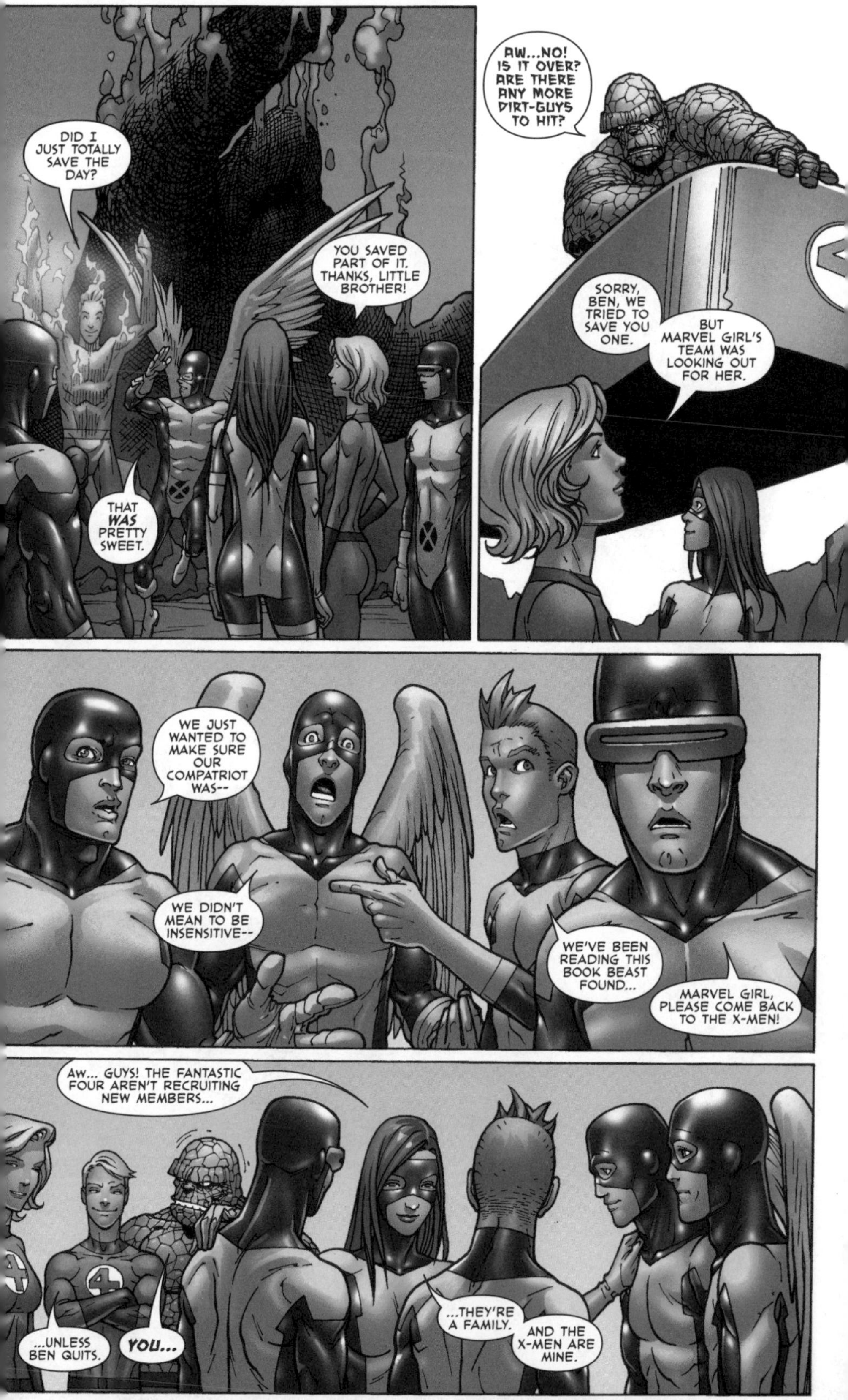
DID I JUST TOTALLY SAVE THE DAY?
YOU SAVED PART OF IT. THANKS, LITTLE BROTHER!
THAT *WAS* PRETTY SWEET.
AW...NO! IS IT OVER? ARE THERE ANY MORE DIRT-GUYS TO HIT?
SORRY, BEN, WE TRIED TO SAVE YOU ONE.
BUT MARVEL GIRL'S TEAM WAS LOOKING OUT FOR HER.
WE JUST WANTED TO MAKE SURE OUR COMPATRIOT WAS--
WE DIDN'T MEAN TO BE INSENSITIVE--
WE'VE BEEN READING THIS BOOK BEAST FOUND...
MARVEL GIRL, PLEASE COME BACK TO THE X-MEN!
AW... GUYS! THE FANTASTIC FOUR AREN'T RECRUITING NEW MEMBERS...
...UNLESS BEN QUITS.
*YOU...*
...THEY'RE A FAMILY.
AND THE X-MEN ARE MINE.

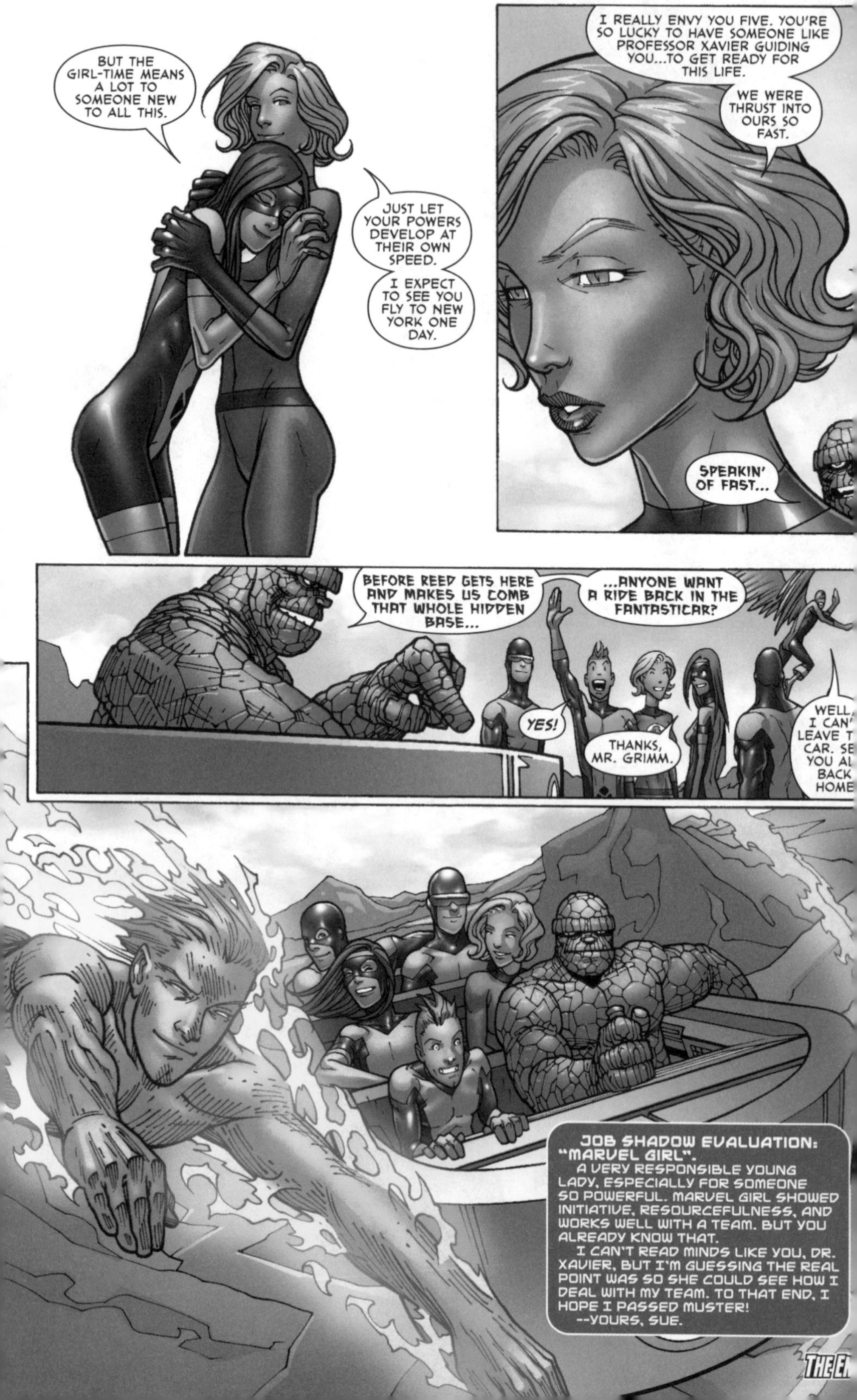

BUT THE GIRL-TIME MEANS A LOT TO SOMEONE NEW TO ALL THIS.
JUST LET YOUR POWERS DEVELOP AT THEIR OWN SPEED.
I EXPECT TO SEE YOU FLY TO NEW YORK ONE DAY.
I REALLY ENVY YOU FIVE. YOU'RE SO LUCKY TO HAVE SOMEONE LIKE PROFESSOR XAVIER GUIDING YOU...TO GET READY FOR THIS LIFE.
WE WERE THRUST INTO OURS SO FAST.
SPEAKIN' OF FAST...
BEFORE REED GETS HERE AND MAKES US COMB THAT WHOLE HIDDEN BASE...
...ANYONE WANT A RIDE BACK IN THE FANTASTICAR?
YES!
THANKS, MR. GRIMM.
WELL, I CAN' LEAVE T CAR. SE YOU AL BACK HOME
JOB SHADOW EVALUATION: "MARVEL GIRL".
A VERY RESPONSIBLE YOUNG LADY, ESPECIALLY FOR SOMEONE SO POWERFUL. MARVEL GIRL SHOWED INITIATIVE, RESOURCEFULNESS, AND WORKS WELL WITH A TEAM. BUT YOU ALREADY KNOW THAT.
I CAN'T READ MINDS LIKE YOU, DR. XAVIER, BUT I'M GUESSING THE REAL POINT WAS SO SHE COULD SEE HOW I DEAL WITH MY TEAM. TO THAT END, I HOPE I PASSED MUSTER!
--YOURS, SUE.

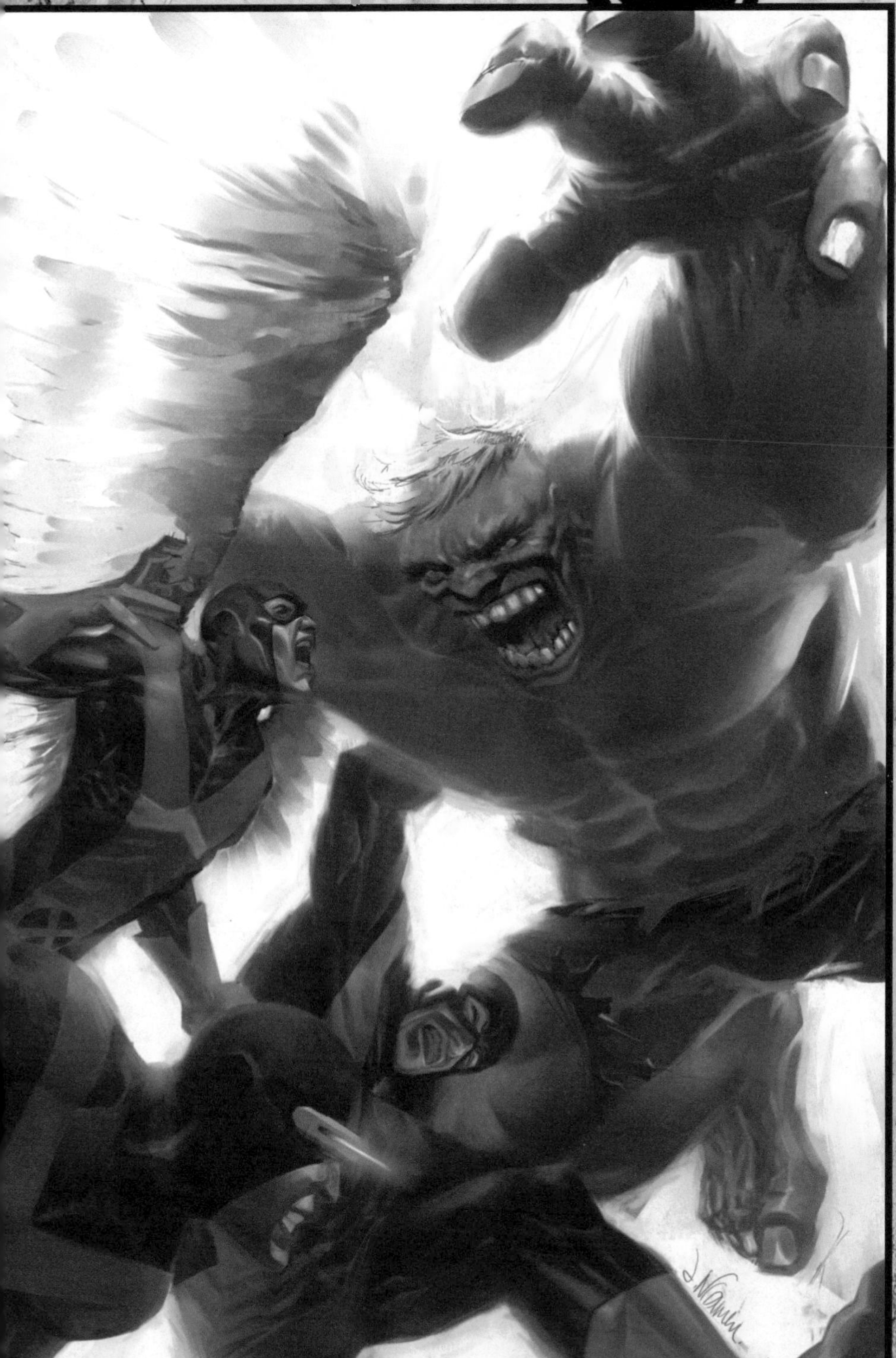

X-Men: First Class (2007) **#5**

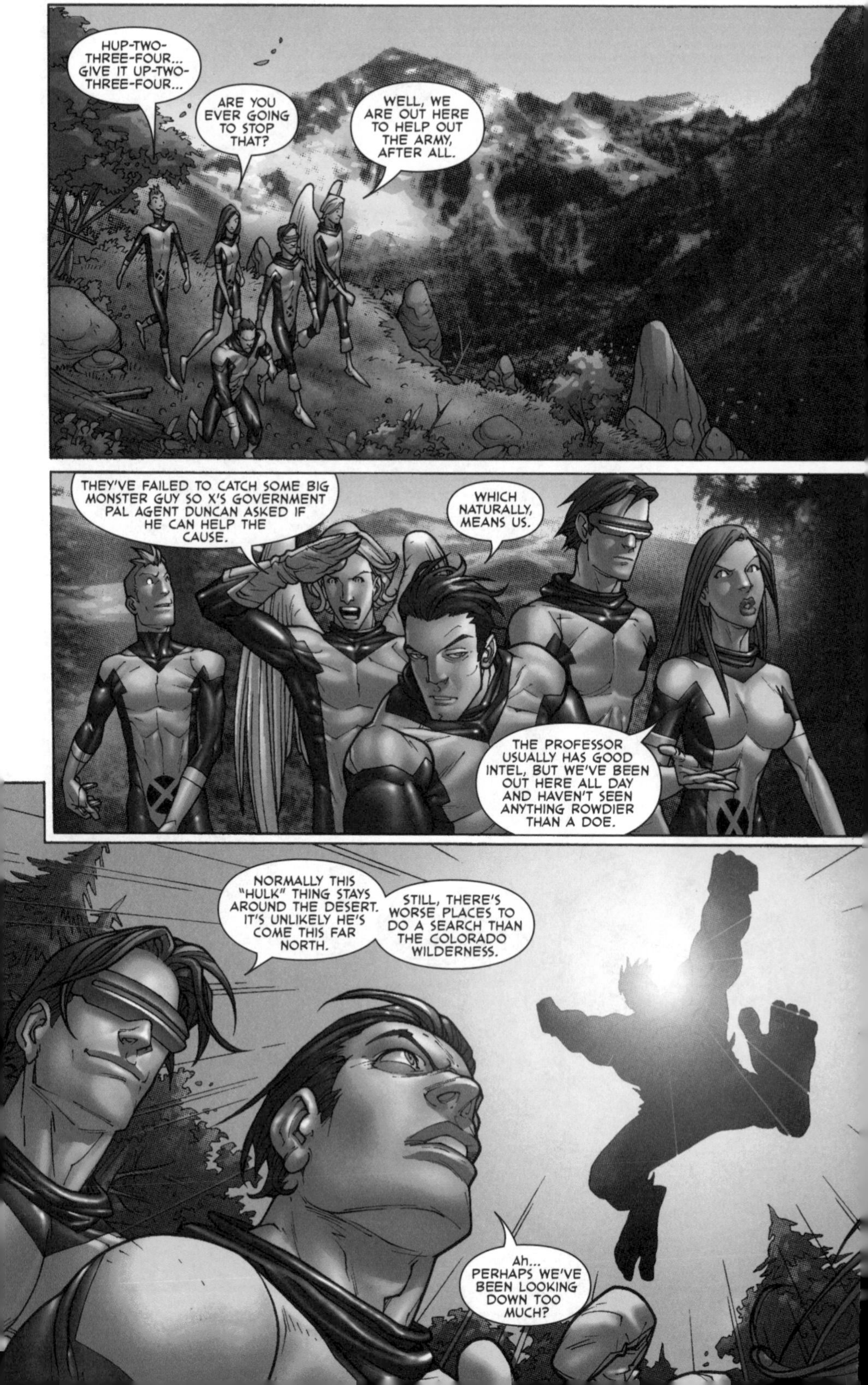
HUP-TWO-THREE-FOUR... GIVE IT UP-TWO-THREE-FOUR...
ARE YOU EVER GOING TO STOP THAT?
WELL, WE ARE OUT HERE TO HELP OUT THE ARMY, AFTER ALL.
THEY'VE FAILED TO CATCH SOME BIG MONSTER GUY SO X'S GOVERNMENT PAL AGENT DUNCAN ASKED IF HE CAN HELP THE CAUSE.
WHICH NATURALLY, MEANS US.
THE PROFESSOR USUALLY HAS GOOD INTEL, BUT WE'VE BEEN OUT HERE ALL DAY AND HAVEN'T SEEN ANYTHING ROWDIER THAN A DOE.
NORMALLY THIS "HULK" THING STAYS AROUND THE DESERT. IT'S UNLIKELY HE'S COME THIS FAR NORTH.
STILL, THERE'S WORSE PLACES TO DO A SEARCH THAN THE COLORADO WILDERNESS.
Ah... PERHAPS WE'VE BEEN LOOKING DOWN TOO MUCH?

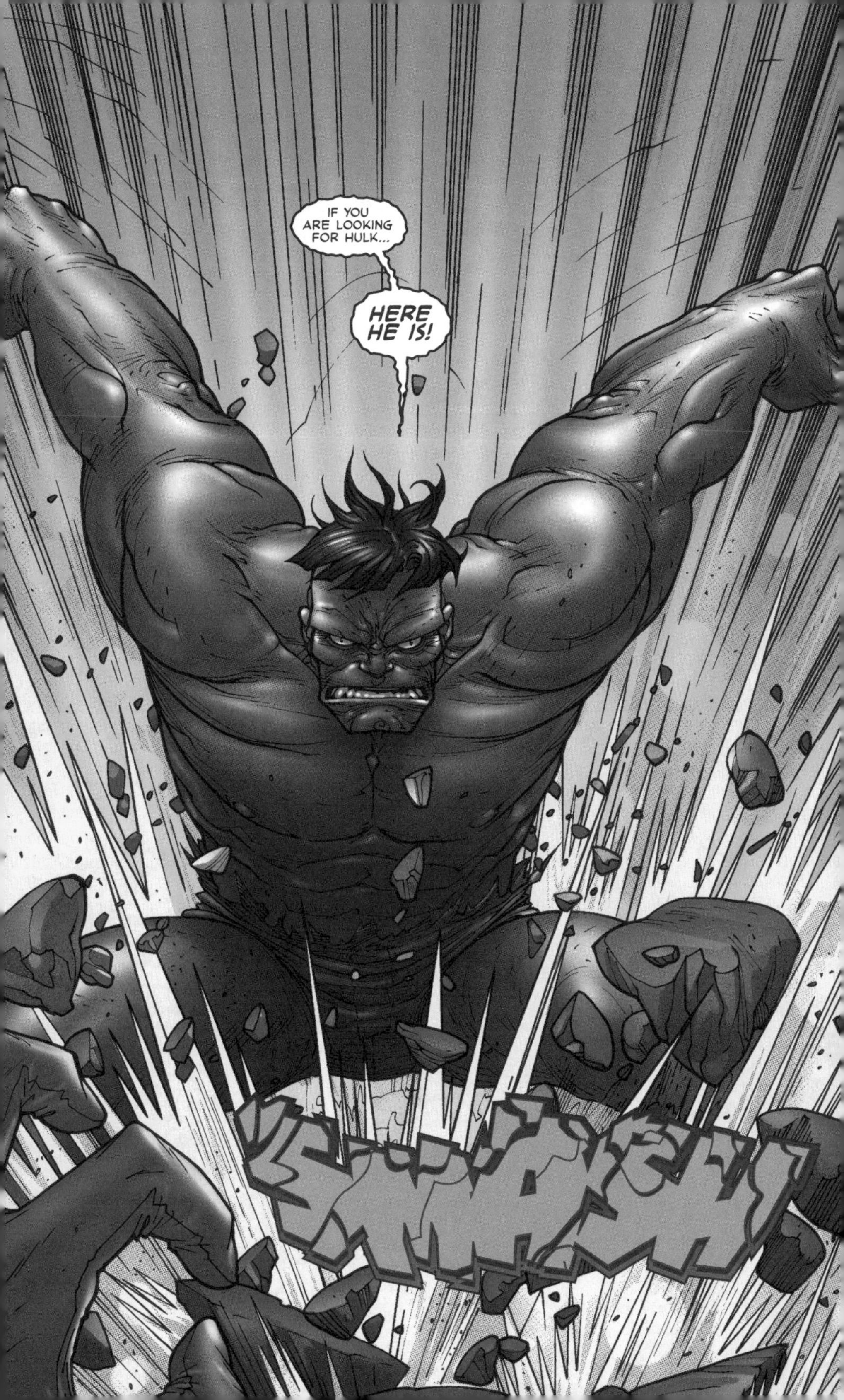
IF YOU ARE LOOKING FOR HULK...
HERE HE IS!

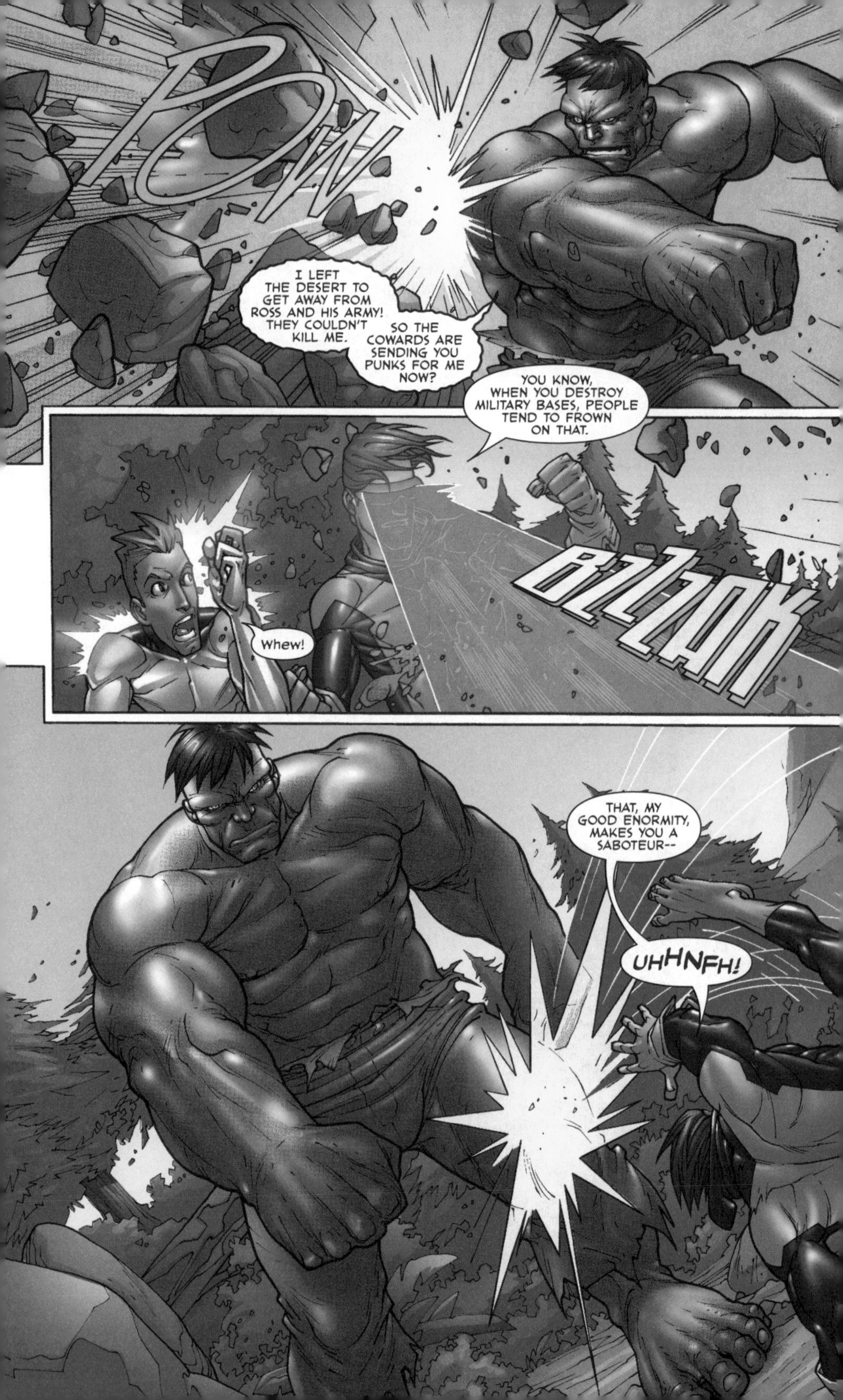
POW
I LEFT THE DESERT TO GET AWAY FROM ROSS AND HIS ARMY! THEY COULDN'T KILL ME.
SO THE COWARDS ARE SENDING YOU PUNKS FOR ME NOW?
YOU KNOW, WHEN YOU DESTROY MILITARY BASES, PEOPLE TEND TO FROWN ON THAT.
BZZZAOK
Whew!
THAT, MY GOOD ENORMITY, MAKES YOU A SABOTEUR--
UHHNFH!

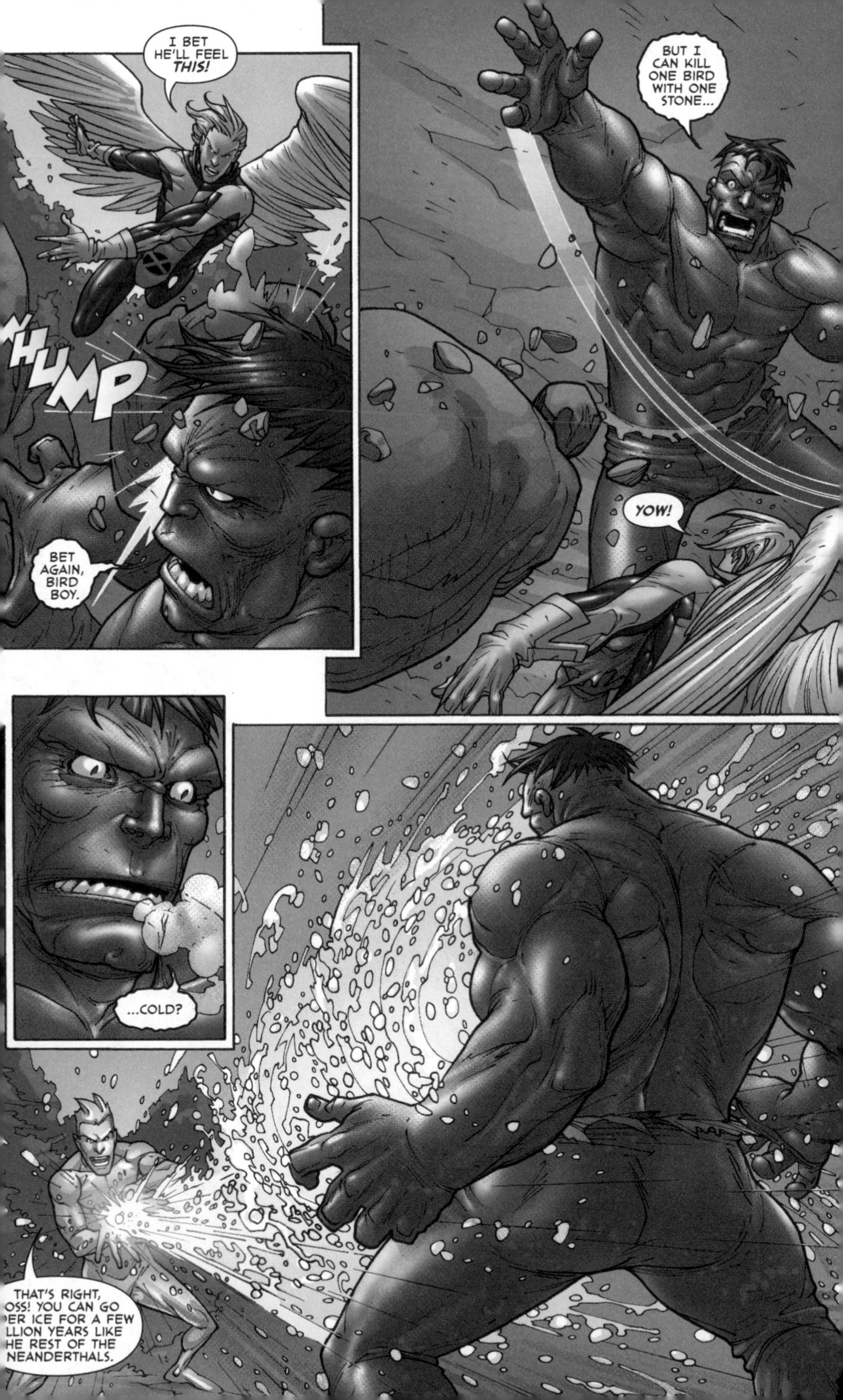
I BET HE'LL FEEL *THIS!*
THUMP
BET AGAIN, BIRD BOY.
BUT I CAN KILL ONE BIRD WITH ONE STONE...
*YOW!*
...COLD?
THAT'S RIGHT, OSS! YOU CAN GO ER ICE FOR A FEW LLION YEARS LIKE HE REST OF THE NEANDERTHALS.

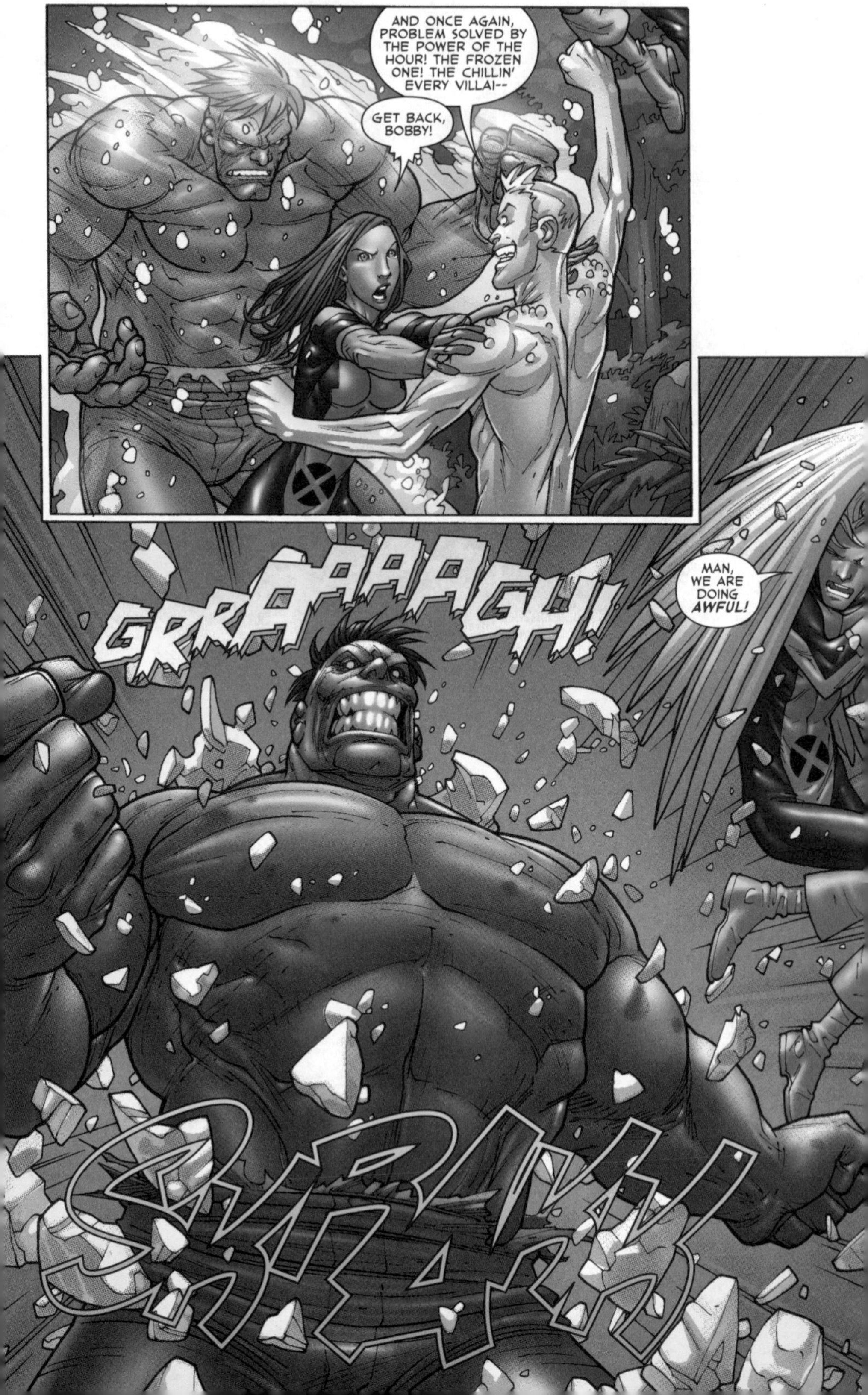
AND ONCE AGAIN, PROBLEM SOLVED BY THE POWER OF THE HOUR! THE FROZEN ONE! THE CHILLIN' EVERY VILLAI--
GET BACK, BOBBY!
GRRAAAAAGH!
MAN, WE ARE DOING AWFUL!

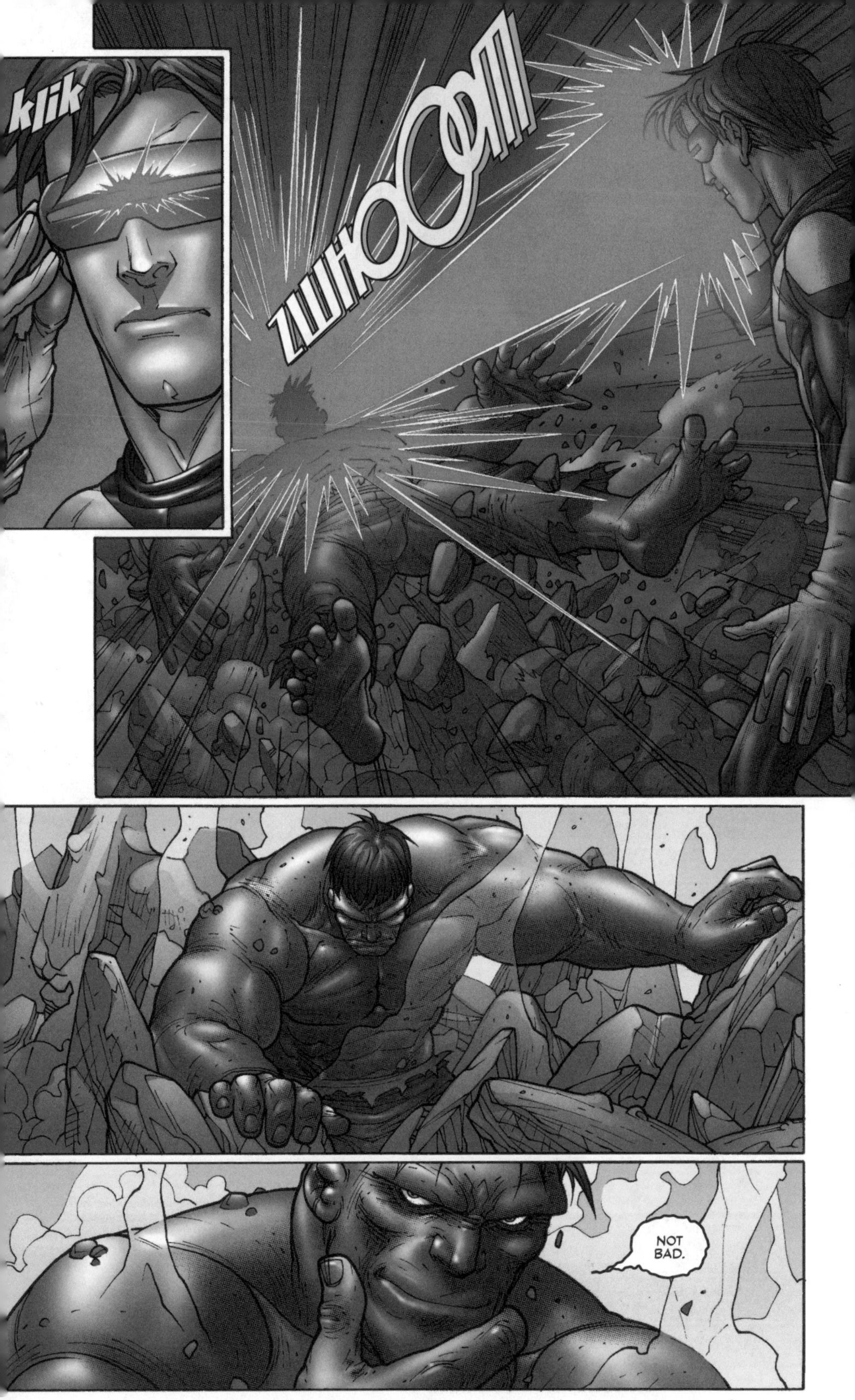
klik
ZWHOOOM
NOT BAD.

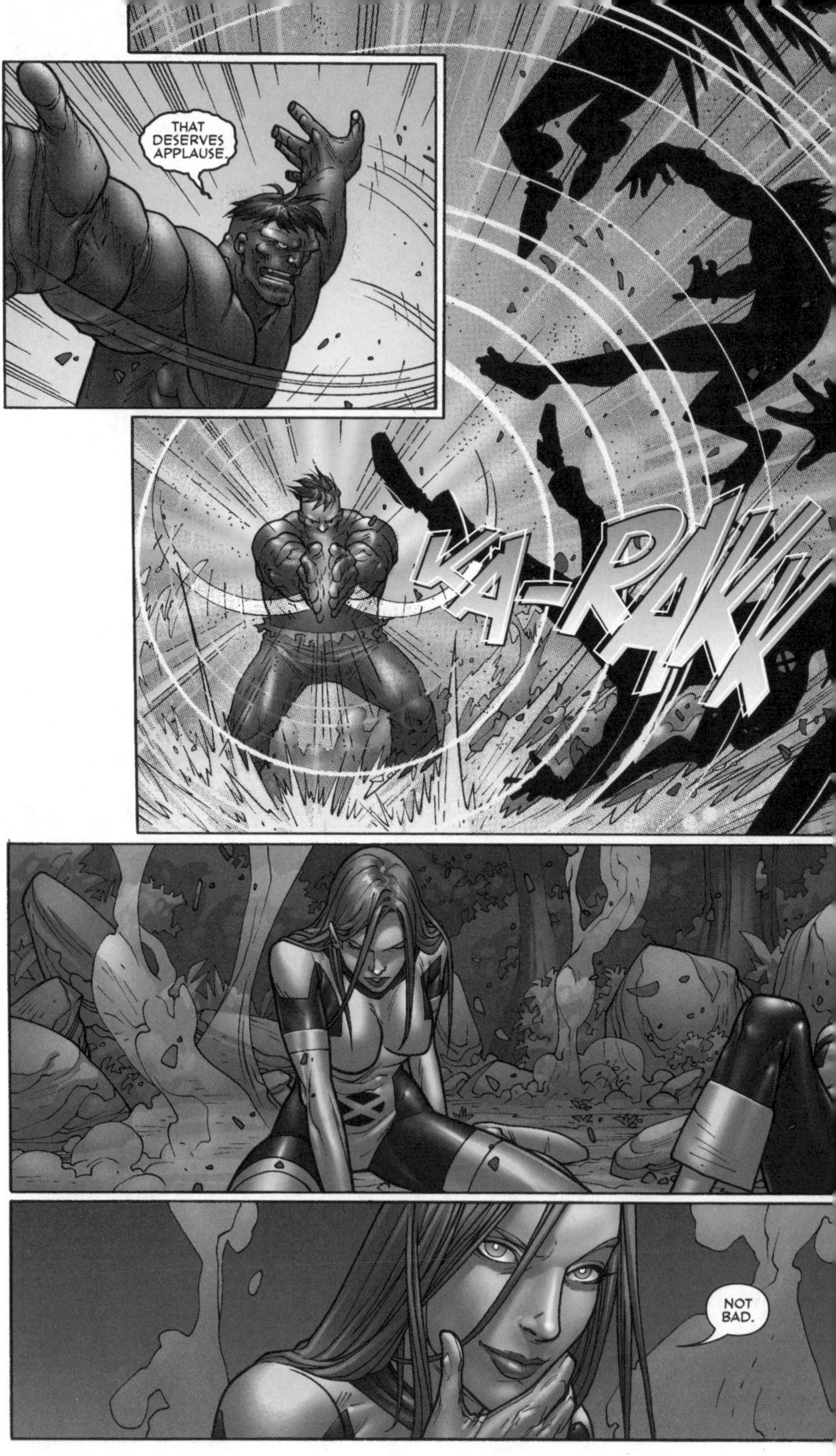
THAT DESERVES APPLAUSE.
KA-RAKK
NOT BAD.

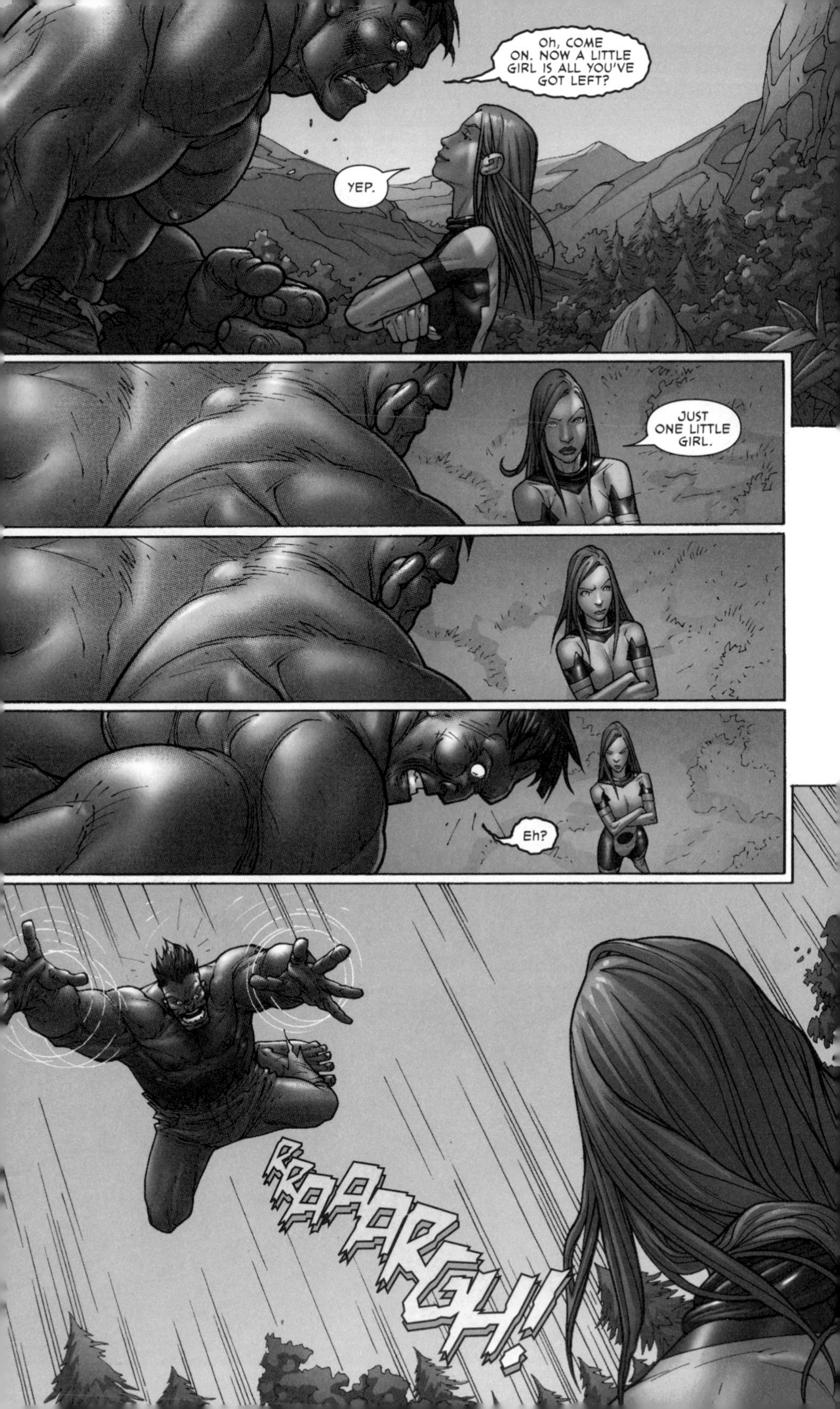

Oh, COME ON. NOW A LITTLE GIRL IS ALL YOU'VE GOT LEFT?
YEP.
JUST ONE LITTLE GIRL.
Eh?
RRAAARRGH!

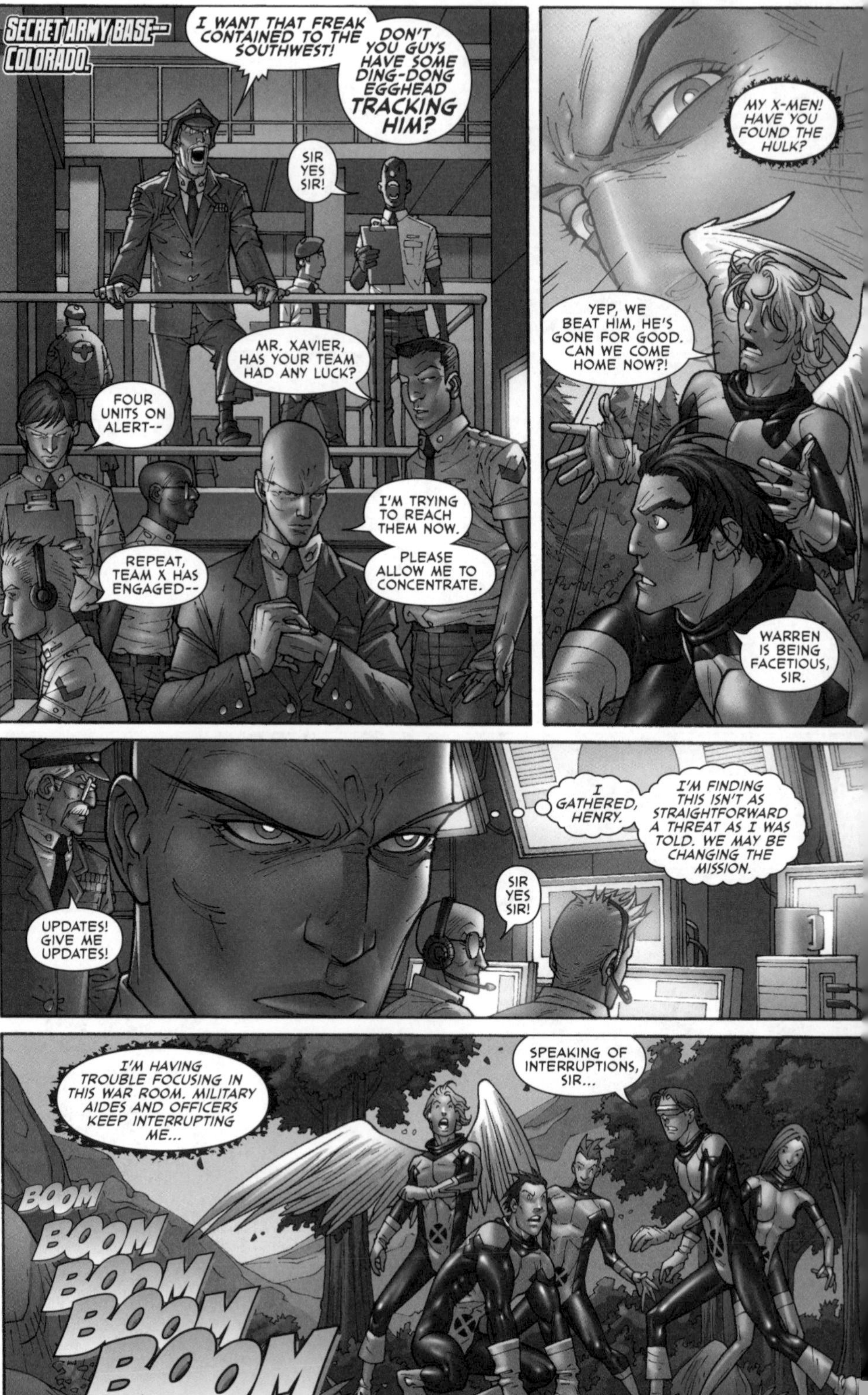
SECRET ARMY BASE-- COLORADO.
I WANT THAT FREAK CONTAINED TO THE SOUTHWEST!
DON'T YOU GUYS HAVE SOME DING-DONG EGGHEAD TRACKING HIM?
SIR YES SIR!
MR. XAVIER, HAS YOUR TEAM HAD ANY LUCK?
FOUR UNITS ON ALERT--
I'M TRYING TO REACH THEM NOW.
PLEASE ALLOW ME TO CONCENTRATE.
REPEAT, TEAM X HAS ENGAGED--
MY X-MEN! HAVE YOU FOUND THE HULK?
YEP, WE BEAT HIM, HE'S GONE FOR GOOD. CAN WE COME HOME NOW?!
WARREN IS BEING FACETIOUS, SIR.
I GATHERED, HENRY.
I'M FINDING THIS ISN'T AS STRAIGHTFORWARD A THREAT AS I WAS TOLD. WE MAY BE CHANGING THE MISSION.
SIR YES SIR!
UPDATES! GIVE ME UPDATES!
I'M HAVING TROUBLE FOCUSING IN THIS WAR ROOM. MILITARY AIDES AND OFFICERS KEEP INTERRUPTING ME...
SPEAKING OF INTERRUPTIONS, SIR...
BOOM
BOOM
BOOM
BOOM
BOOM

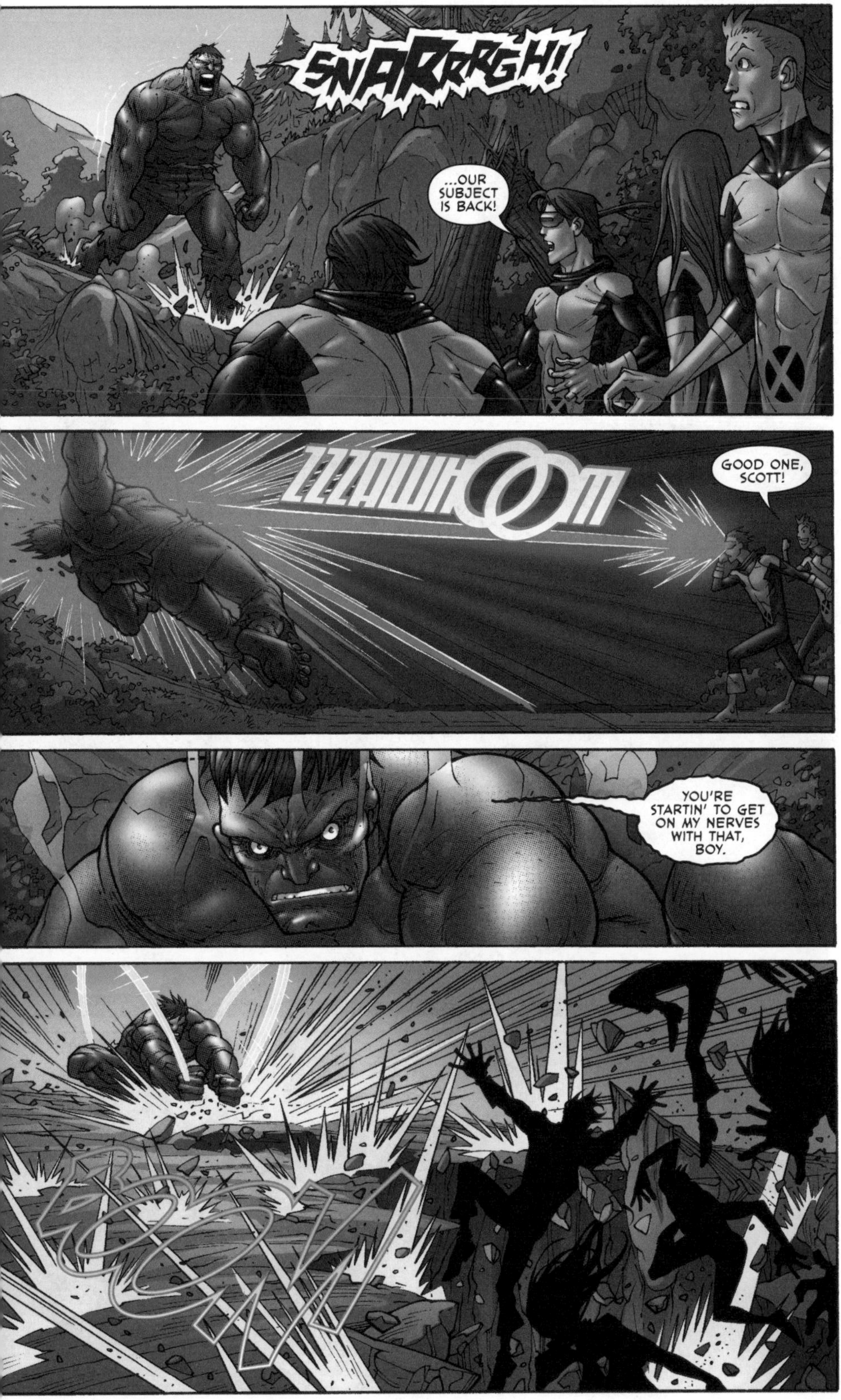
SNARRRGH!
...OUR SUBJECT IS BACK!
ZZZAWHOOM
GOOD ONE, SCOTT!
YOU'RE STARTIN' TO GET ON MY NERVES WITH THAT, BOY.
BOOM

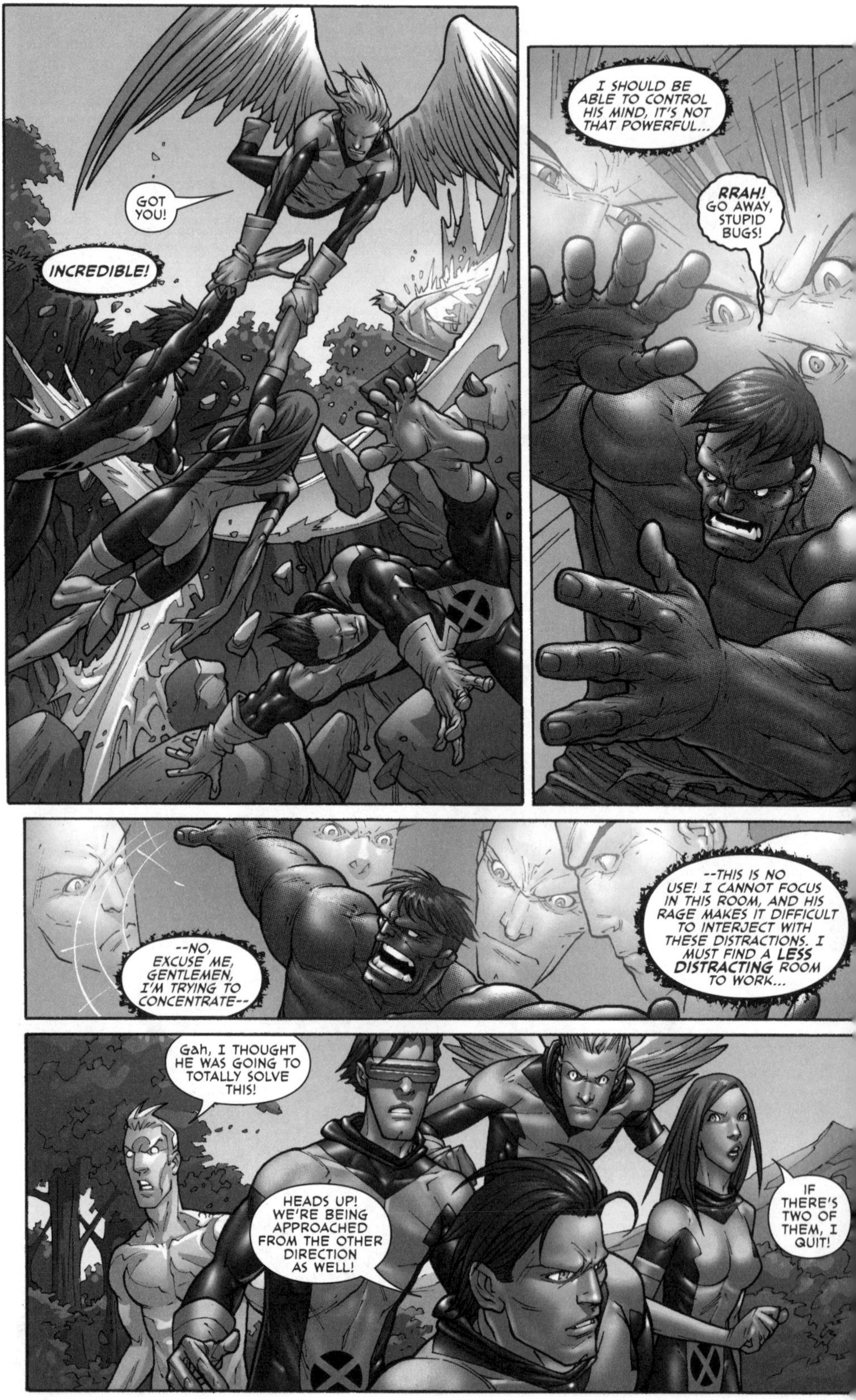
GOT YOU!
INCREDIBLE!
I SHOULD BE ABLE TO CONTROL HIS MIND, IT'S NOT THAT POWERFUL...
RRAH! GO AWAY, STUPID BUGS!
--NO, EXCUSE ME, GENTLEMEN, I'M TRYING TO CONCENTRATE--
--THIS IS NO USE! I CANNOT FOCUS IN THIS ROOM, AND HIS RAGE MAKES IT DIFFICULT TO INTERJECT WITH THESE DISTRACTIONS. I MUST FIND A LESS DISTRACTING ROOM TO WORK...
Gah, I THOUGHT HE WAS GOING TO TOTALLY SOLVE THIS!
HEADS UP! WE'RE BEING APPROACHED FROM THE OTHER DIRECTION AS WELL!
IF THERE'S TWO OF THEM, I QUIT!

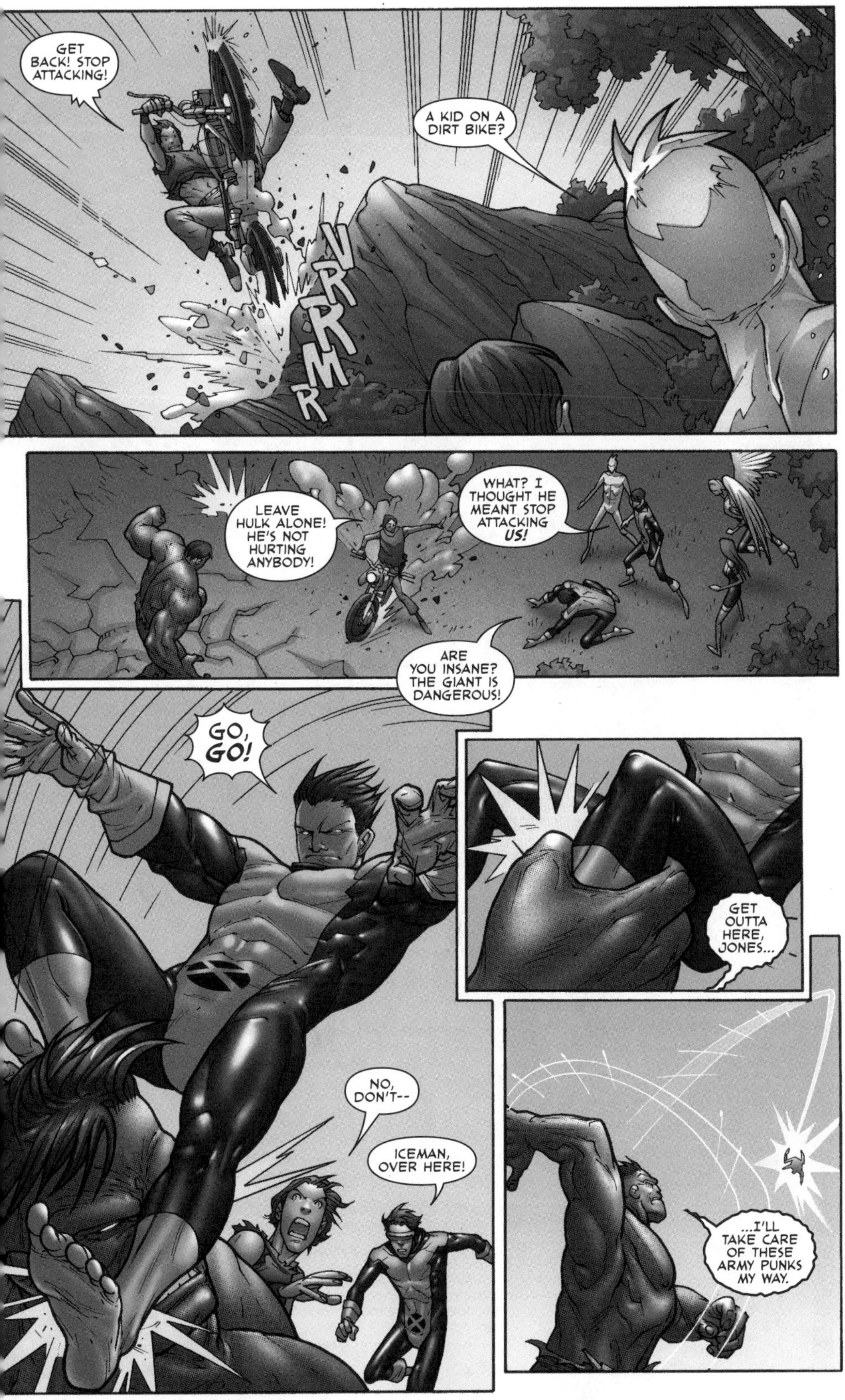
GET BACK! STOP ATTACKING!
A KID ON A DIRT BIKE?
VRRRMRR
LEAVE HULK ALONE! HE'S NOT HURTING ANYBODY!
WHAT? I THOUGHT HE MEANT STOP ATTACKING US!
ARE YOU INSANE? THE GIANT IS DANGEROUS!
GO, GO!
NO, DON'T--
ICEMAN, OVER HERE!
GET OUTTA HERE, JONES...
...I'LL TAKE CARE OF THESE ARMY PUNKS MY WAY.

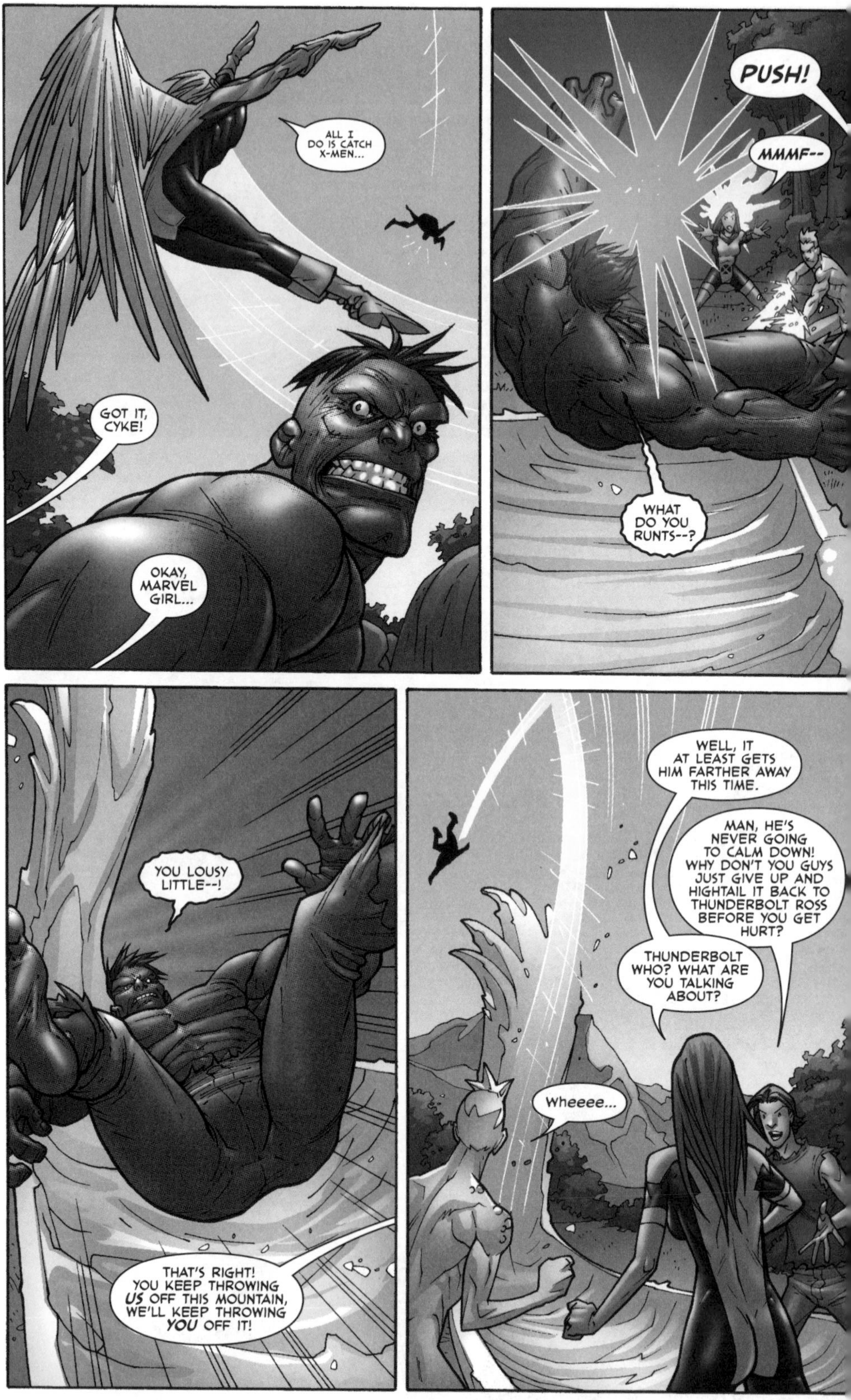
ALL I DO IS CATCH X-MEN...
GOT IT, CYKE!
OKAY, MARVEL GIRL...
PUSH!
MMMF--
WHAT DO YOU RUNTS--?
YOU LOUSY LITTLE--!
THAT'S RIGHT! YOU KEEP THROWING *US* OFF THIS MOUNTAIN, WE'LL KEEP THROWING *YOU* OFF IT!
WELL, IT AT LEAST GETS HIM FARTHER AWAY THIS TIME.
MAN, HE'S NEVER GOING TO CALM DOWN! WHY DON'T YOU GUYS JUST GIVE UP AND HIGHTAIL IT BACK TO THUNDERBOLT ROSS BEFORE YOU GET HURT?
THUNDERBOLT WHO? WHAT ARE YOU TALKING ABOUT?
Wheeee...

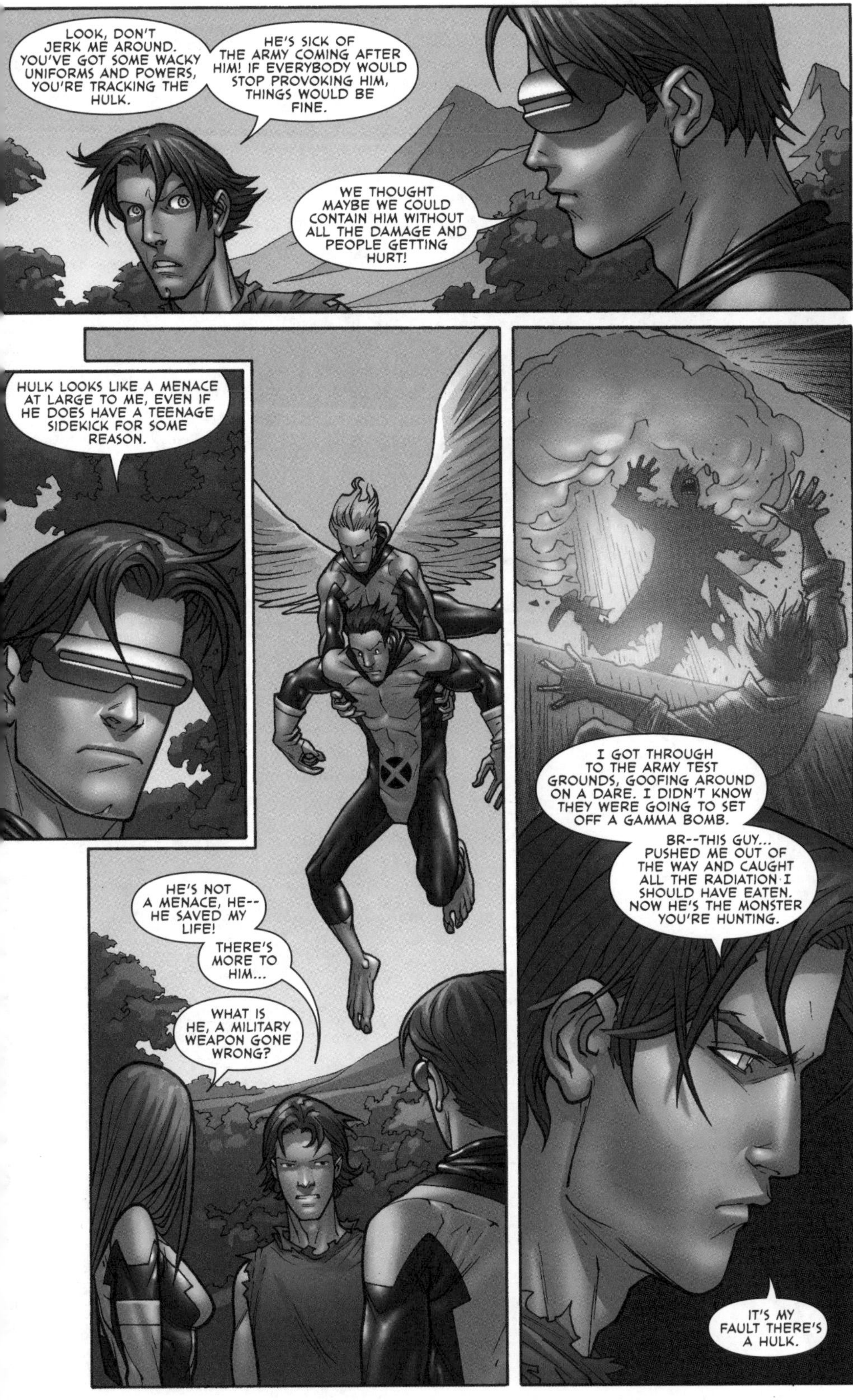
LOOK, DON'T JERK ME AROUND. YOU'VE GOT SOME WACKY UNIFORMS AND POWERS, YOU'RE TRACKING THE HULK.
HE'S SICK OF THE ARMY COMING AFTER HIM! IF EVERYBODY WOULD STOP PROVOKING HIM, THINGS WOULD BE FINE.
WE THOUGHT MAYBE WE COULD CONTAIN HIM WITHOUT ALL THE DAMAGE AND PEOPLE GETTING HURT!
HULK LOOKS LIKE A MENACE AT LARGE TO ME, EVEN IF HE DOES HAVE A TEENAGE SIDEKICK FOR SOME REASON.
HE'S NOT A MENACE, HE-- HE SAVED MY LIFE!
THERE'S MORE TO HIM...
WHAT IS HE, A MILITARY WEAPON GONE WRONG?
I GOT THROUGH TO THE ARMY TEST GROUNDS, GOOFING AROUND ON A DARE. I DIDN'T KNOW THEY WERE GOING TO SET OFF A GAMMA BOMB.
BR--THIS GUY... PUSHED ME OUT OF THE WAY AND CAUGHT ALL THE RADIATION I SHOULD HAVE EATEN. NOW HE'S THE MONSTER YOU'RE HUNTING.
IT'S MY FAULT THERE'S A HULK.

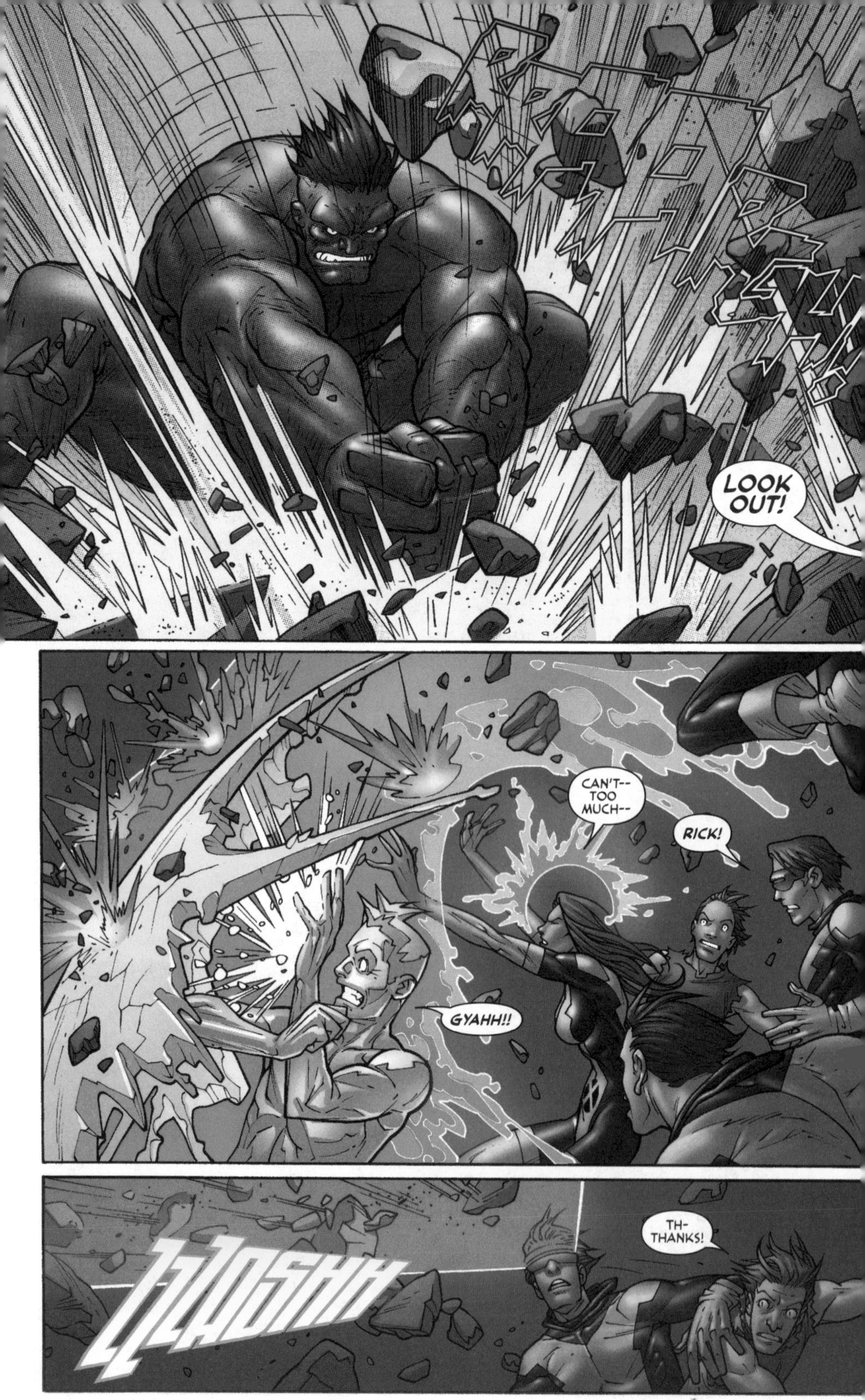
LOOK OUT!
CAN'T-- TOO MUCH--
RICK!
GYAHH!!
TH- THANKS!

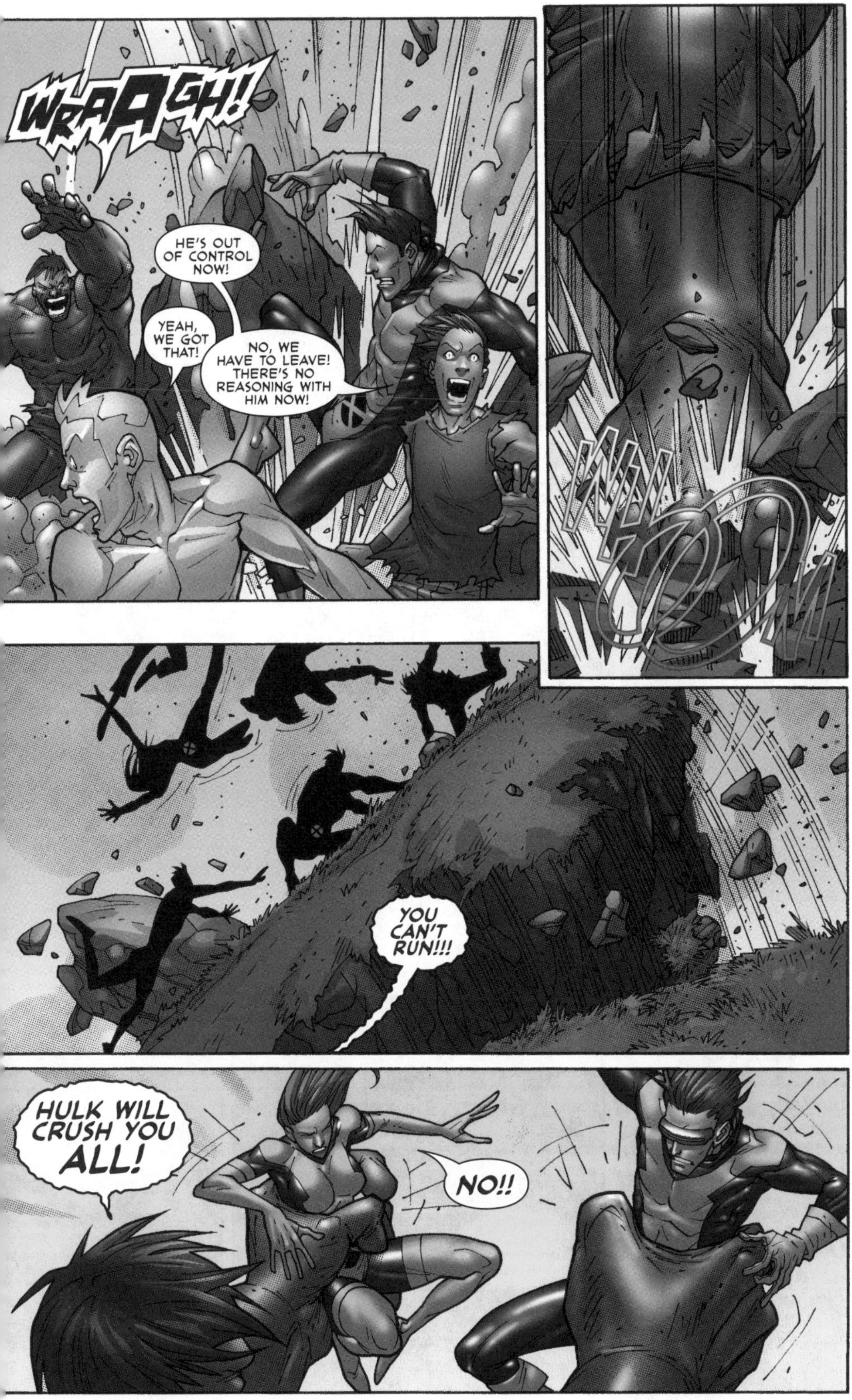

WRAAGH!!
HE'S OUT OF CONTROL NOW!
YEAH, WE GOT THAT!
NO, WE HAVE TO LEAVE! THERE'S NO REASONING WITH HIM NOW!
YOU CAN'T RUN!!!
HULK WILL CRUSH YOU ALL!
NO!!

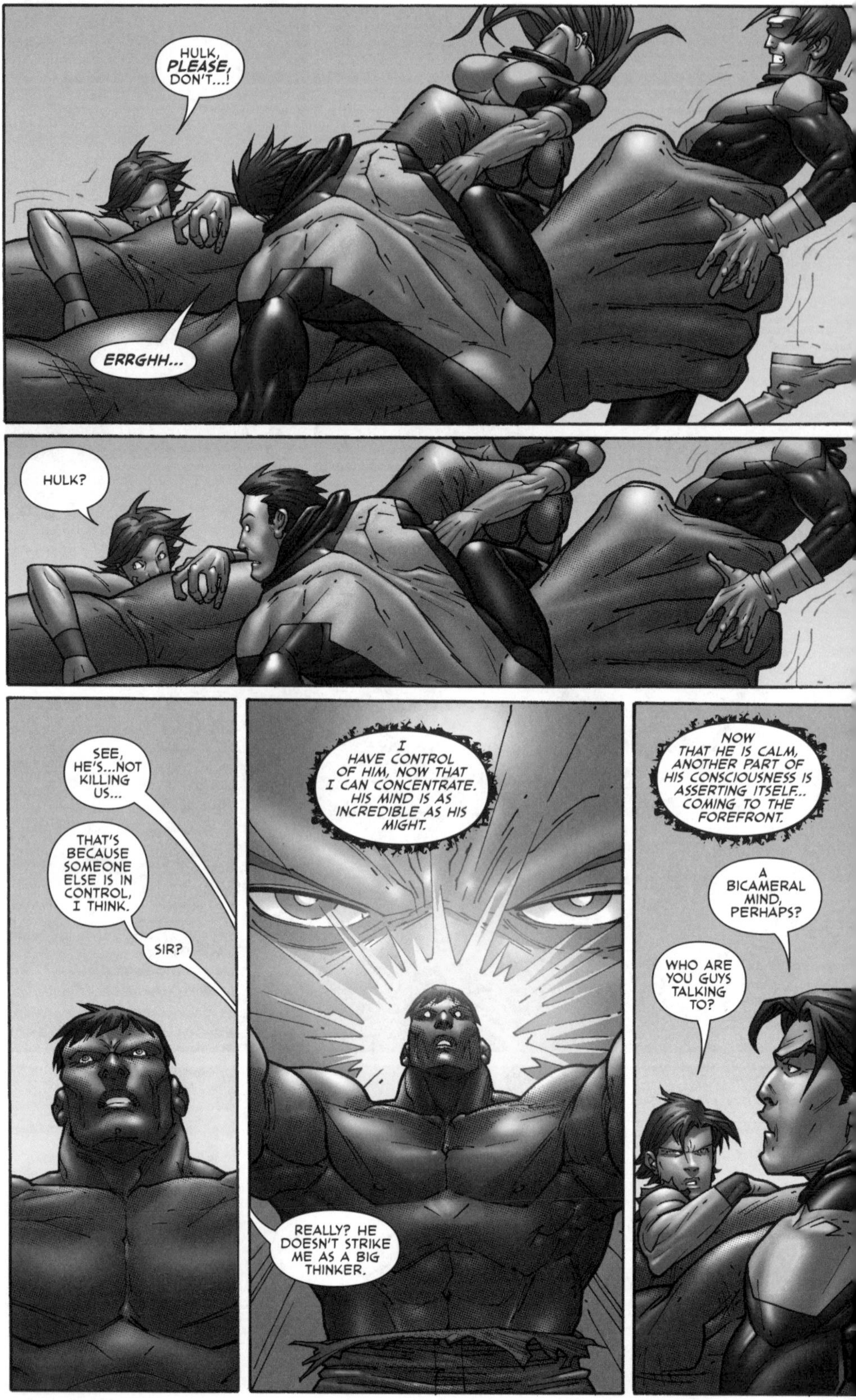

HULK, *PLEASE,* DON'T...!
*ERRGHH...*
HULK?
SEE, HE'S...NOT KILLING US...
THAT'S BECAUSE SOMEONE ELSE IS IN CONTROL, I THINK.
SIR?
I HAVE CONTROL OF HIM, NOW THAT I CAN CONCENTRATE. HIS MIND IS AS INCREDIBLE AS HIS MIGHT.
REALLY? HE DOESN'T STRIKE ME AS A BIG THINKER.
NOW THAT HE IS CALM, ANOTHER PART OF HIS CONSCIOUSNESS IS ASSERTING ITSELF... COMING TO THE FOREFRONT.
A BICAMERAL MIND, PERHAPS?
WHO ARE YOU GUYS TALKING TO?

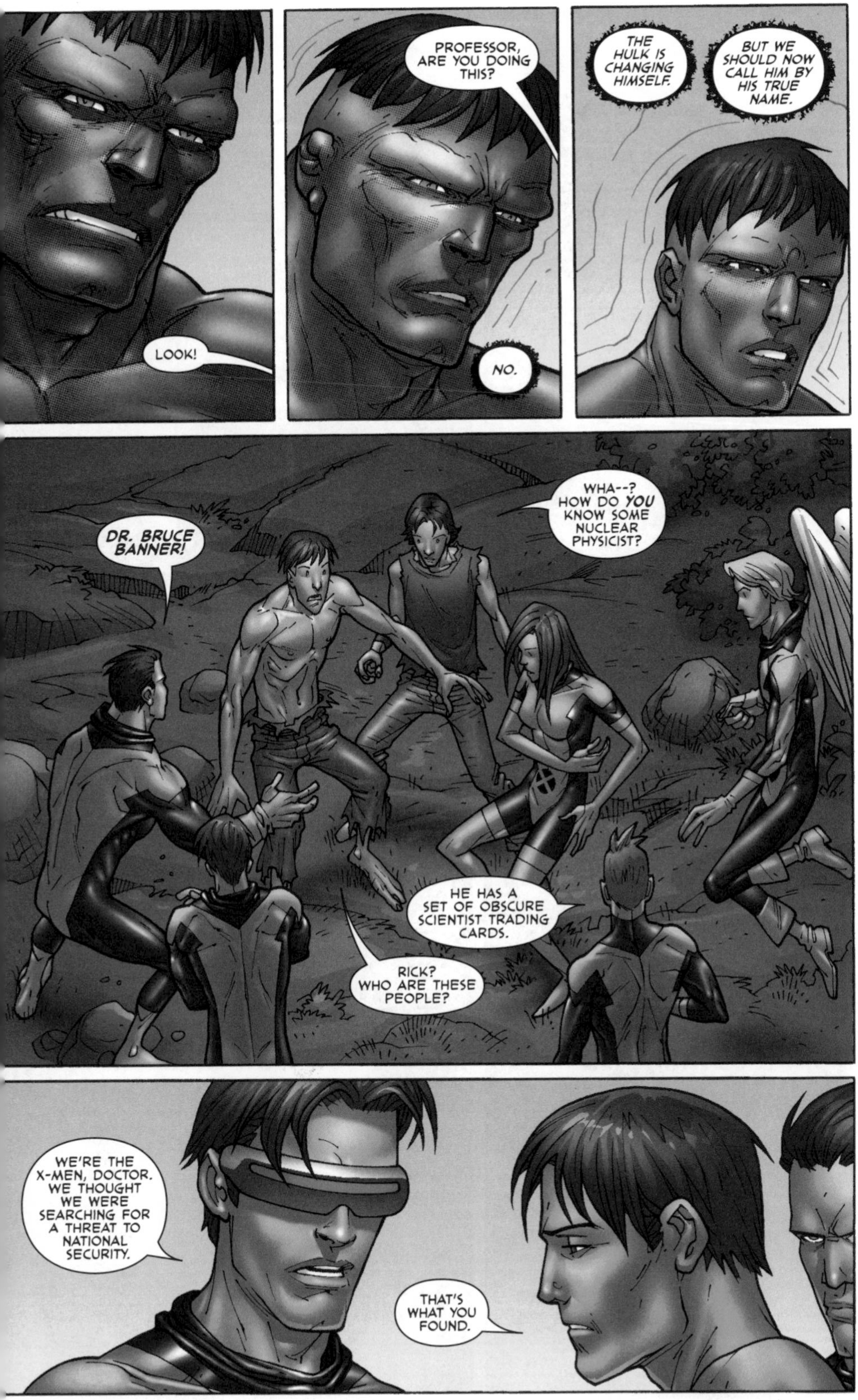

LOOK!
PROFESSOR, ARE YOU DOING THIS?
NO.
THE HULK IS CHANGING HIMSELF.
BUT WE SHOULD NOW CALL HIM BY HIS TRUE NAME.
DR. BRUCE BANNER!
WHA--? HOW DO YOU KNOW SOME NUCLEAR PHYSICIST?
HE HAS A SET OF OBSCURE SCIENTIST TRADING CARDS.
RICK? WHO ARE THESE PEOPLE?
WE'RE THE X-MEN, DOCTOR. WE THOUGHT WE WERE SEARCHING FOR A THREAT TO NATIONAL SECURITY.
THAT'S WHAT YOU FOUND.

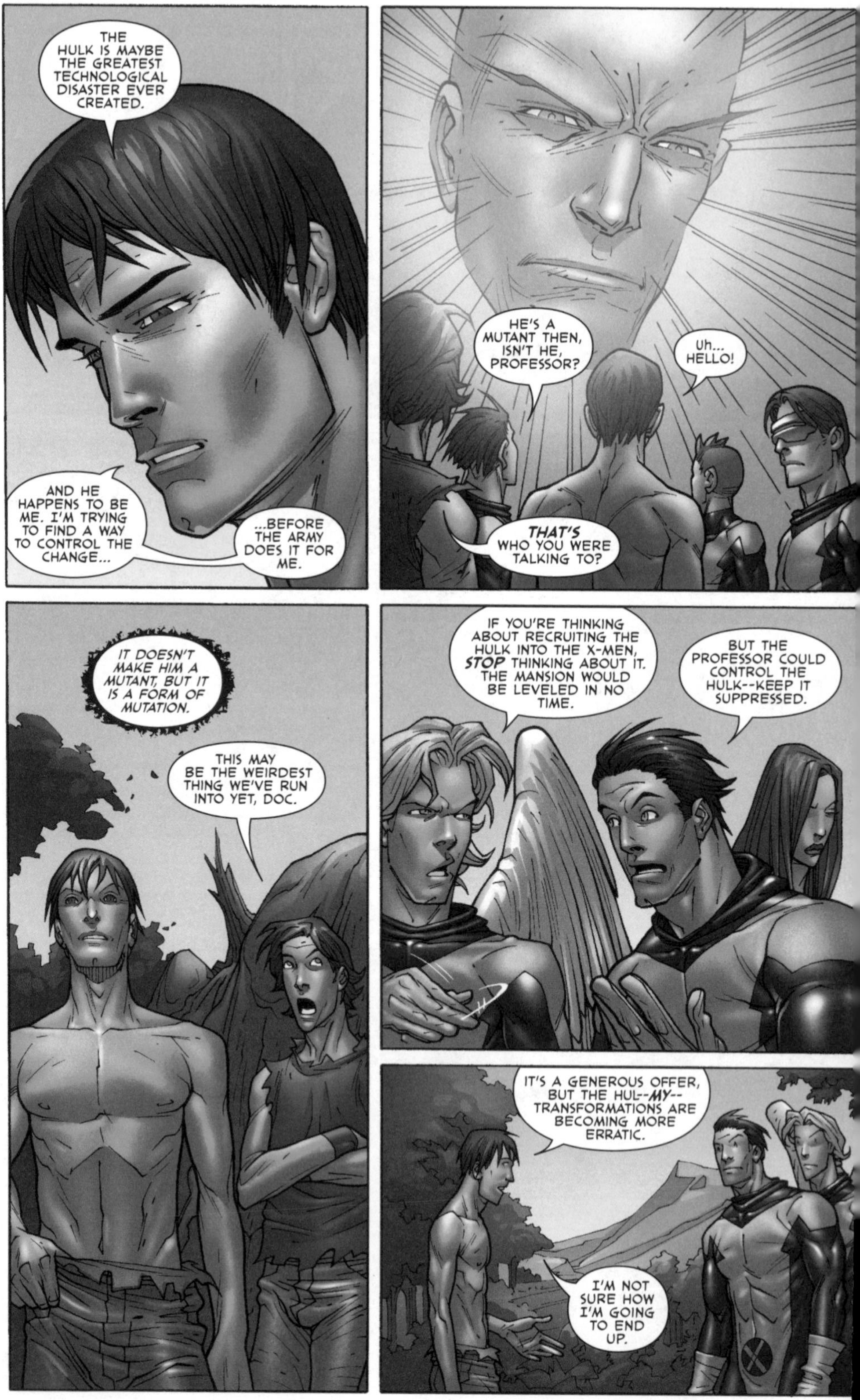

THE HULK IS MAYBE THE GREATEST TECHNOLOGICAL DISASTER EVER CREATED.
AND HE HAPPENS TO BE ME. I'M TRYING TO FIND A WAY TO CONTROL THE CHANGE...
...BEFORE THE ARMY DOES IT FOR ME.
HE'S A MUTANT THEN, ISN'T HE, PROFESSOR?
Uh... HELLO!
THAT'S WHO YOU WERE TALKING TO?
IT DOESN'T MAKE HIM A MUTANT, BUT IT IS A FORM OF MUTATION.
THIS MAY BE THE WEIRDEST THING WE'VE RUN INTO YET, DOC.
IF YOU'RE THINKING ABOUT RECRUITING THE HULK INTO THE X-MEN, STOP THINKING ABOUT IT. THE MANSION WOULD BE LEVELED IN NO TIME.
BUT THE PROFESSOR COULD CONTROL THE HULK--KEEP IT SUPPRESSED.
IT'S A GENEROUS OFFER, BUT THE HUL--MY--TRANSFORMATIONS ARE BECOMING MORE ERRATIC.
I'M NOT SURE HOW I'M GOING TO END UP.

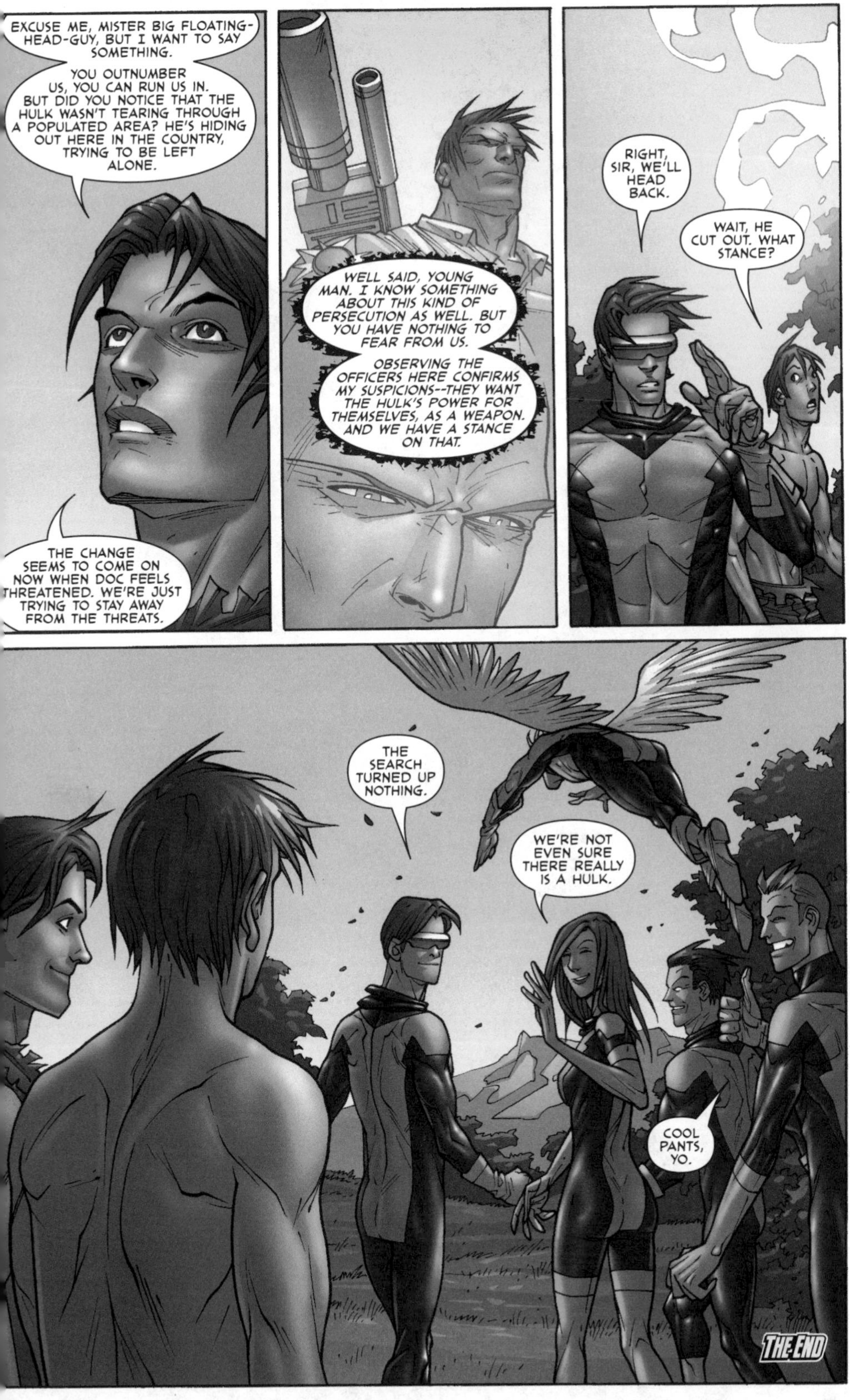
EXCUSE ME, MISTER BIG FLOATING-HEAD-GUY, BUT I WANT TO SAY SOMETHING.
YOU OUTNUMBER US, YOU CAN RUN US IN. BUT DID YOU NOTICE THAT THE HULK WASN'T TEARING THROUGH A POPULATED AREA? HE'S HIDING OUT HERE IN THE COUNTRY, TRYING TO BE LEFT ALONE.
THE CHANGE SEEMS TO COME ON NOW WHEN DOC FEELS THREATENED. WE'RE JUST TRYING TO STAY AWAY FROM THE THREATS.
WELL SAID, YOUNG MAN. I KNOW SOMETHING ABOUT THIS KIND OF PERSECUTION AS WELL. BUT YOU HAVE NOTHING TO FEAR FROM US.
OBSERVING THE OFFICERS HERE CONFIRMS MY SUSPICIONS--THEY WANT THE HULK'S POWER FOR THEMSELVES, AS A WEAPON. AND WE HAVE A STANCE ON THAT.
RIGHT, SIR, WE'LL HEAD BACK.
WAIT, HE CUT OUT. WHAT STANCE?
THE SEARCH TURNED UP NOTHING.
WE'RE NOT EVEN SURE THERE REALLY IS A HULK.
COOL PANTS, YO.
THE END

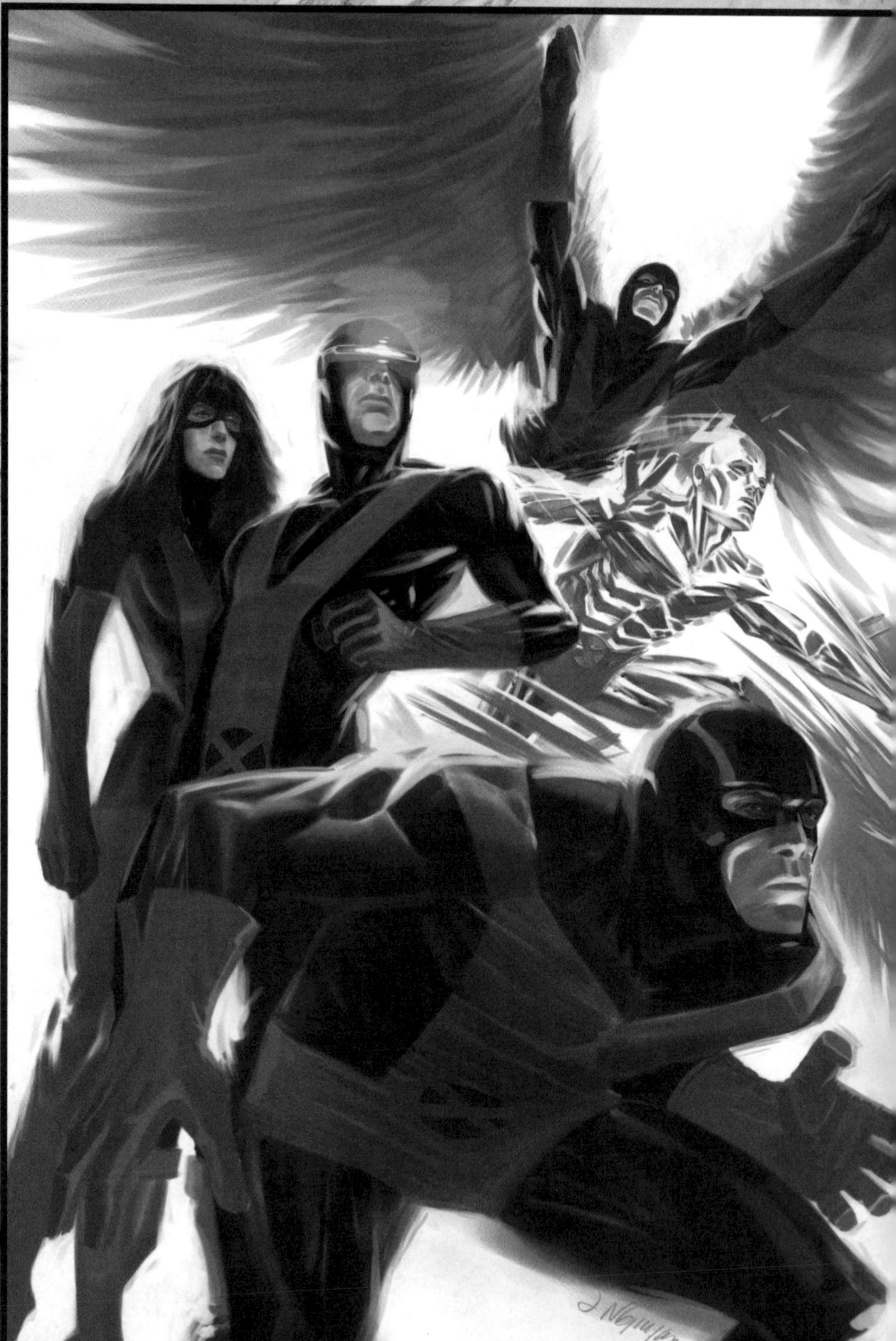

X-Men: First Class (2007) **#6**

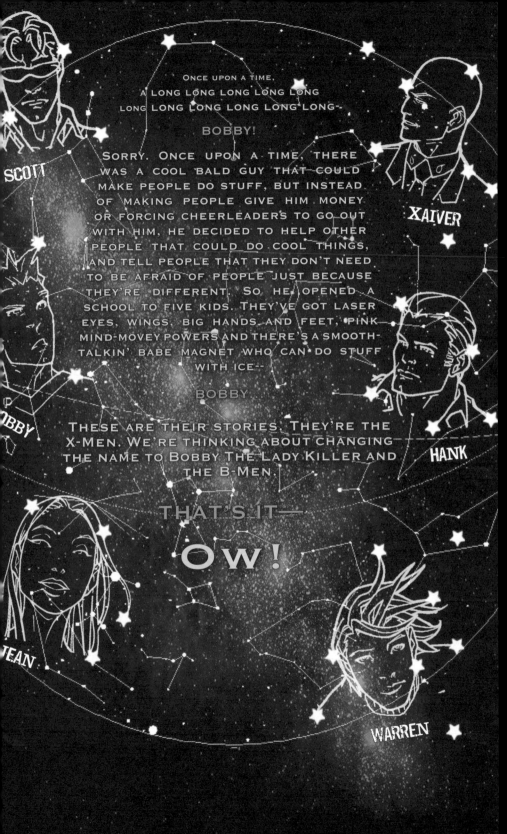

ONCE UPON A TIME,
A LONG LONG LONG LONG LONG
LONG LONG LONG LONG LONG LONG—

BOBBY!

SORRY. ONCE UPON A TIME, THERE
WAS A COOL BALD GUY THAT COULD
MAKE PEOPLE DO STUFF, BUT INSTEAD
OF MAKING PEOPLE GIVE HIM MONEY
OR FORCING CHEERLEADER'S TO GO OUT
WITH HIM, HE DECIDED TO HELP OTHER
PEOPLE THAT COULD DO COOL THINGS,
AND TELL PEOPLE THAT THEY DON'T NEED
TO BE AFRAID OF PEOPLE JUST BECAUSE
THEY'RE DIFFERENT. SO HE OPENED A
SCHOOL TO FIVE KIDS. THEY'VE GOT LASER
EYES, WINGS, BIG HANDS AND FEET, PINK
MIND-MOVEY POWERS AND THERE'S A SMOOTH-
TALKIN' BABE MAGNET WHO CAN DO STUFF
WITH ICE--

BOBBY...

THESE ARE THEIR STORIES. THEY'RE THE
X-MEN. WE'RE THINKING ABOUT CHANGING
THE NAME TO BOBBY THE LADY KILLER AND
THE B-MEN.

THAT'S IT—

OW!

SCOTT

XAIVER

BOBBY

HANK

JEAN

WARREN

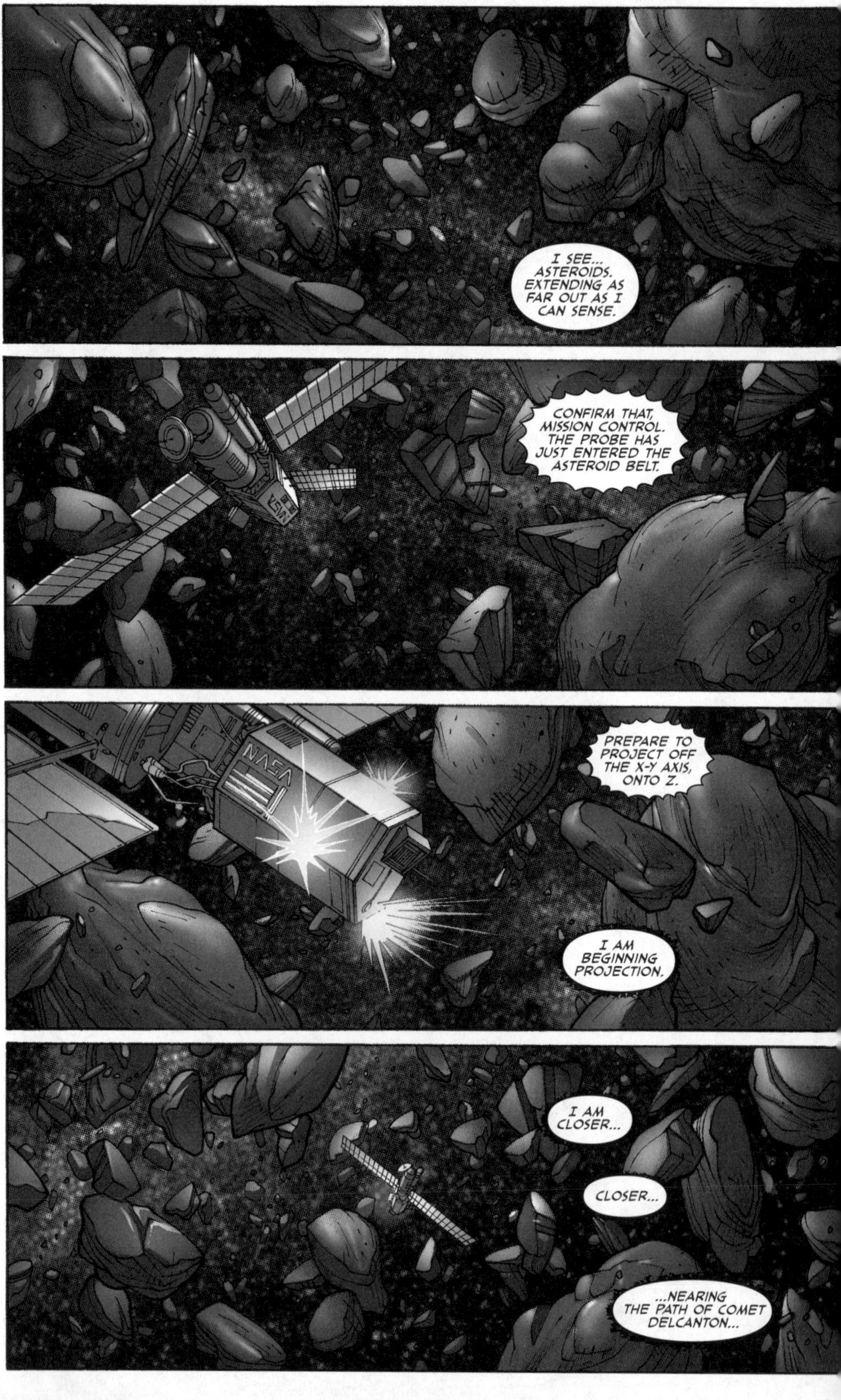
I SEE... ASTEROIDS. EXTENDING AS FAR OUT AS I CAN SENSE.
CONFIRM THAT, MISSION CONTROL. THE PROBE HAS JUST ENTERED THE ASTEROID BELT.
NASA
PREPARE TO PROJECT OFF THE X-Y AXIS, ONTO Z.
I AM BEGINNING PROJECTION.
I AM CLOSER...
CLOSER...
...NEARING THE PATH OF COMET DELCANTON...

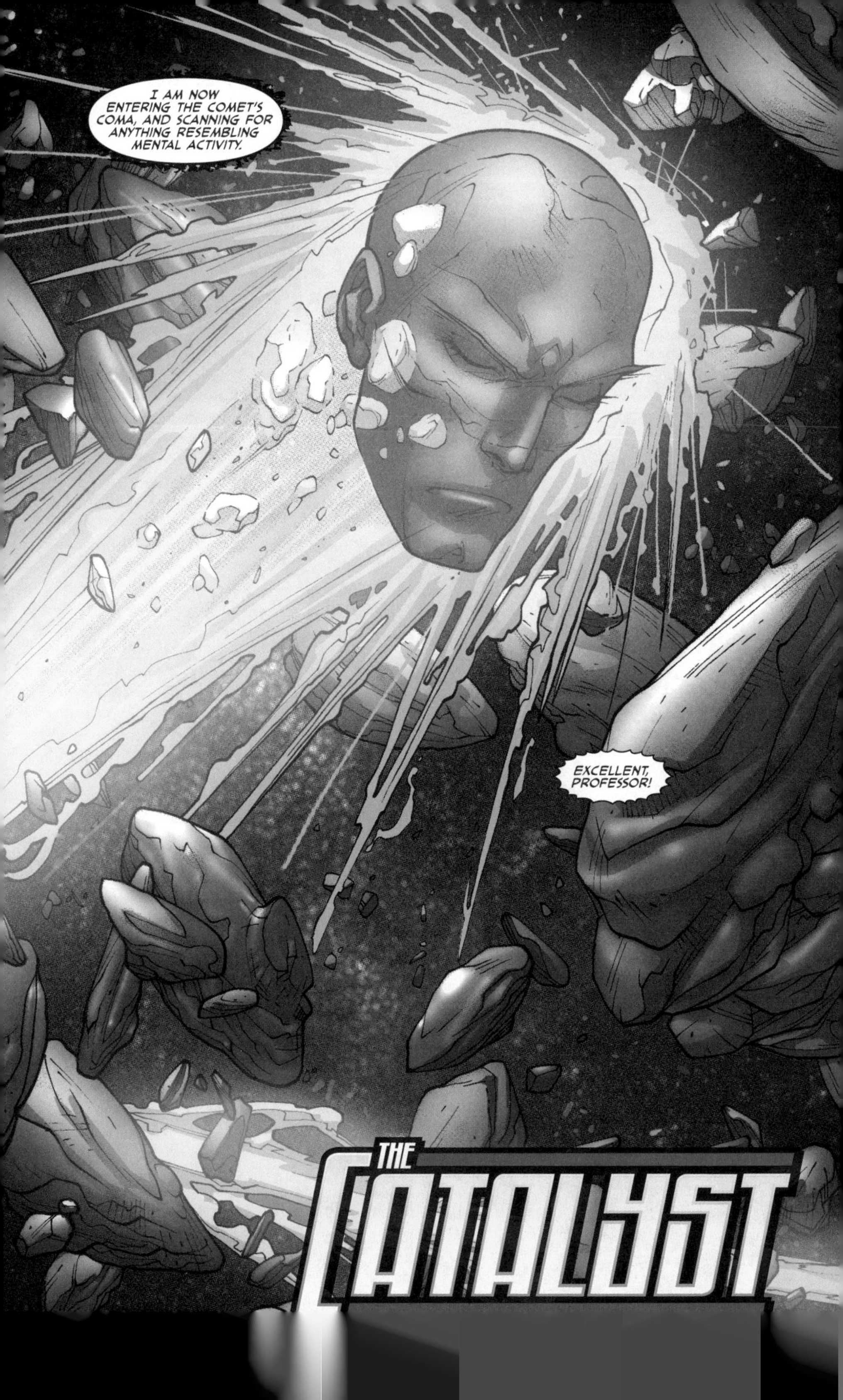
I AM NOW ENTERING THE COMET'S COMA, AND SCANNING FOR ANYTHING RESEMBLING MENTAL ACTIVITY.
EXCELLENT, PROFESSOR!
THE CATALYST

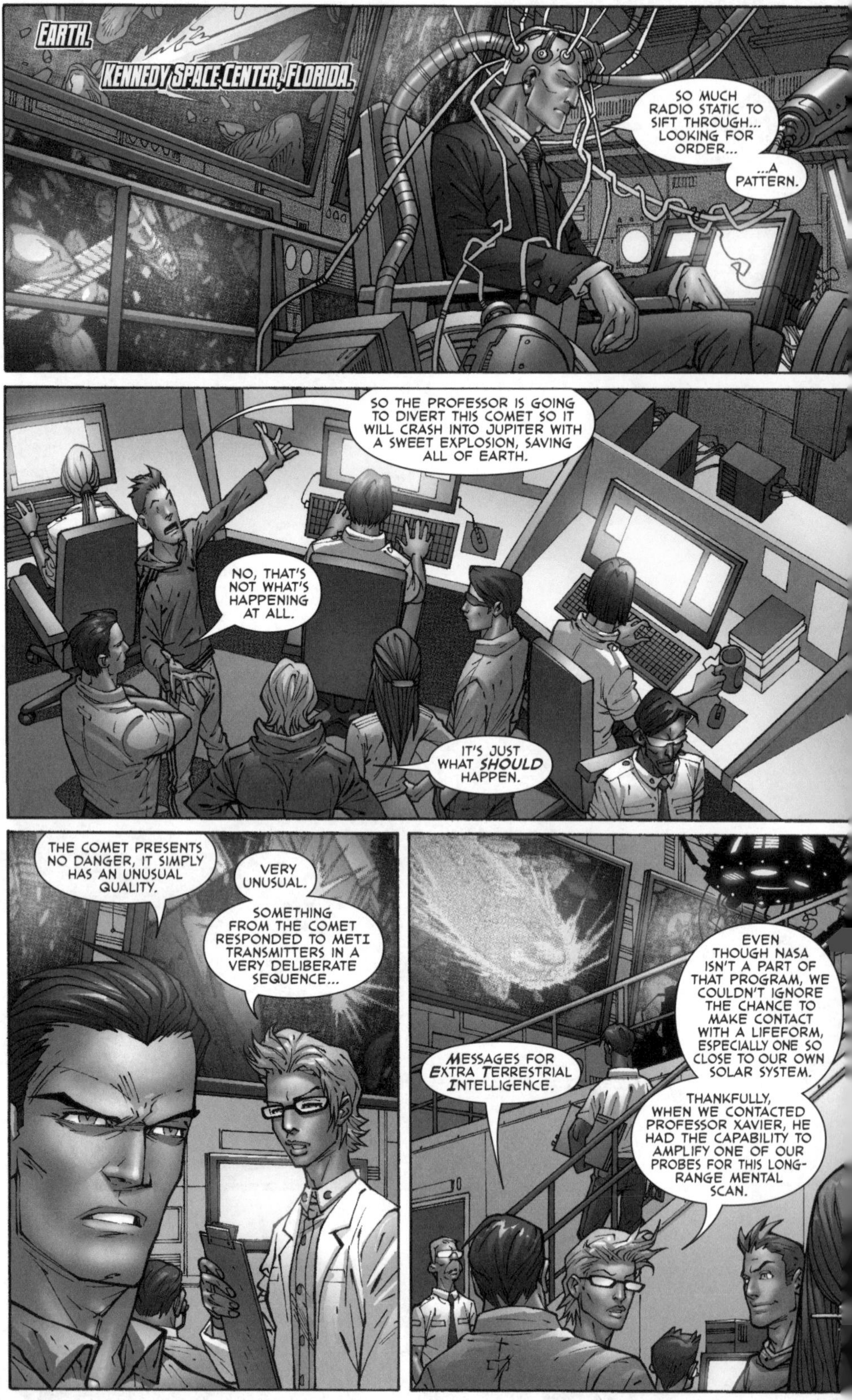
EARTH.
KENNEDY SPACE CENTER, FLORIDA.
SO MUCH RADIO STATIC TO SIFT THROUGH... LOOKING FOR ORDER...
...A PATTERN.
SO THE PROFESSOR IS GOING TO DIVERT THIS COMET SO IT WILL CRASH INTO JUPITER WITH A SWEET EXPLOSION, SAVING ALL OF EARTH.
NO, THAT'S NOT WHAT'S HAPPENING AT ALL.
IT'S JUST WHAT *SHOULD* HAPPEN.
THE COMET PRESENTS NO DANGER, IT SIMPLY HAS AN UNUSUAL QUALITY.
VERY UNUSUAL.
SOMETHING FROM THE COMET RESPONDED TO METI TRANSMITTERS IN A VERY DELIBERATE SEQUENCE...
MESSAGES FOR EXTRA TERRESTRIAL INTELLIGENCE.
EVEN THOUGH NASA ISN'T A PART OF THAT PROGRAM, WE COULDN'T IGNORE THE CHANCE TO MAKE CONTACT WITH A LIFEFORM, ESPECIALLY ONE SO CLOSE TO OUR OWN SOLAR SYSTEM.
THANKFULLY, WHEN WE CONTACTED PROFESSOR XAVIER, HE HAD THE CAPABILITY TO AMPLIFY ONE OF OUR PROBES FOR THIS LONG-RANGE MENTAL SCAN.

OF COURSE HE DEMANDED TO BECOME THE FIRST "CEREBE-NAUT."

STILL, HE'S MADE SOME GOOD FINDS ALONG THE WAY, I GUESS.

CAN LIFE EXIST INSIDE A COMET?

NOT AS WE WOULD RECOGNIZE IT. HOPEFULLY YOUR TEACHER'S INCREDIBLE MIND WILL FIND WHAT OUR EQUIPMENT CAN'T.

THERE'S EVEN THE POSSIBILITY THAT WHAT ANSWERED OUR SIGNALS HAD A SHORT LIFESPAN AND IS ALREADY DEAD BY NOW.

I CAN'T PROJECT ANY FURTHER, IT'S LEAVING ME...

THE PROBE IS DRIFTING OUT OF RANGE.

PROFESSOR XAVIER, YOU MAY NEED TO BREAK YOUR CONNECTION BEFORE--

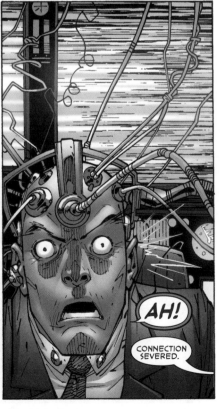

AH!

CONNECTION SEVERED.

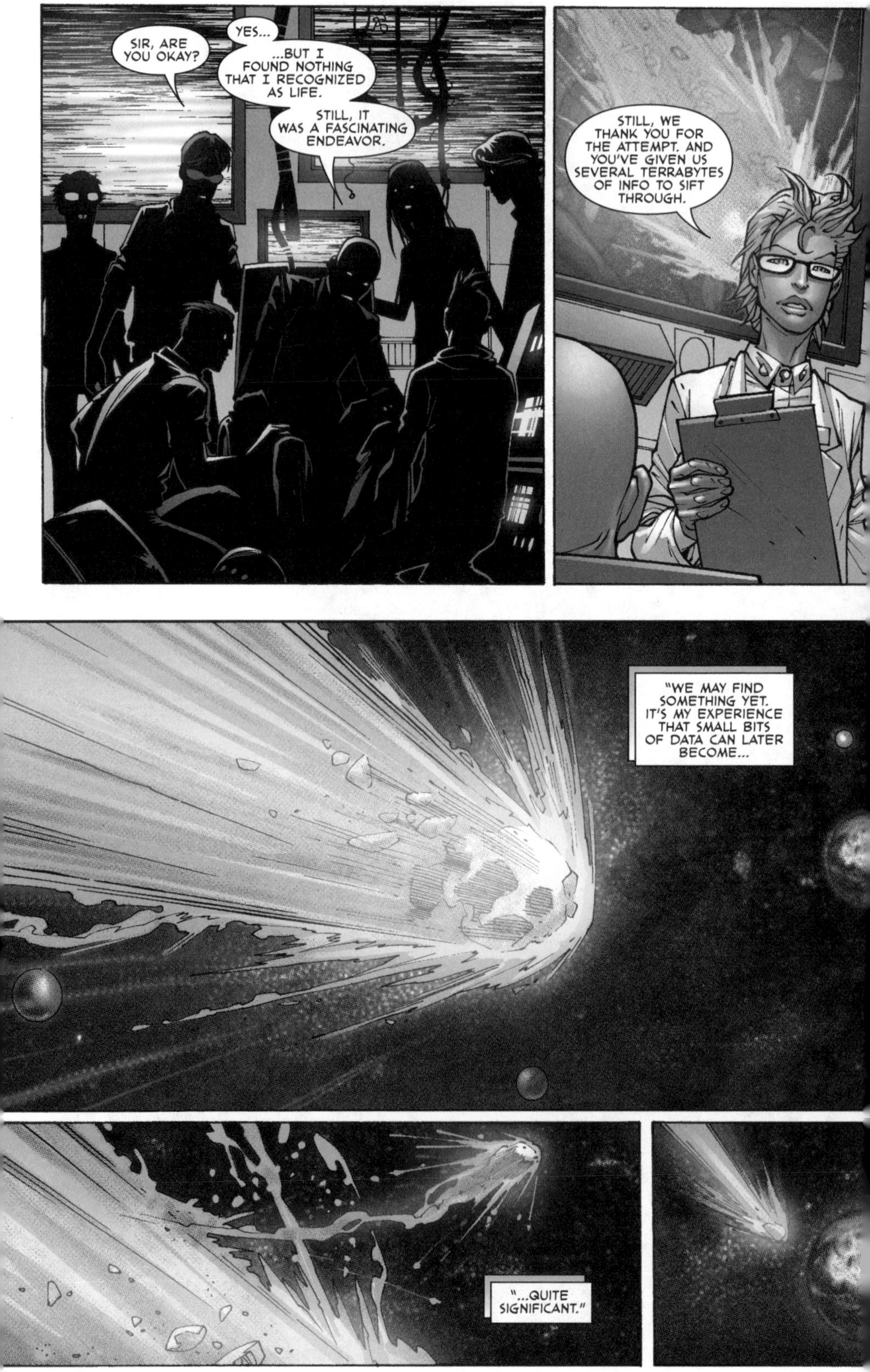
SIR, ARE YOU OKAY?
YES...
...BUT I FOUND NOTHING THAT I RECOGNIZED AS LIFE.
STILL, IT WAS A FASCINATING ENDEAVOR.
STILL, WE THANK YOU FOR THE ATTEMPT. AND YOU'VE GIVEN US SEVERAL TERRABYTES OF INFO TO SIFT THROUGH.
"WE MAY FIND SOMETHING YET. IT'S MY EXPERIENCE THAT SMALL BITS OF DATA CAN LATER BECOME...
"...QUITE SIGNIFICANT."

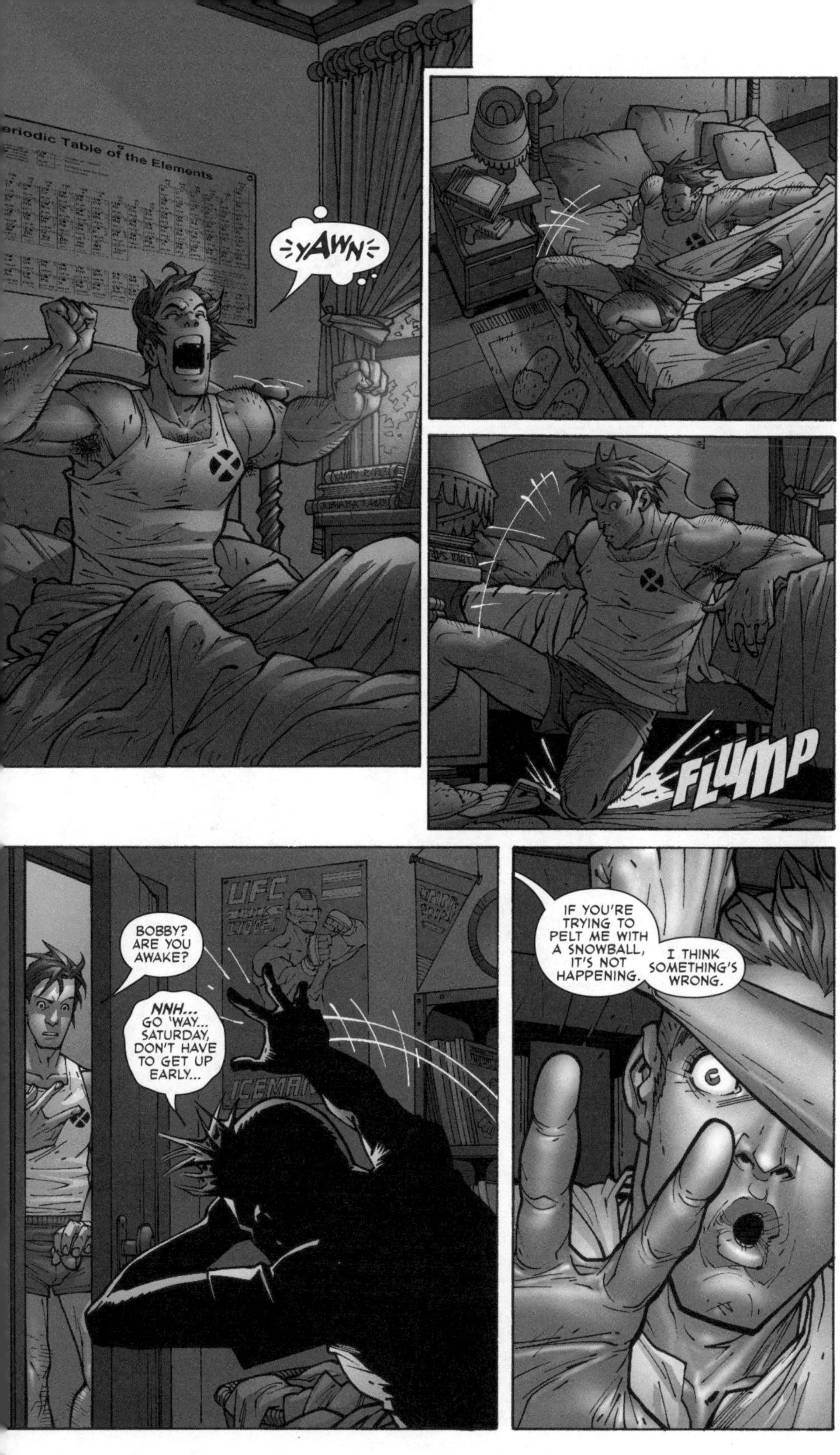

Periodic Table of the Elements
YAWN
FLUMP
UFC
ICEMAN
BOBBY? ARE YOU AWAKE?
NNH... GO 'WAY... SATURDAY, DON'T HAVE TO GET UP EARLY...
IF YOU'RE TRYING TO PELT ME WITH A SNOWBALL, IT'S NOT HAPPENING.
I THINK SOMETHING'S WRONG.

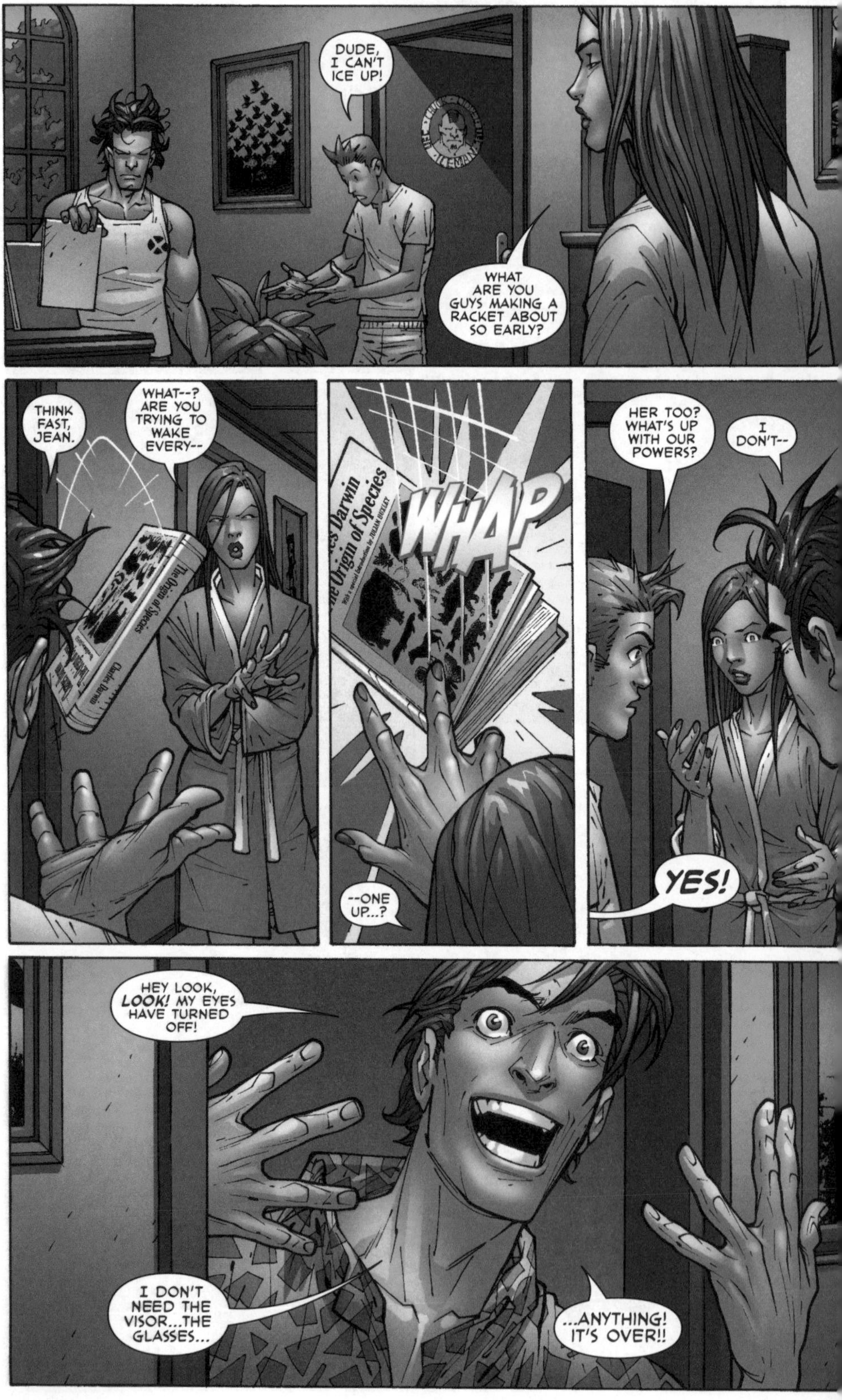
DUDE, I CAN'T ICE UP!
WHAT ARE YOU GUYS MAKING A RACKET ABOUT SO EARLY?
THINK FAST, JEAN.
WHAT--? ARE YOU TRYING TO WAKE EVERY--
The Origin of Species
Charles Darwin
WHAP
--ONE UP...?
HER TOO? WHAT'S UP WITH OUR POWERS?
I DON'T--
YES!
HEY LOOK, LOOK! MY EYES HAVE TURNED OFF!
I DON'T NEED THE VISOR...THE GLASSES...
...ANYTHING! IT'S OVER!!

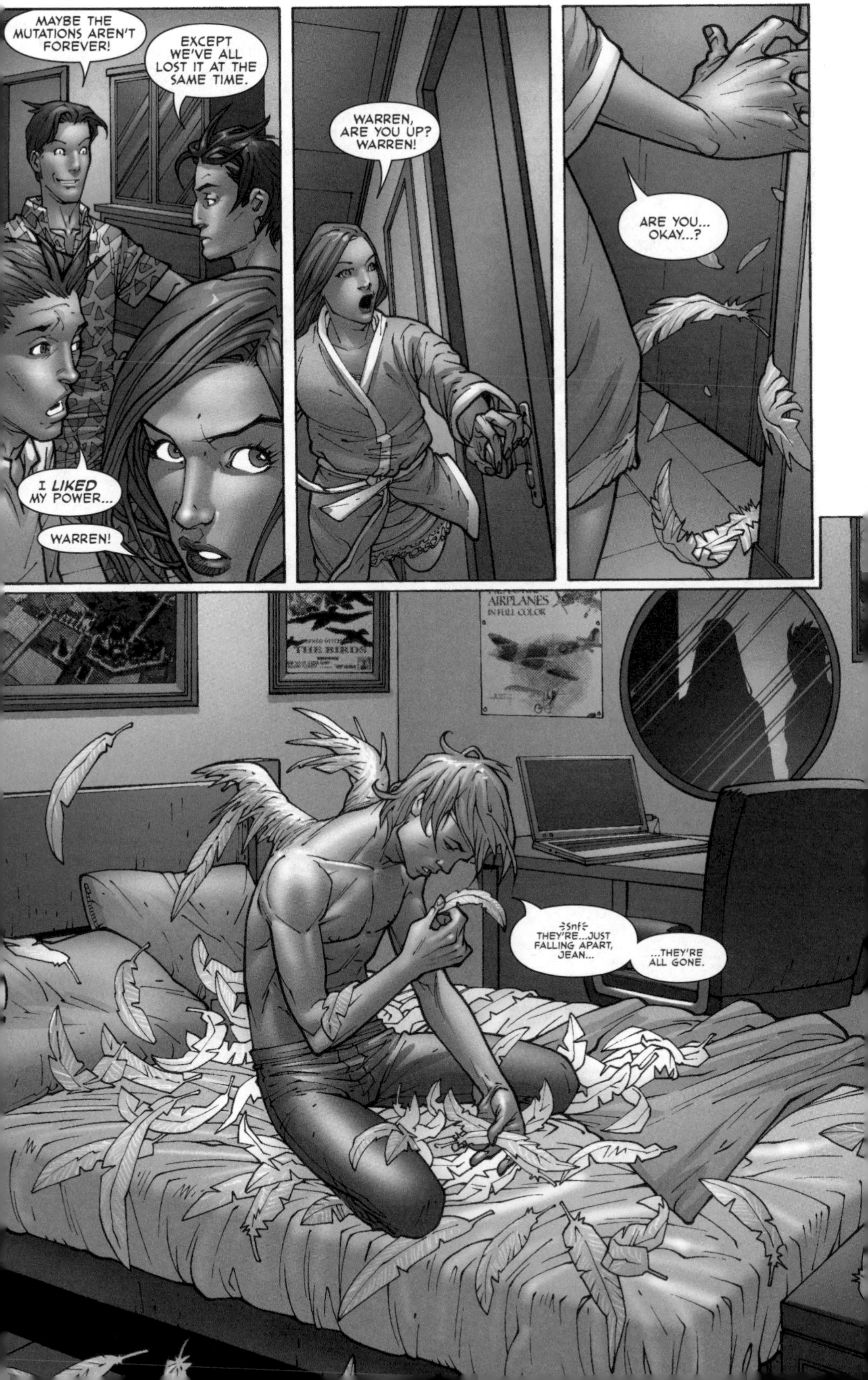
MAYBE THE MUTATIONS AREN'T FOREVER!
EXCEPT WE'VE ALL LOST IT AT THE SAME TIME.
I LIKED MY POWER...
WARREN!
WARREN, ARE YOU UP? WARREN!
ARE YOU... OKAY...?
AIRPLANES IN FULL COLOR
THE BIRDS
Snf THEY'RE...JUST FALLING APART, JEAN...
...THEY'RE ALL GONE.

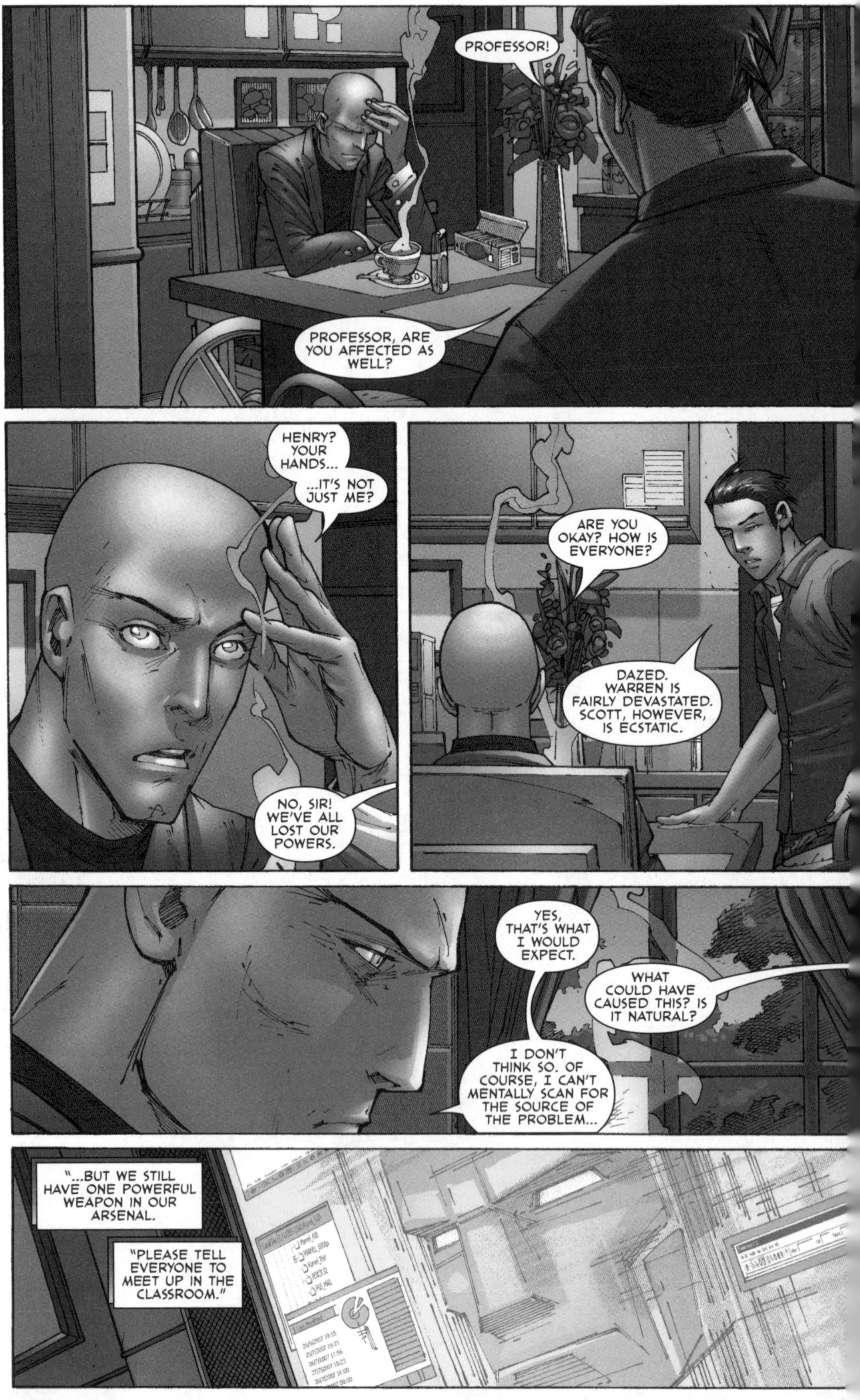
PROFESSOR!
PROFESSOR, ARE YOU AFFECTED AS WELL?
HENRY? YOUR HANDS...
...IT'S NOT JUST ME?
NO, SIR! WE'VE ALL LOST OUR POWERS.
ARE YOU OKAY? HOW IS EVERYONE?
DAZED. WARREN IS FAIRLY DEVASTATED. SCOTT, HOWEVER, IS ECSTATIC.
YES, THAT'S WHAT I WOULD EXPECT.
WHAT COULD HAVE CAUSED THIS? IS IT NATURAL?
I DON'T THINK SO. OF COURSE, I CAN'T MENTALLY SCAN FOR THE SOURCE OF THE PROBLEM...
"...BUT WE STILL HAVE ONE POWERFUL WEAPON IN OUR ARSENAL.
"PLEASE TELL EVERYONE TO MEET UP IN THE CLASSROOM."

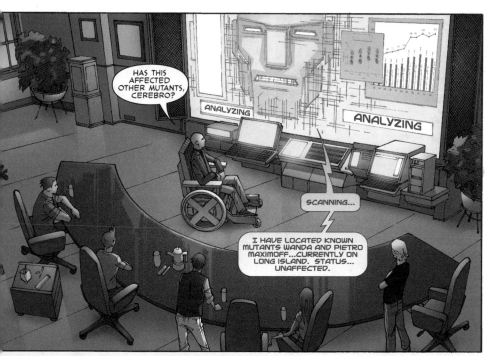

HAS THIS AFFECTED OTHER MUTANTS, CEREBRO?

ANALYZING

ANALYZING

SCANNING...

I HAVE LOCATED KNOWN MUTANTS WANDA AND PIETRO MAXIMOFF...CURRENTLY ON LONG ISLAND. STATUS... UNAFFECTED.

THEN IT'S A LOCAL PHENOMENON.

CAN YOU DETERMINE ANY SOURCE THAT MAY HAVE AFFECTED OUR GENETICS?

I WANT YOU TO DEVOTE ALL PROCESSORS SOLELY TO THIS, AND ANALYZE ALL AVAILABLE DATA PERTINENT TO LAST NIGHT.

CEREBRO HAS NO APPROPRIATE DATA.

SYSTEMS REGISTERED NO UNUSUAL ACTIVITY DURING THE NIGHT...

...RE-ANALYZING DATA...

RE-ANALYZING

CEREBRO JUST ISN'T DESIGNED FOR THIS. IT'S MY FAULT, I'VE GEARED ALL OF HIS SYSTEMS TOWARDS MUTANT DETECTION.

I CAN'T THINK OF ANY OF OUR ENEMIES WHO COULD PULL THIS OFF.

THE SCARIER THING IS THAT IT MAY NOT INVOLVE ENEMIES AT ALL.

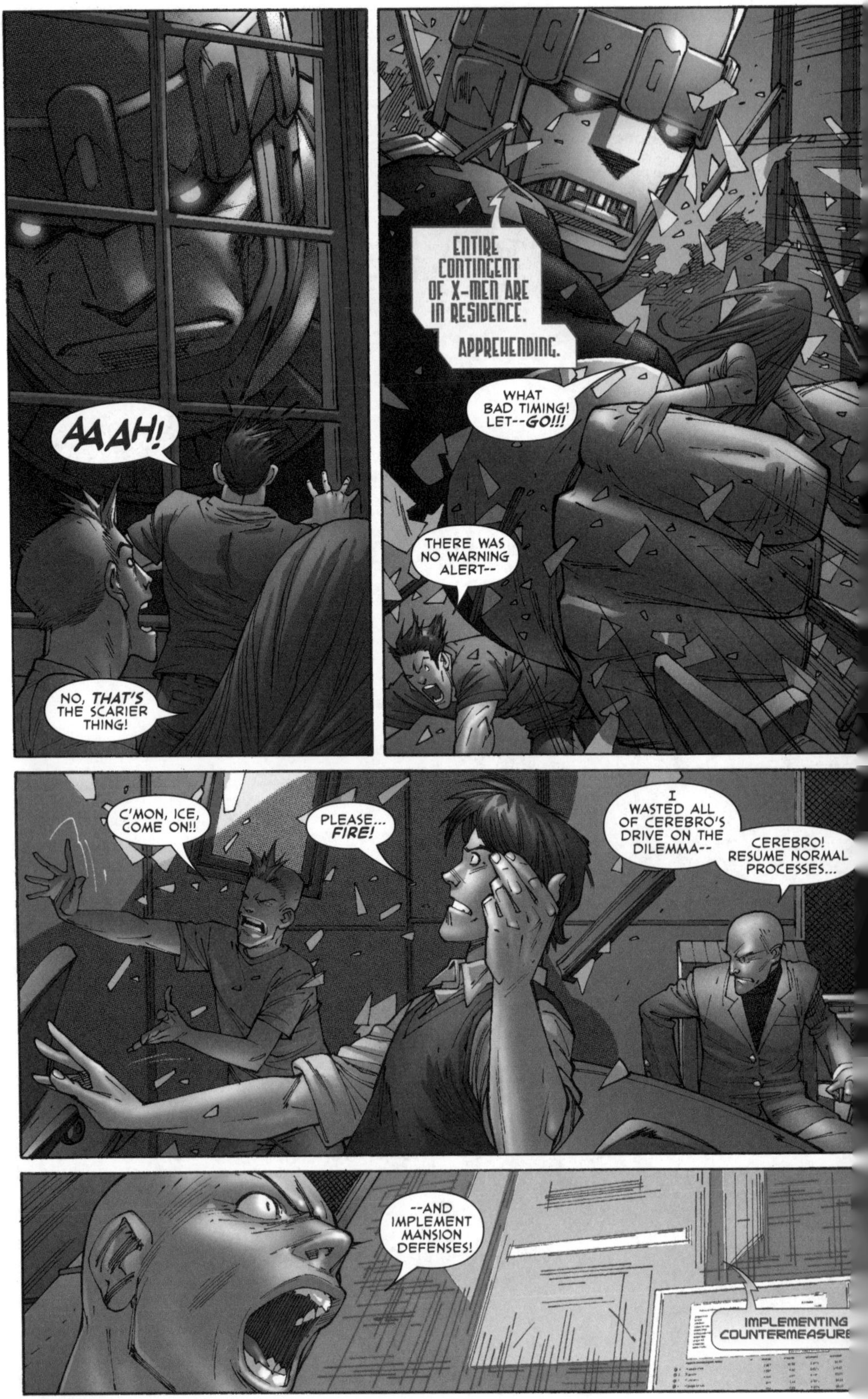

AAAH!
NO, THAT'S THE SCARIER THING!
ENTIRE CONTINGENT OF X-MEN ARE IN RESIDENCE.
APPREHENDING.
WHAT BAD TIMING! LET--GO!!!
THERE WAS NO WARNING ALERT--
C'MON, ICE, COME ON!!
PLEASE... FIRE!
I WASTED ALL OF CEREBRO'S DRIVE ON THE DILEMMA--
CEREBRO! RESUME NORMAL PROCESSES...
--AND IMPLEMENT MANSION DEFENSES!
IMPLEMENTING COUNTERMEASURE

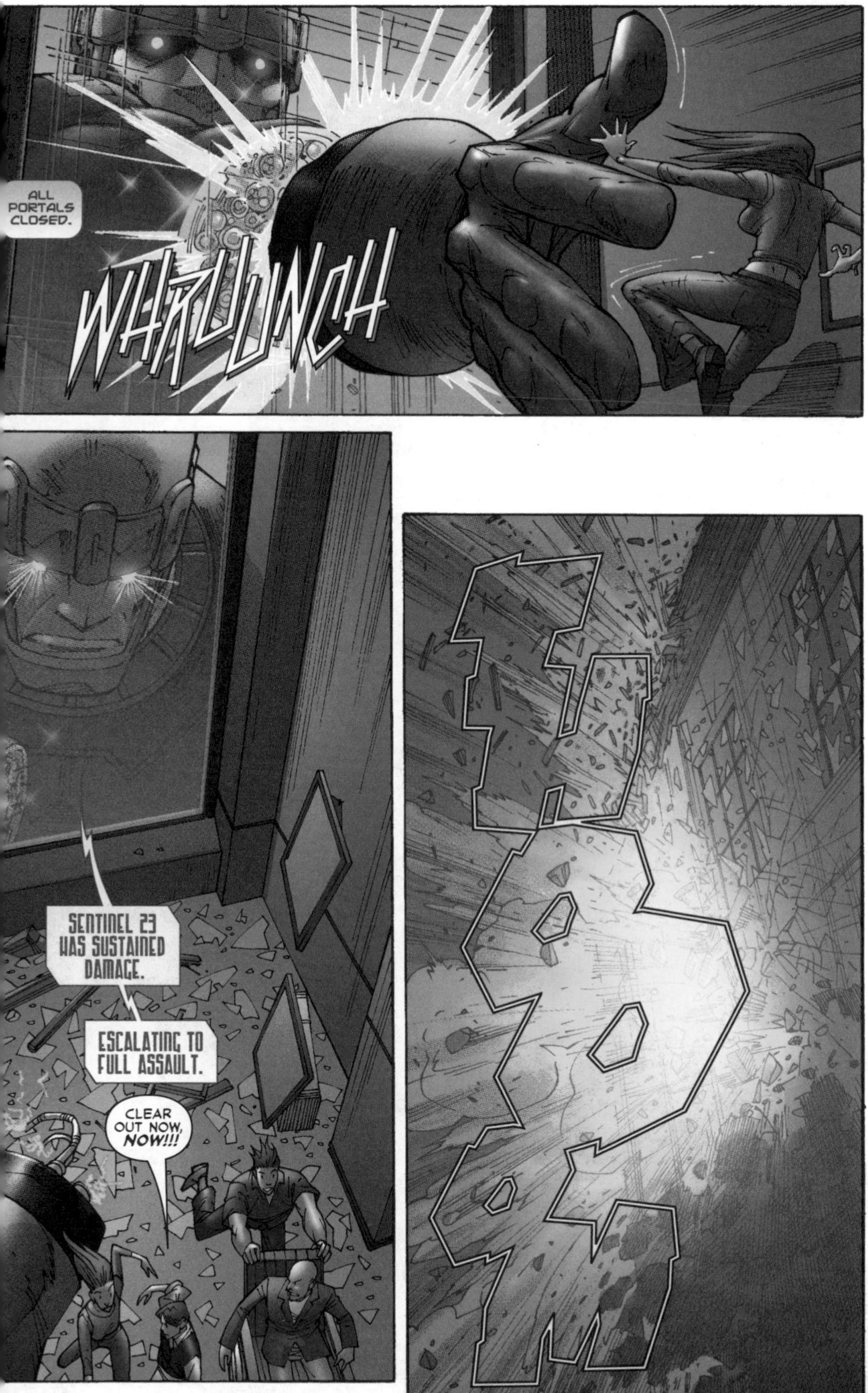
ALL PORTALS CLOSED.
WHRUUNCH
SENTINEL 23 HAS SUSTAINED DAMAGE.
ESCALATING TO FULL ASSAULT.
CLEAR OUT NOW, NOW!!!

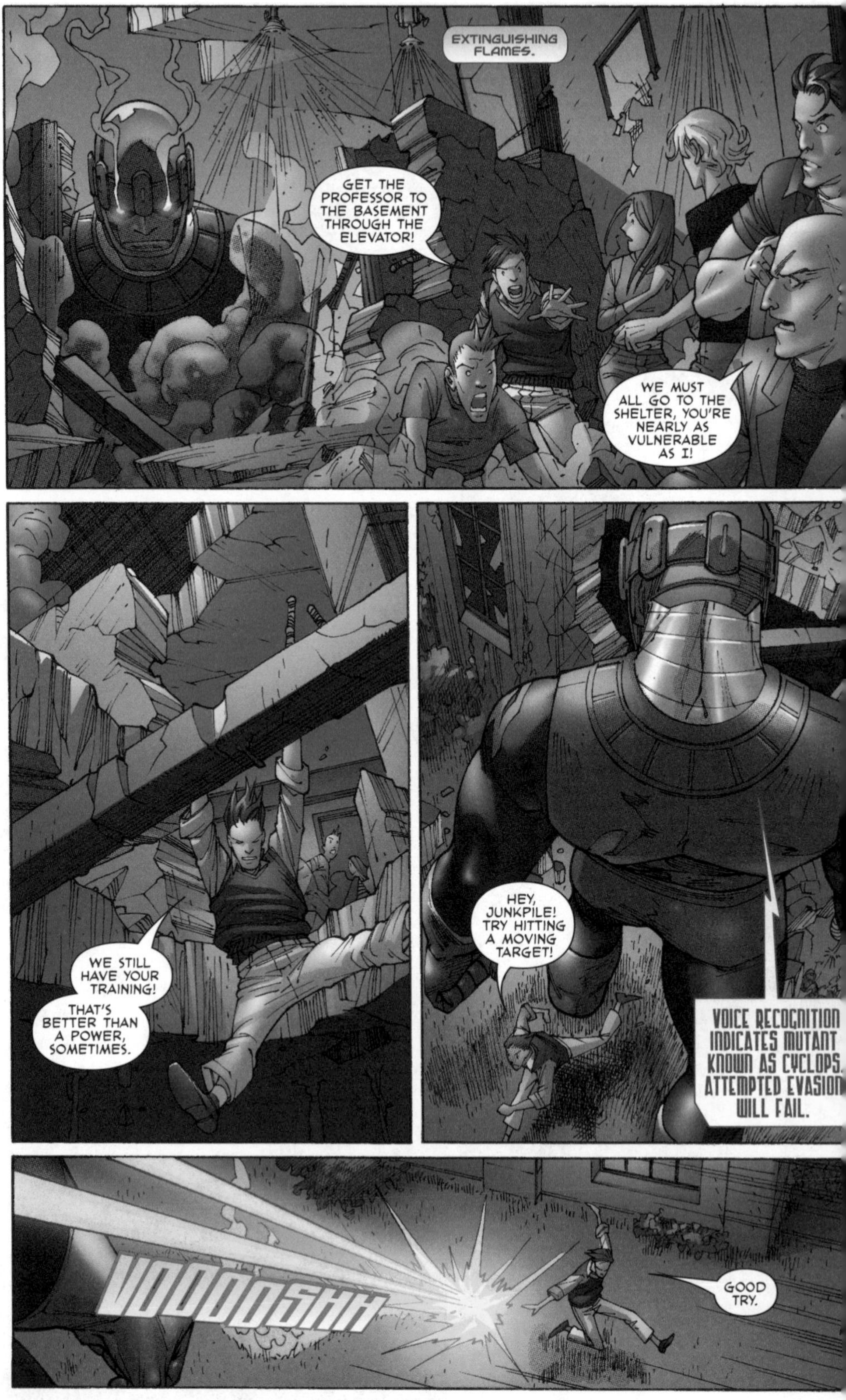
EXTINGUISHING FLAMES.
GET THE PROFESSOR TO THE BASEMENT THROUGH THE ELEVATOR!
WE MUST ALL GO TO THE SHELTER, YOU'RE NEARLY AS VULNERABLE AS I!
WE STILL HAVE YOUR TRAINING!
THAT'S BETTER THAN A POWER, SOMETIMES.
HEY, JUNKPILE! TRY HITTING A MOVING TARGET!
VOICE RECOGNITION INDICATES MUTANT KNOWN AS CYCLOPS. ATTEMPTED EVASION WILL FAIL.
VOOOOSHH
GOOD TRY.

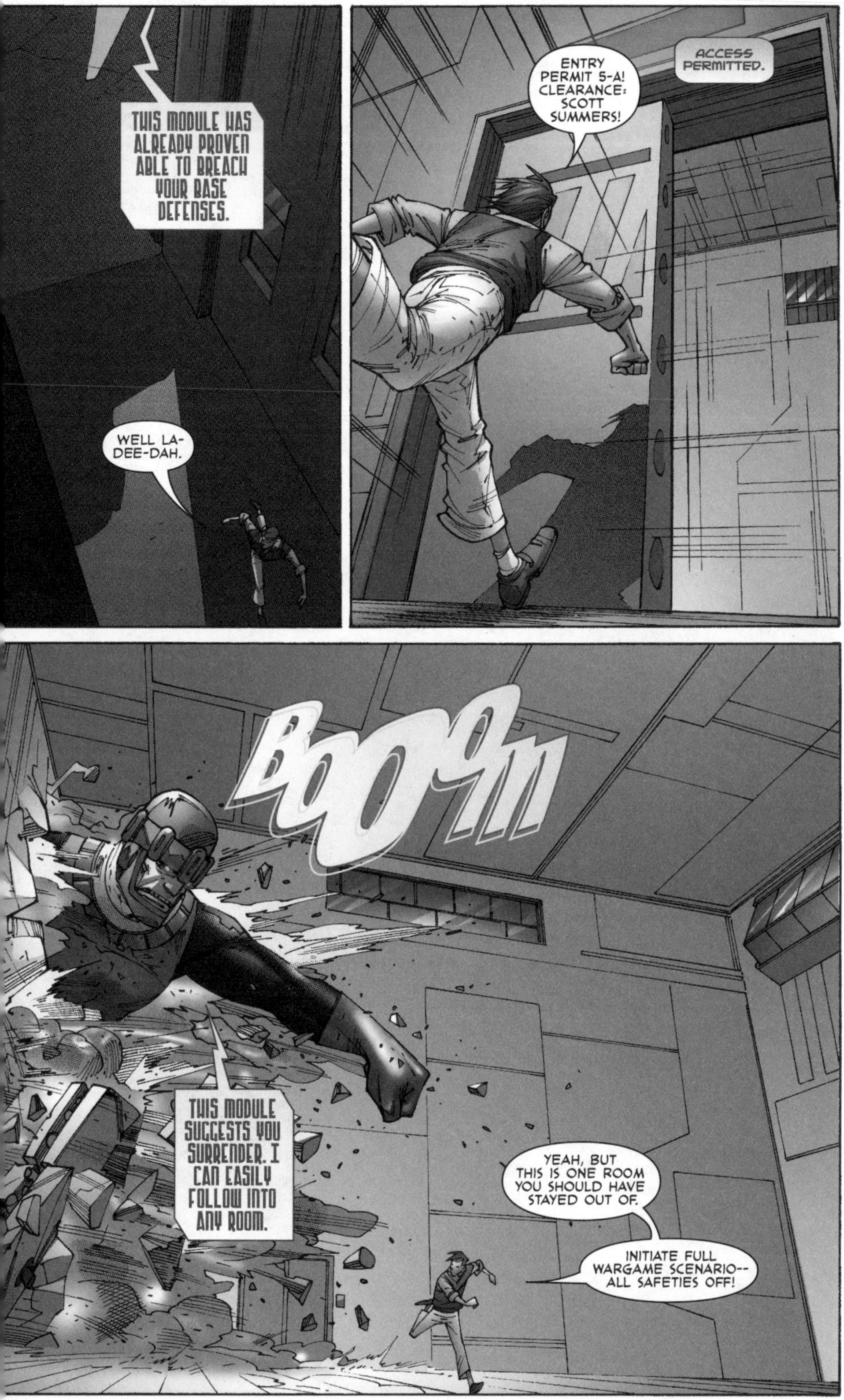

THIS MODULE HAS ALREADY PROVEN ABLE TO BREACH YOUR BASE DEFENSES.
WELL LA-DEE-DAH.
ENTRY PERMIT 5-A! CLEARANCE: SCOTT SUMMERS!
ACCESS PERMITTED.
BOOOM
THIS MODULE SUGGESTS YOU SURRENDER. I CAN EASILY FOLLOW INTO ANY ROOM.
YEAH, BUT THIS IS ONE ROOM YOU SHOULD HAVE STAYED OUT OF.
INITIATE FULL WARGAME SCENARIO--ALL SAFETIES OFF!

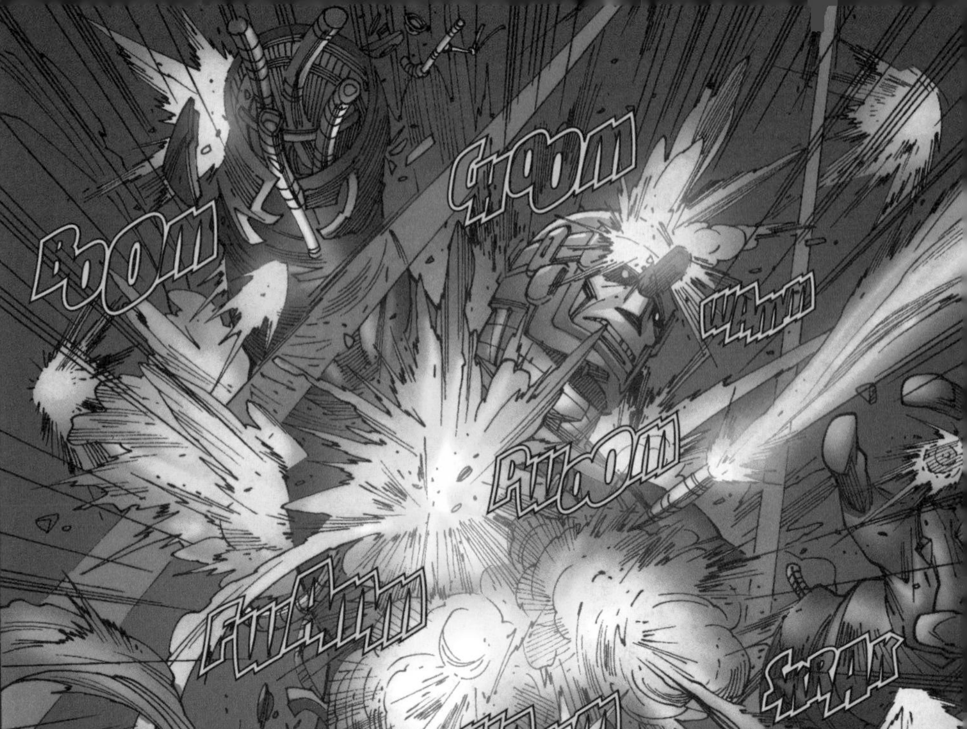
BOOM
GROOM
WAMM
FWOOM
FWAMM
SKRAK
WAMM
IF YOU'RE STILL RECORDING DATA ON US, WE CALL THIS...
...THE DANGER ROOM.

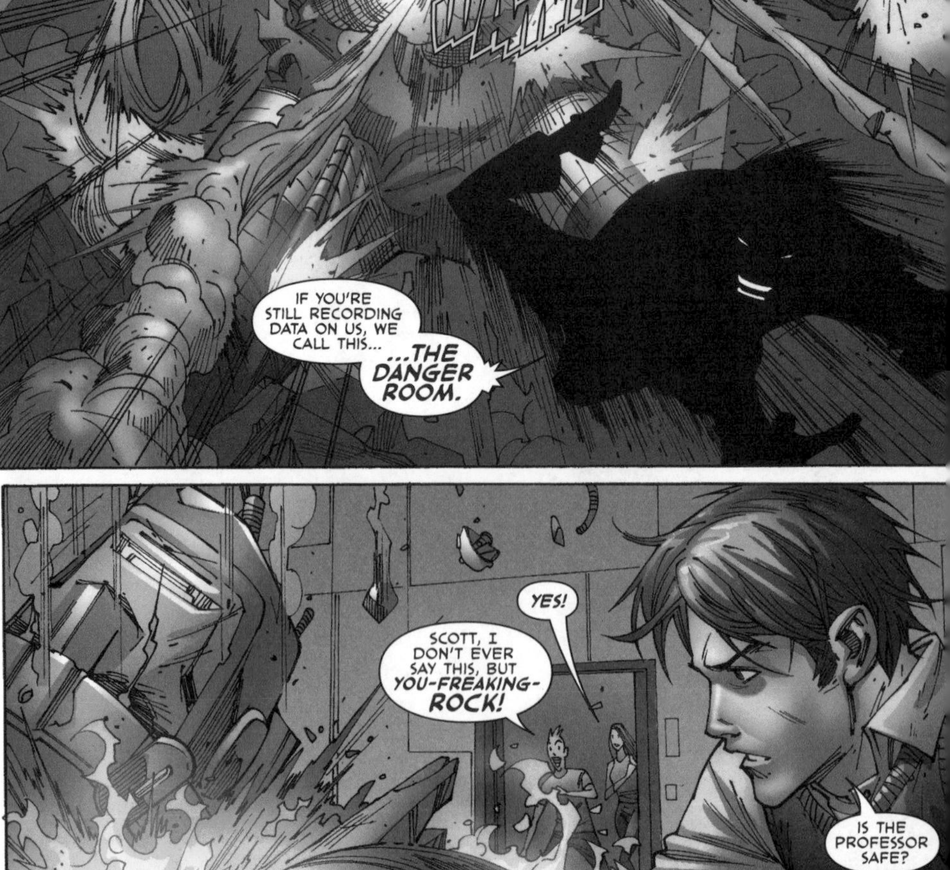
YES!
SCOTT, I DON'T EVER SAY THIS, BUT YOU-FREAKING-ROCK!
IS THE PROFESSOR SAFE?

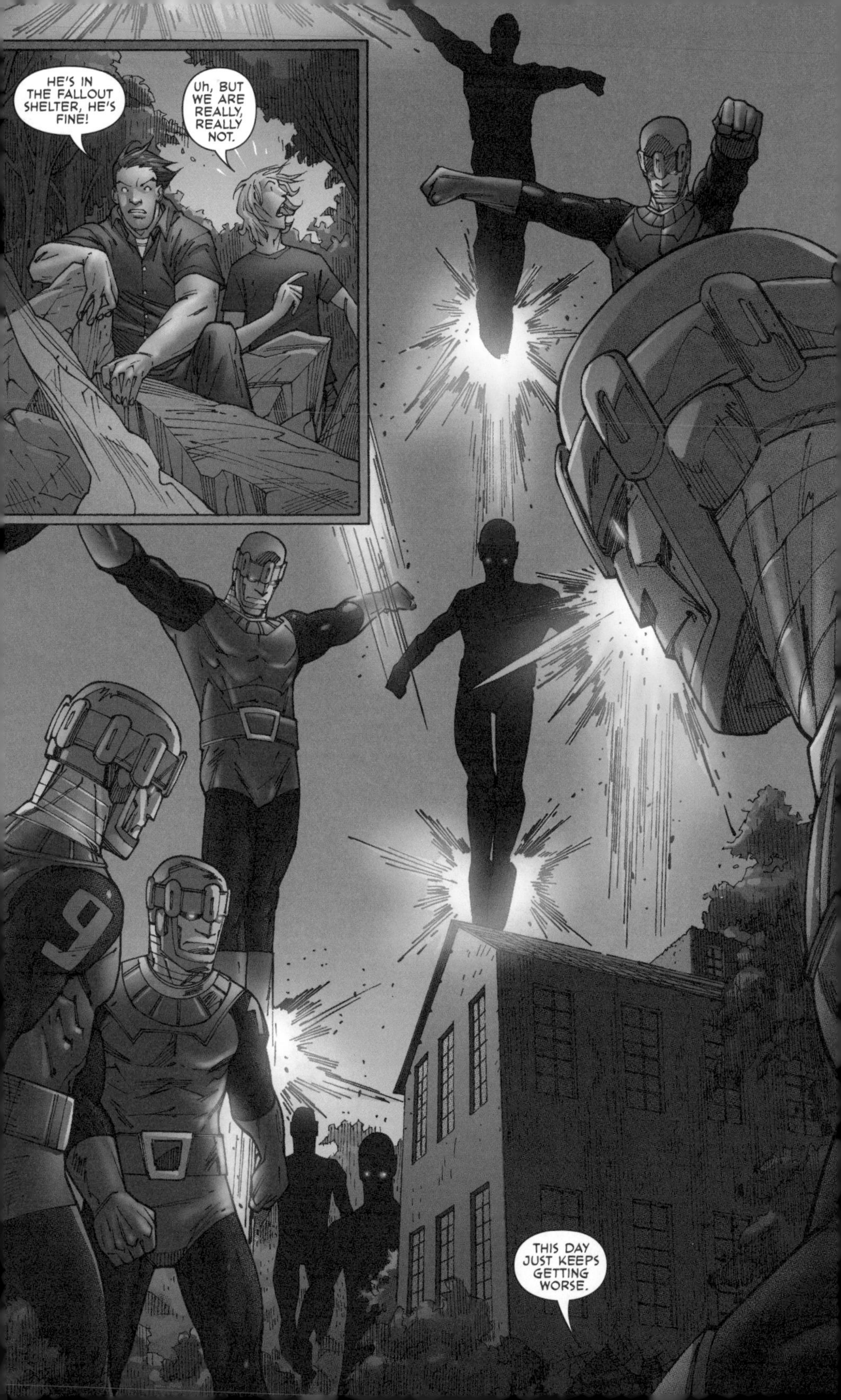
HE'S IN THE FALLOUT SHELTER, HE'S FINE!
Uh, BUT WE ARE REALLY, REALLY NOT.
THIS DAY JUST KEEPS GETTING WORSE.

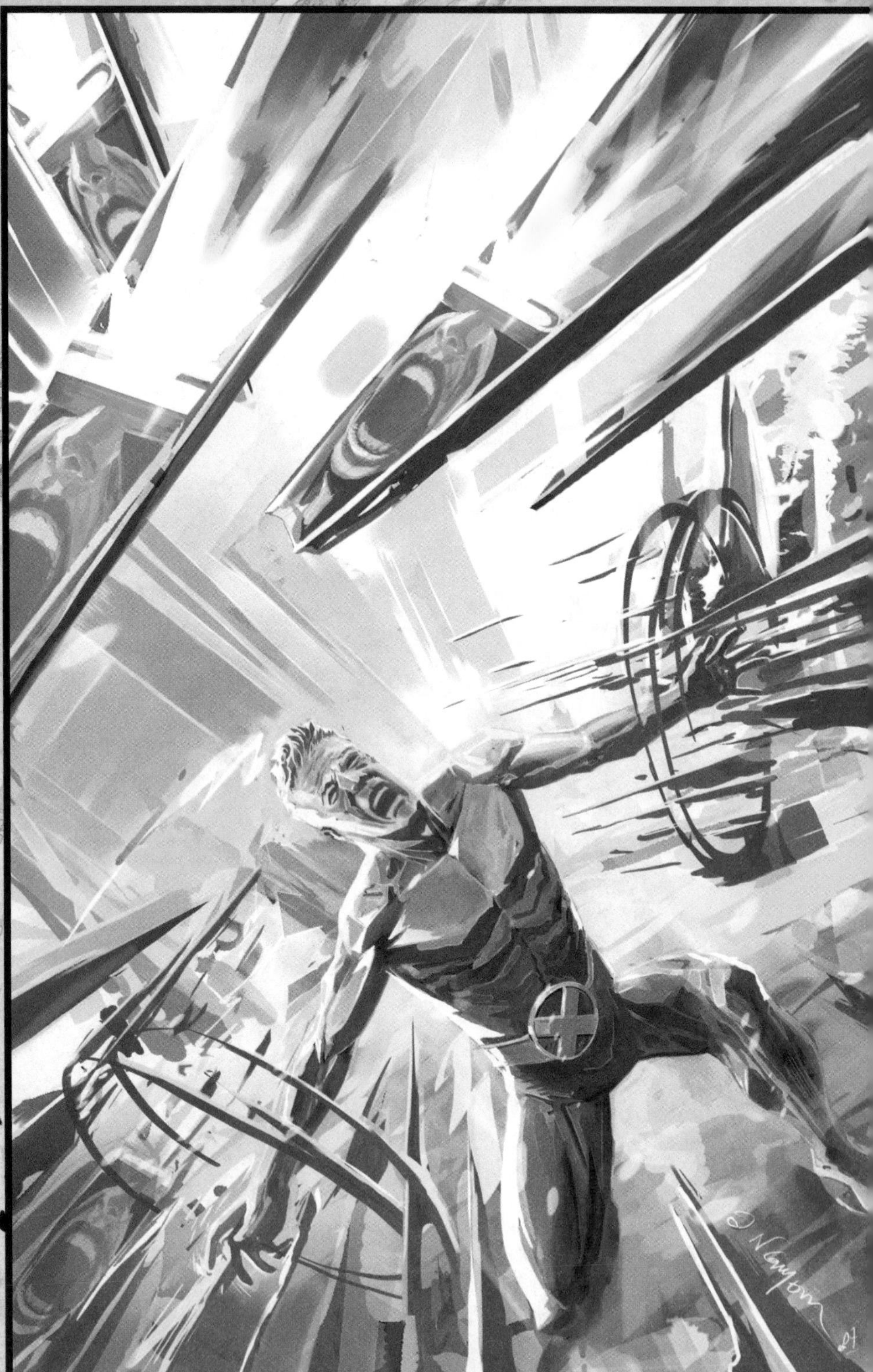

X-Men: First Class (2007) **#7**

# -MEN vs. SENTINELS: A COMPARATIVE ANALYSIS

by Henry P. McCoy

**THE X-MEN vs.**
**A SENTINEL (IN THE OFF POSITION)**

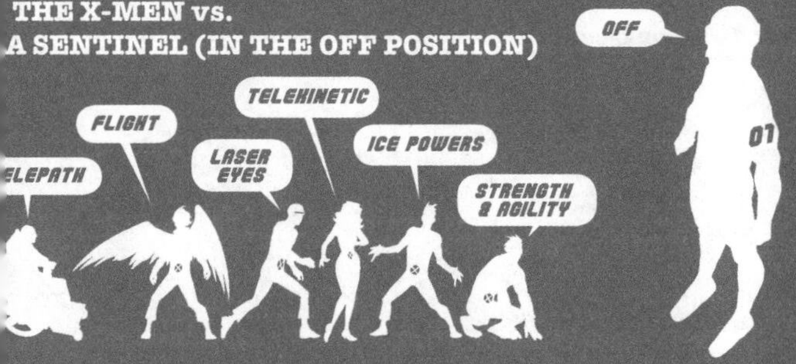

OFF
TELEKINETIC
FLIGHT
ICE POWERS
LASER EYES
ELEPATH
STRENGTH & AGILITY
01


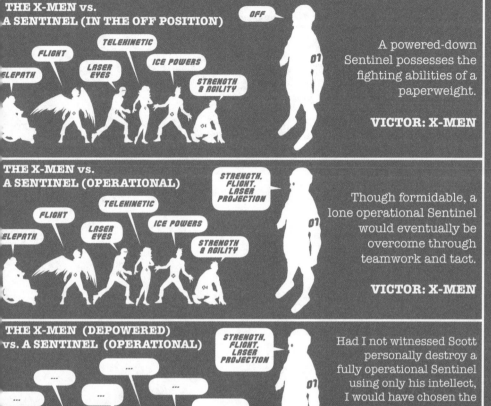

A powered-down Sentinel possesses the fighting abilities of a paperweight.

**VICTOR: X-MEN**

**THE X-MEN vs.**
**A SENTINEL (OPERATIONAL)**

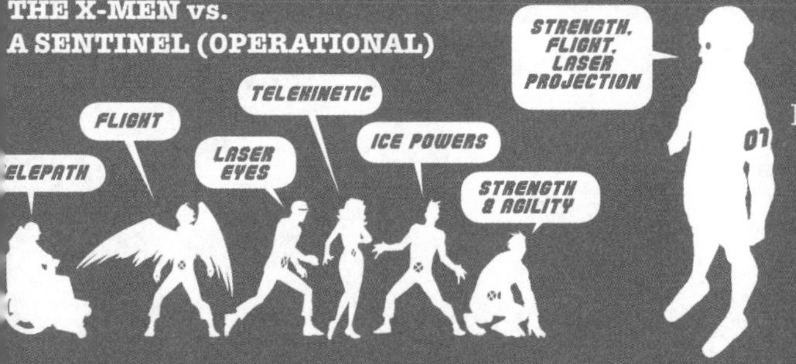

STRENGTH, FLIGHT, LASER PROJECTION
TELEKINETIC
FLIGHT
LASER EYES
ICE POWERS
ELEPATH
STRENGTH & AGILITY
01


Though formidable, a lone operational Sentinel would eventually be overcome through teamwork and tact.

**VICTOR: X-MEN**

**THE X-MEN (DEPOWERED)**
**vs. A SENTINEL (OPERATIONAL)**

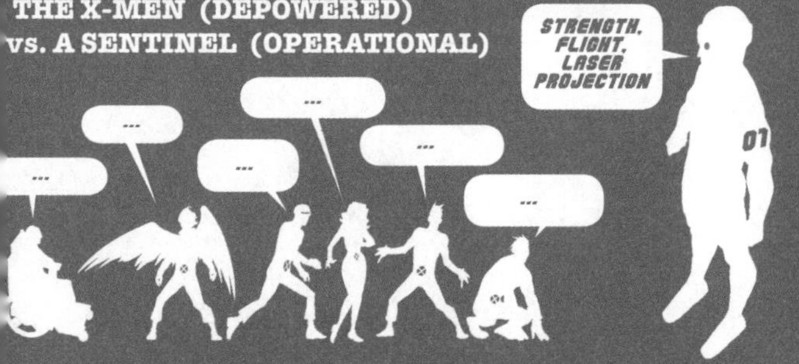

STRENGTH, FLIGHT, LASER PROJECTION
...
...
...
...
...
...
01


Had I not witnessed Scott personally destroy a fully operational Sentinel using only his intellect, I would have chosen the Sentinel. But theoreticals are postulated to be disproven...

**VICTOR: X-MEN**

**THE X-MEN (DEPOWERED)**
**vs. 99 SENTINELS (OPERATIONAL)**

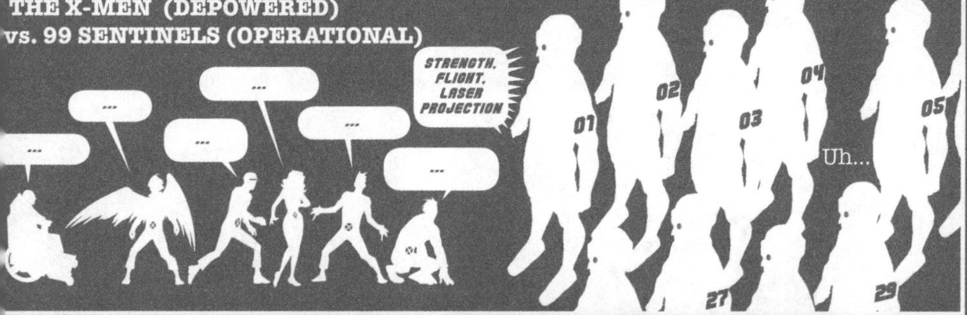

STRENGTH, FLIGHT, LASER PROJECTION
...
...
...
...
...
...
01
02
03
04
05
Uh...
27
29

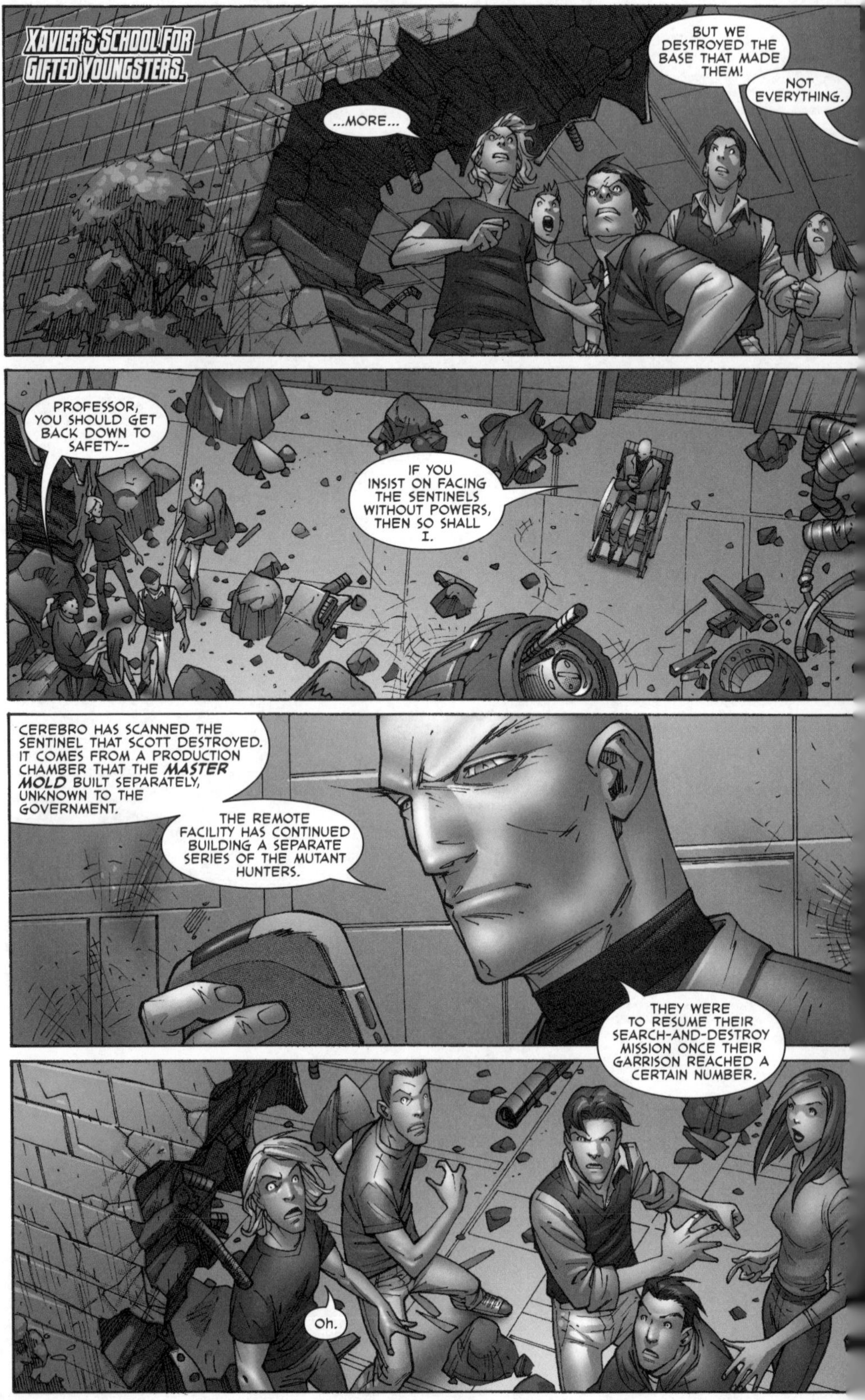
XAVIER'S SCHOOL FOR GIFTED YOUNGSTERS.
...MORE...
BUT WE DESTROYED THE BASE THAT MADE THEM!
NOT EVERYTHING.
PROFESSOR, YOU SHOULD GET BACK DOWN TO SAFETY--
IF YOU INSIST ON FACING THE SENTINELS WITHOUT POWERS, THEN SO SHALL I.
CEREBRO HAS SCANNED THE SENTINEL THAT SCOTT DESTROYED. IT COMES FROM A PRODUCTION CHAMBER THAT THE MASTER MOLD BUILT SEPARATELY, UNKNOWN TO THE GOVERNMENT.
THE REMOTE FACILITY HAS CONTINUED BUILDING A SEPARATE SERIES OF THE MUTANT HUNTERS.
THEY WERE TO RESUME THEIR SEARCH-AND-DESTROY MISSION ONCE THEIR GARRISON REACHED A CERTAIN NUMBER.
Oh.

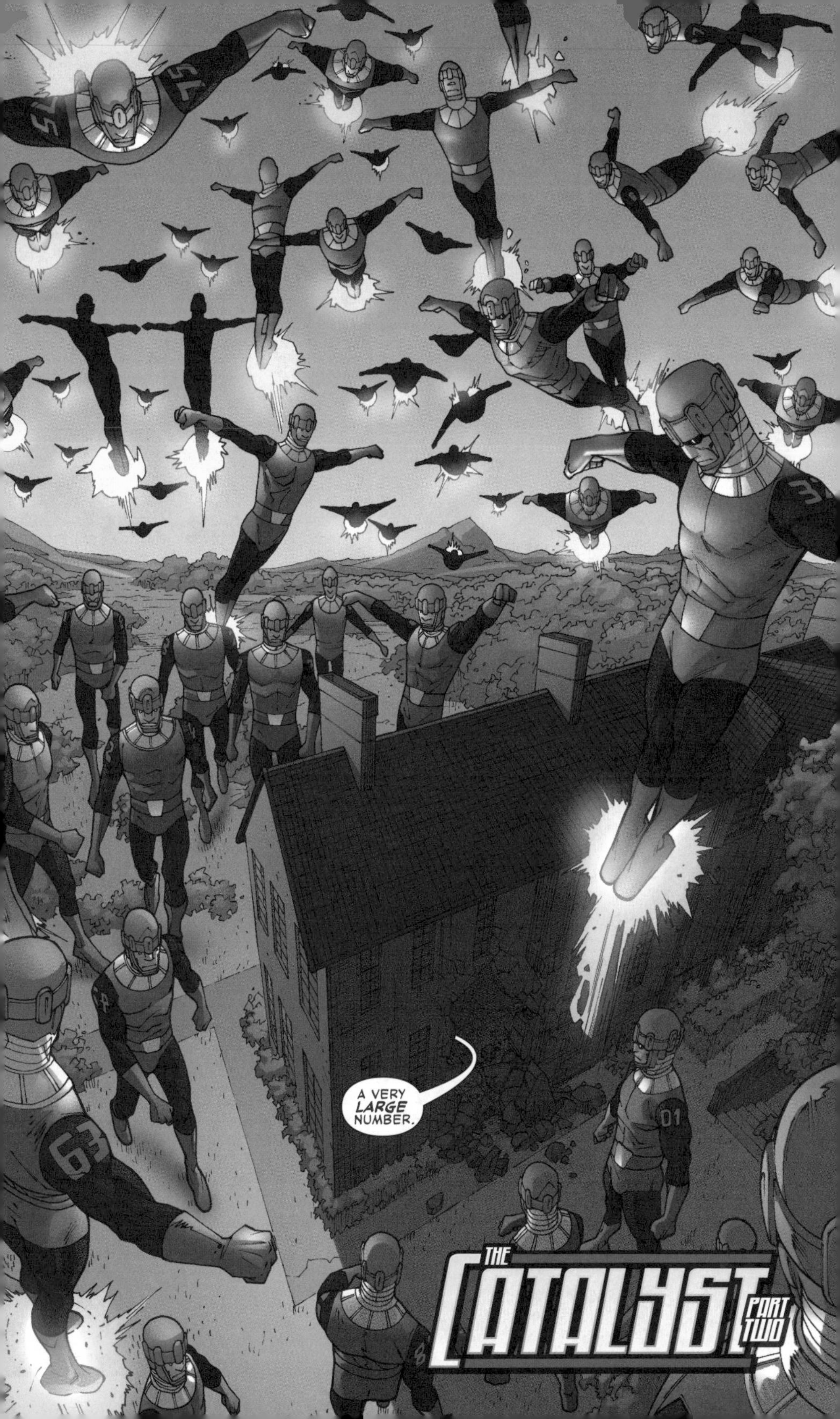
A VERY LARGE NUMBER.
THE CATALYST PART TWO

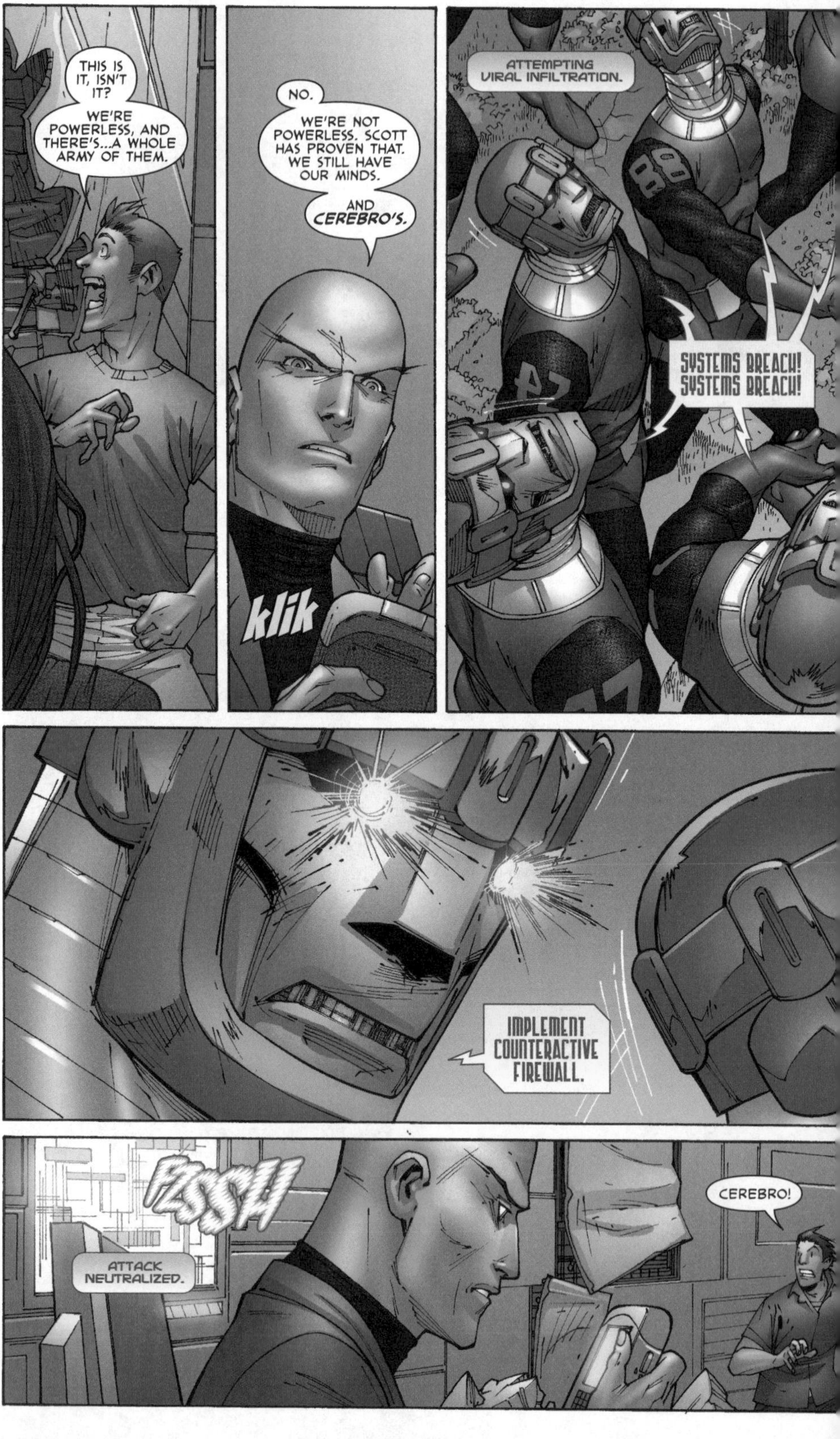
THIS IS IT, ISN'T IT?
WE'RE POWERLESS, AND THERE'S...A WHOLE ARMY OF THEM.
NO.
WE'RE NOT POWERLESS. SCOTT HAS PROVEN THAT. WE STILL HAVE OUR MINDS.
AND CEREBRO'S.
klik
ATTEMPTING VIRAL INFILTRATION.
SYSTEMS BREACH! SYSTEMS BREACH!
IMPLEMENT COUNTERACTIVE FIREWALL.
FZSSH
ATTACK NEUTRALIZED.
CEREBRO!

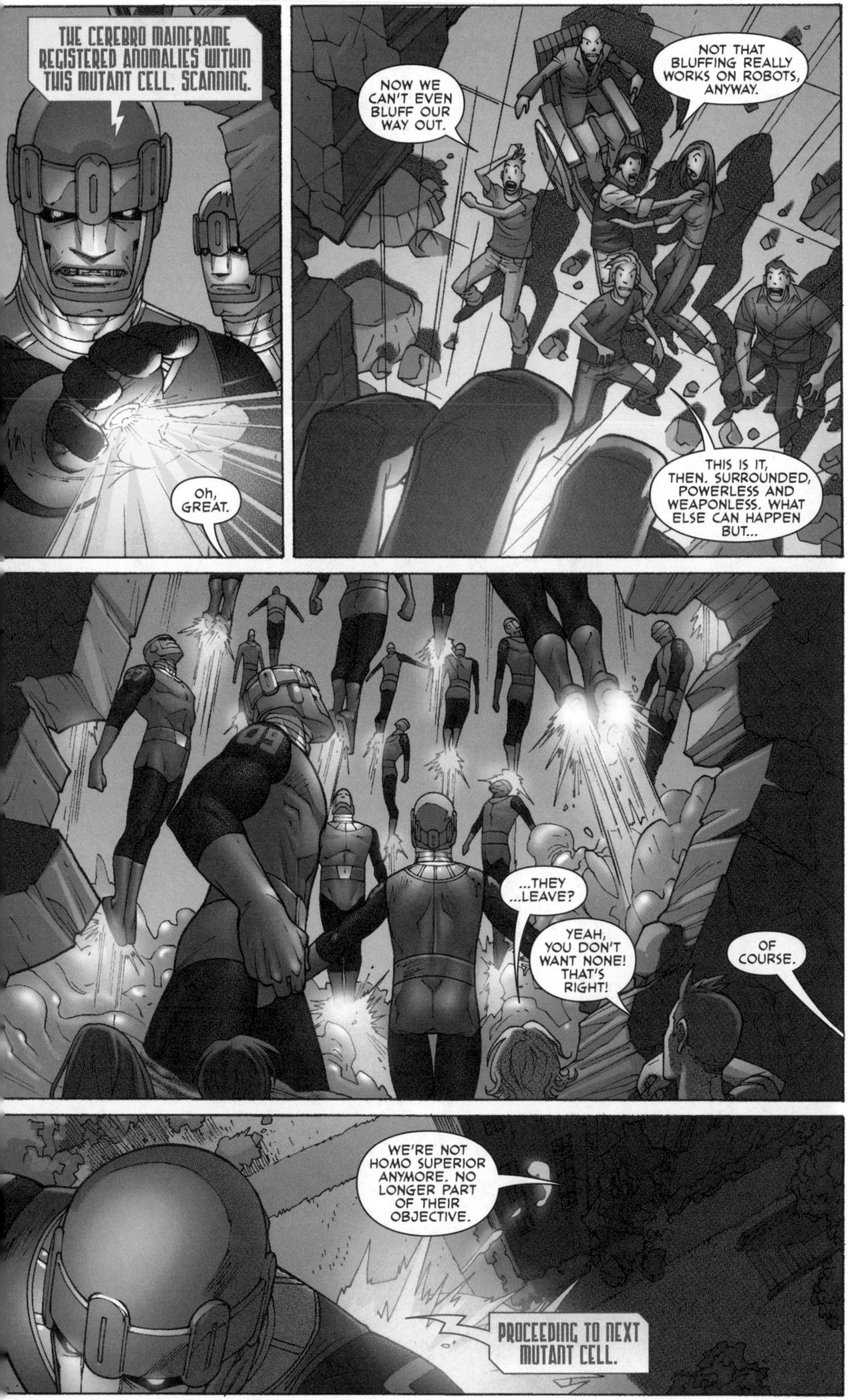

THE CEREBRO MAINFRAME REGISTERED ANOMALIES WITHIN THIS MUTANT CELL. SCANNING.
Oh, GREAT.
NOW WE CAN'T EVEN BLUFF OUR WAY OUT.
NOT THAT BLUFFING REALLY WORKS ON ROBOTS, ANYWAY.
THIS IS IT, THEN. SURROUNDED, POWERLESS AND WEAPONLESS. WHAT ELSE CAN HAPPEN BUT...
...THEY ...LEAVE?
YEAH, YOU DON'T WANT NONE! THAT'S RIGHT!
OF COURSE.
WE'RE NOT HOMO SUPERIOR ANYMORE. NO LONGER PART OF THEIR OBJECTIVE.
PROCEEDING TO NEXT MUTANT CELL.

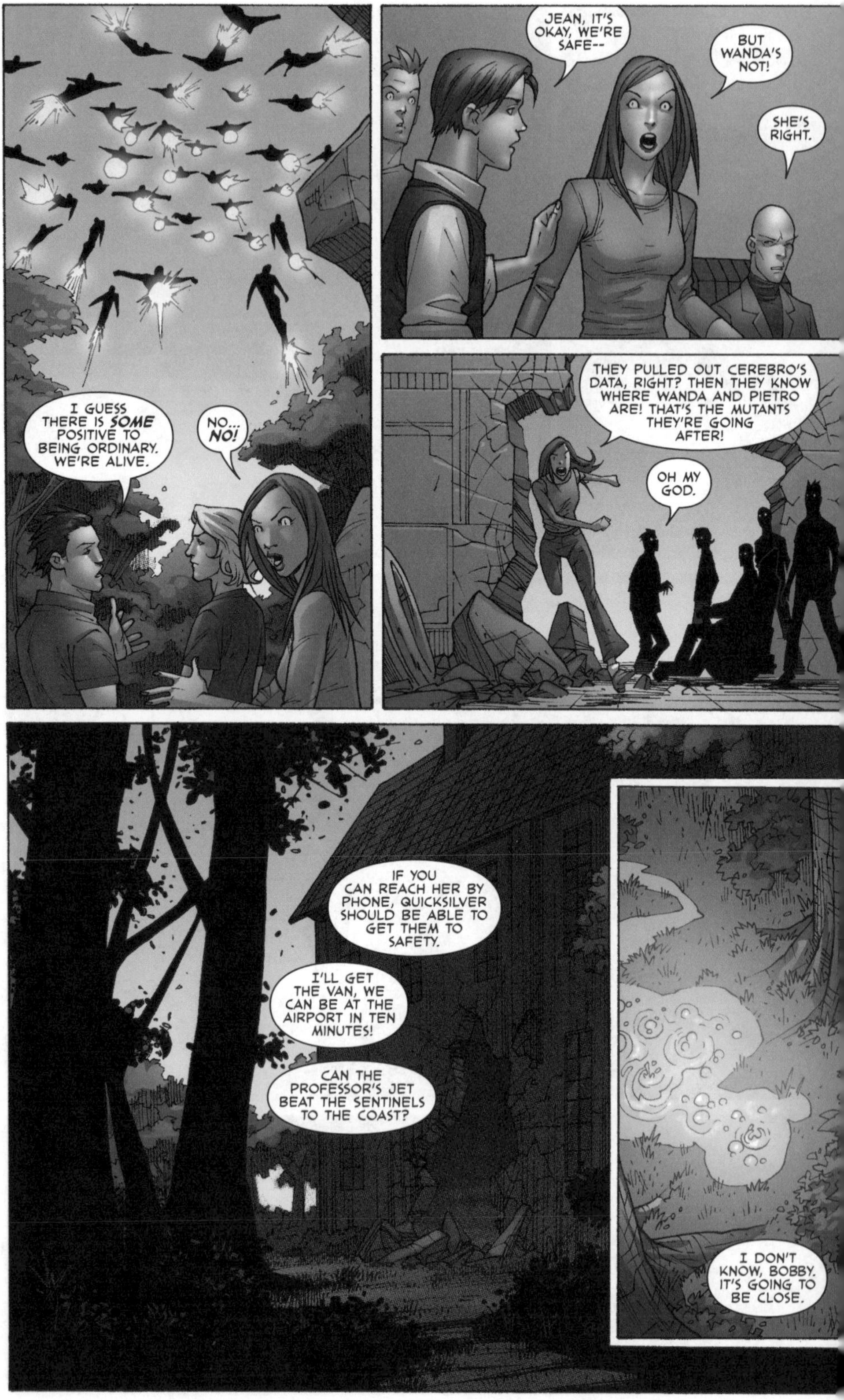
I GUESS THERE IS *SOME* POSITIVE TO BEING ORDINARY. WE'RE ALIVE.
NO... *NO!*
JEAN, IT'S OKAY, WE'RE SAFE--
BUT WANDA'S NOT!
SHE'S RIGHT.
THEY PULLED OUT CEREBRO'S DATA, RIGHT? THEN THEY KNOW WHERE WANDA AND PIETRO ARE! THAT'S THE MUTANTS THEY'RE GOING AFTER!
OH MY GOD.
IF YOU CAN REACH HER BY PHONE, QUICKSILVER SHOULD BE ABLE TO GET THEM TO SAFETY.
I'LL GET THE VAN, WE CAN BE AT THE AIRPORT IN TEN MINUTES!
CAN THE PROFESSOR'S JET BEAT THE SENTINELS TO THE COAST?
I DON'T KNOW, BOBBY. IT'S GOING TO BE CLOSE.

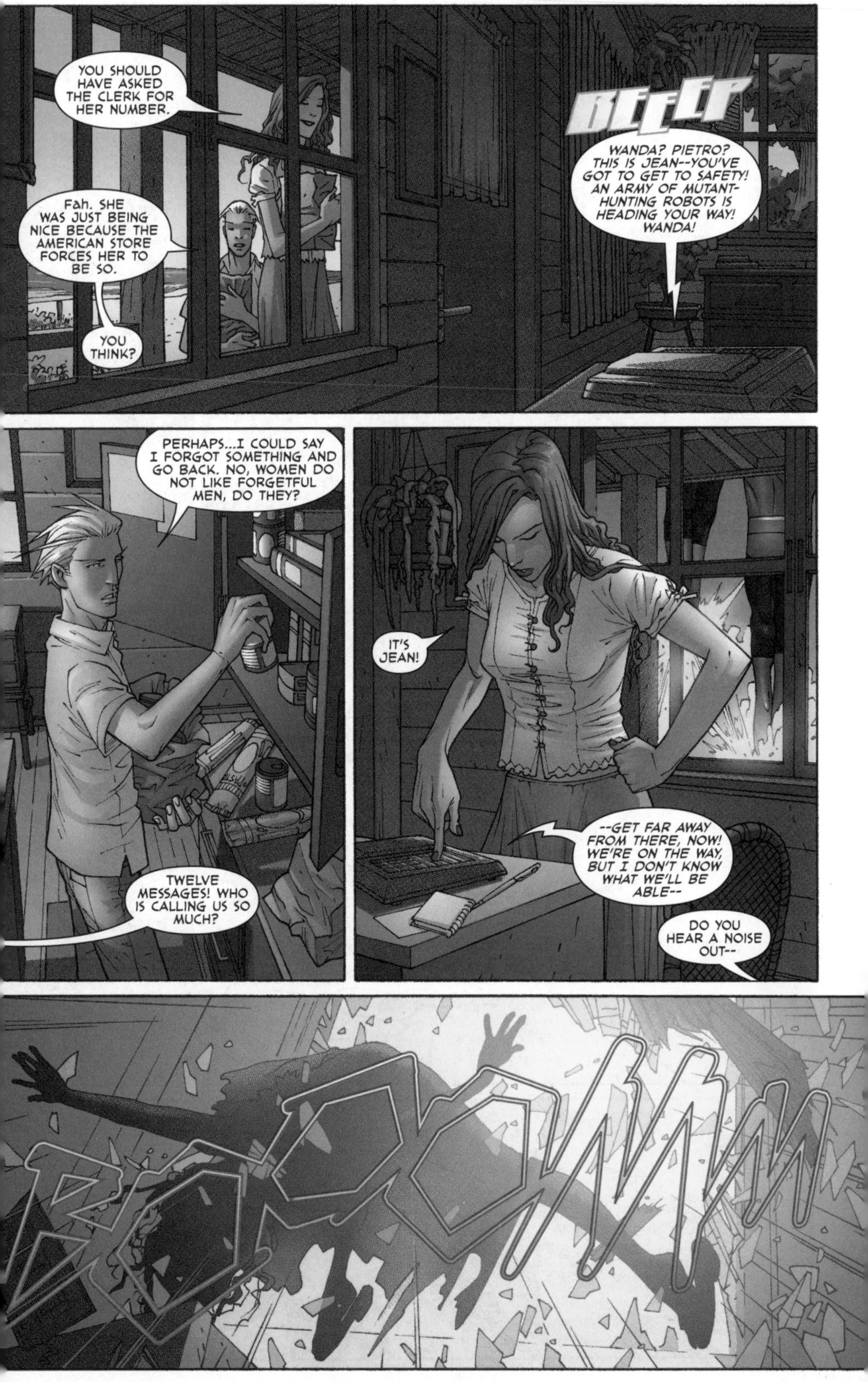

YOU SHOULD HAVE ASKED THE CLERK FOR HER NUMBER.
Fah. SHE WAS JUST BEING NICE BECAUSE THE AMERICAN STORE FORCES HER TO BE SO.
YOU THINK?
BEEEP
WANDA? PIETRO? THIS IS JEAN--YOU'VE GOT TO GET TO SAFETY! AN ARMY OF MUTANT-HUNTING ROBOTS IS HEADING YOUR WAY! WANDA!
PERHAPS...I COULD SAY I FORGOT SOMETHING AND GO BACK. NO, WOMEN DO NOT LIKE FORGETFUL MEN, DO THEY?
TWELVE MESSAGES! WHO IS CALLING US SO MUCH?
IT'S JEAN!
--GET FAR AWAY FROM THERE, NOW! WE'RE ON THE WAY, BUT I DON'T KNOW WHAT WE'LL BE ABLE--
DO YOU HEAR A NOISE OUT--
BOOOMMM

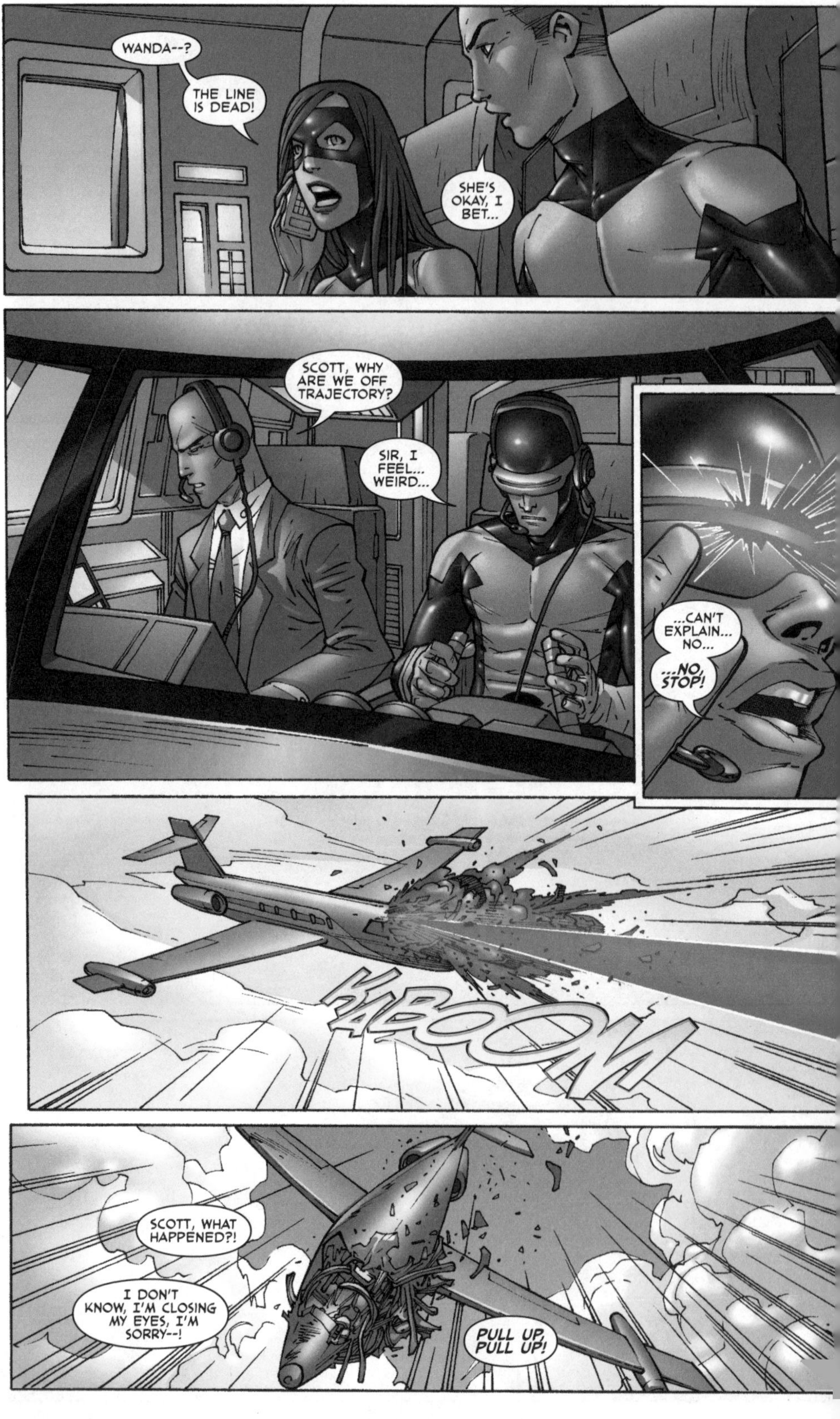
WANDA--?
THE LINE IS DEAD!
SHE'S OKAY, I BET...
SCOTT, WHY ARE WE OFF TRAJECTORY?
SIR, I FEEL... WEIRD...
...CAN'T EXPLAIN... NO...
...NO, STOP!
KABOOM
SCOTT, WHAT HAPPENED?!
I DON'T KNOW, I'M CLOSING MY EYES, I'M SORRY--!
PULL UP, PULL UP!

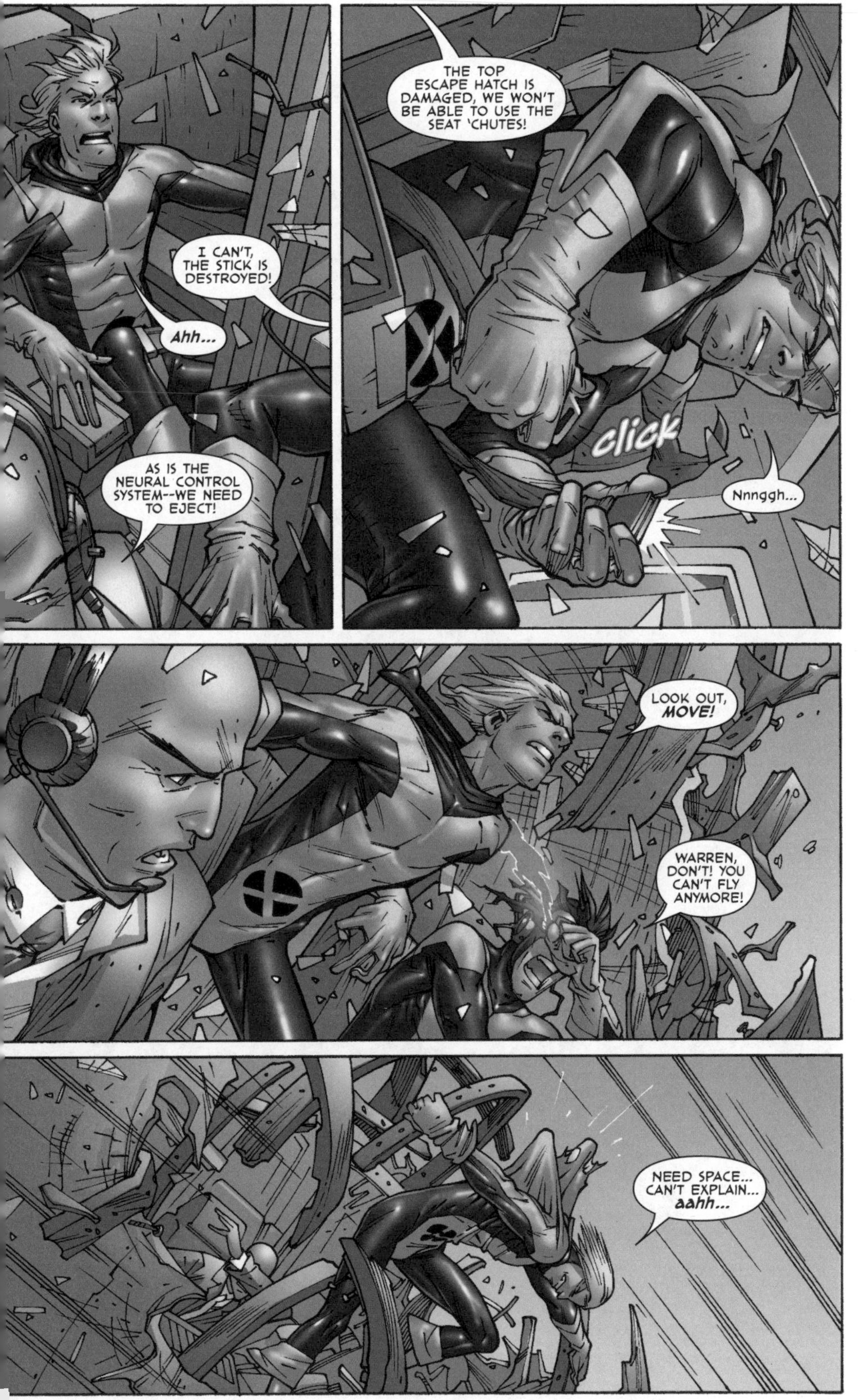
I CAN'T, THE STICK IS DESTROYED!
Ahh...
AS IS THE NEURAL CONTROL SYSTEM--WE NEED TO EJECT!
THE TOP ESCAPE HATCH IS DAMAGED, WE WON'T BE ABLE TO USE THE SEAT 'CHUTES!
click
Nnnggh...
LOOK OUT, MOVE!
WARREN, DON'T! YOU CAN'T FLY ANYMORE!
NEED SPACE... CAN'T EXPLAIN... aahh...

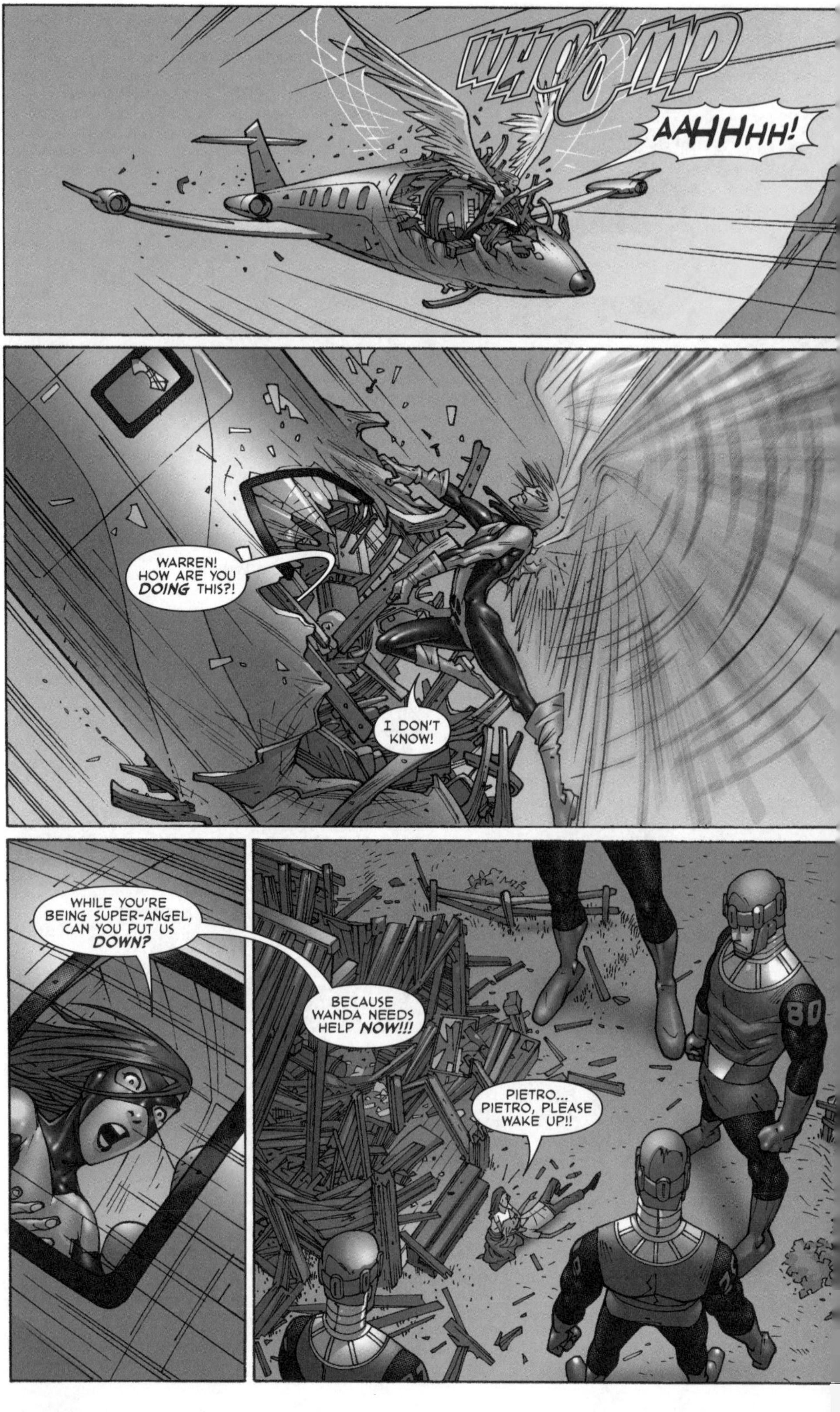
WHOOMP
AAHHHH!
WARREN! HOW ARE YOU DOING THIS?!
I DON'T KNOW!
WHILE YOU'RE BEING SUPER-ANGEL, CAN YOU PUT US DOWN?
BECAUSE WANDA NEEDS HELP NOW!!!
PIETRO... PIETRO, PLEASE WAKE UP!!
80

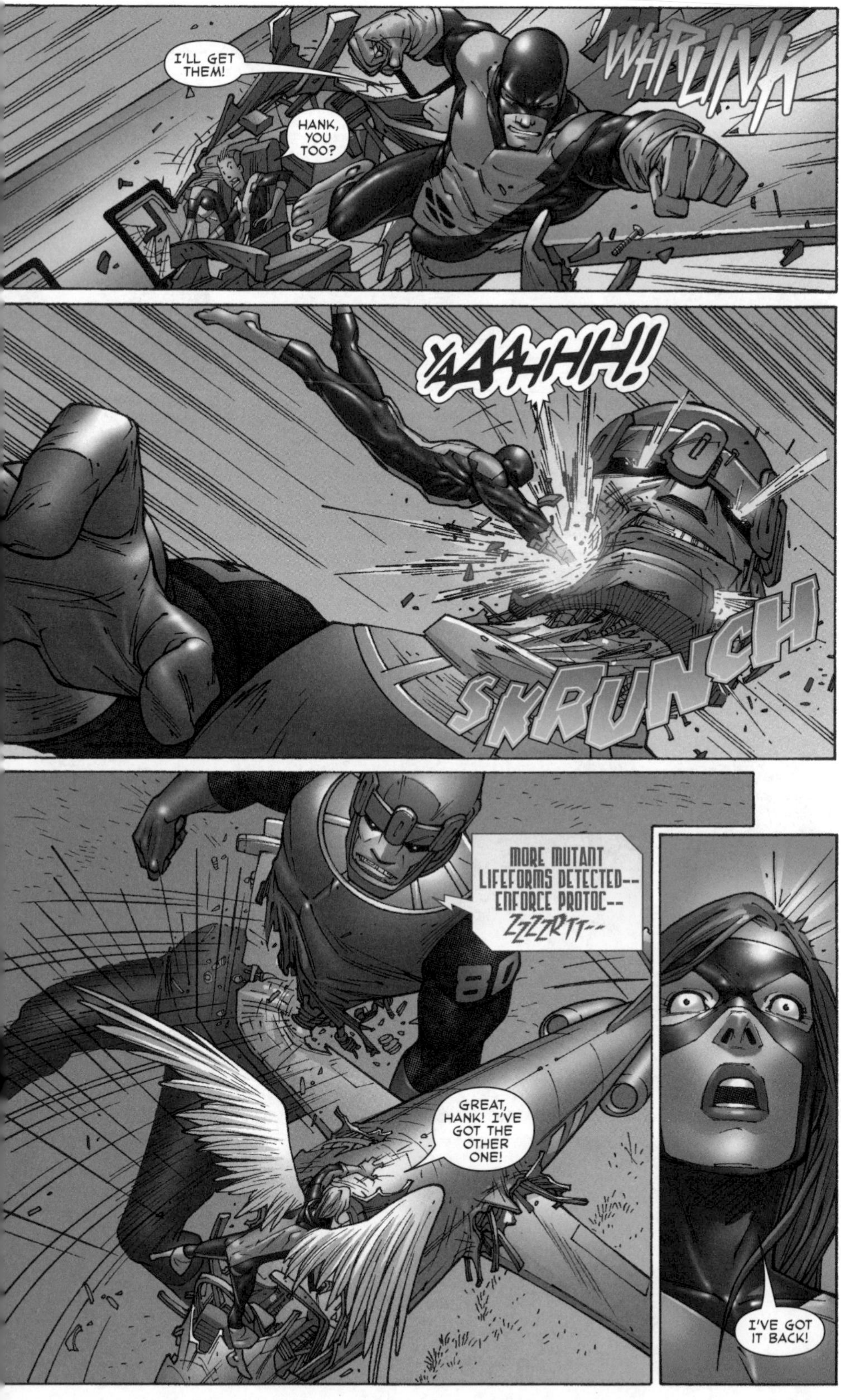
I'LL GET THEM!
HANK, YOU TOO?
WHRUNK
YAAAHH!
SKRUNCH
MORE MUTANT LIFEFORMS DETECTED-- ENFORCE PROTOC-- ZZZZRTT--
GREAT, HANK! I'VE GOT THE OTHER ONE!
I'VE GOT IT BACK!

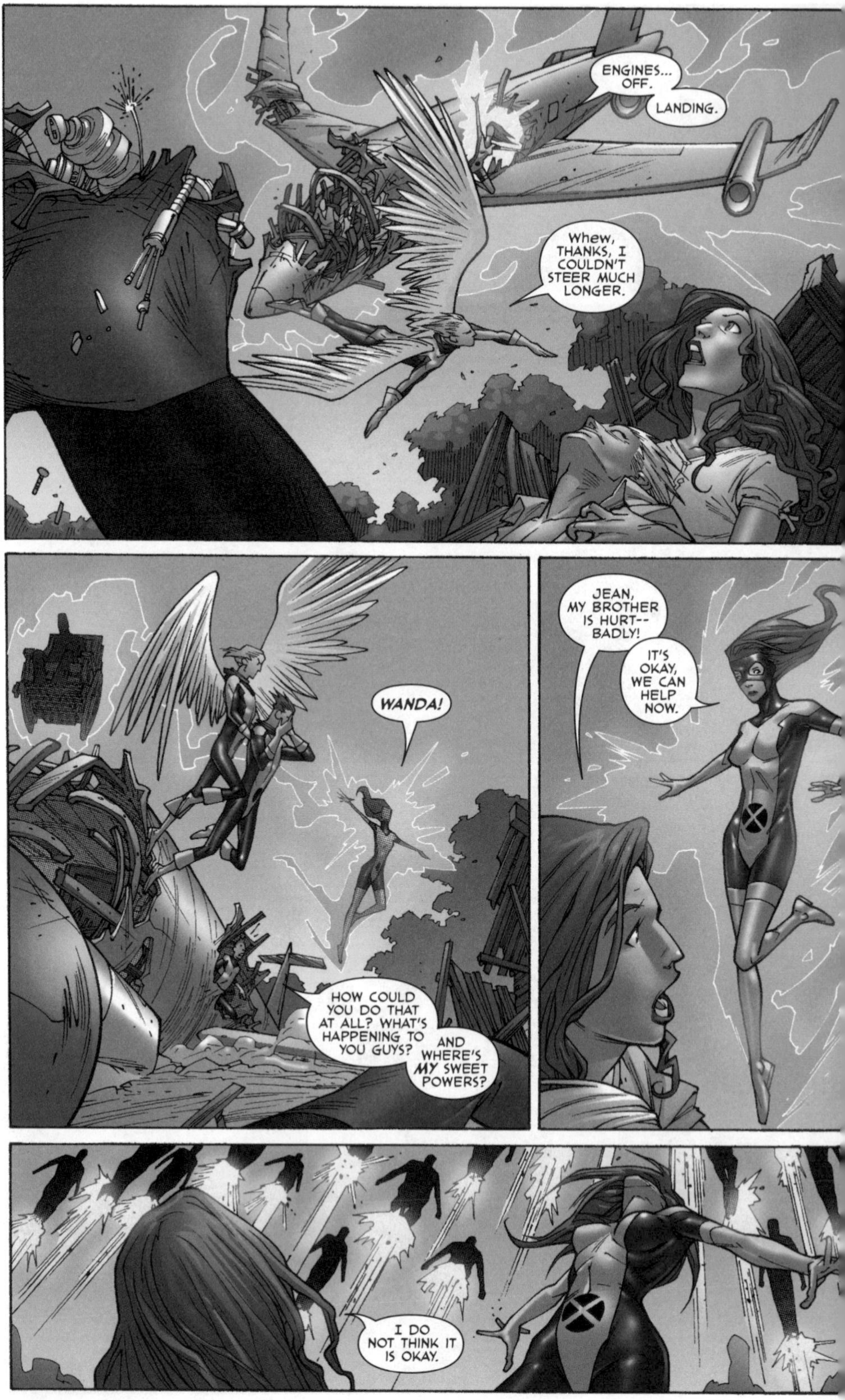
ENGINES... OFF.
LANDING.
Whew, THANKS, I COULDN'T STEER MUCH LONGER.
WANDA!
HOW COULD YOU DO THAT AT ALL? WHAT'S HAPPENING TO YOU GUYS?
AND WHERE'S MY SWEET POWERS?
JEAN, MY BROTHER IS HURT-- BADLY!
IT'S OKAY, WE CAN HELP NOW.
I DO NOT THINK IT IS OKAY.

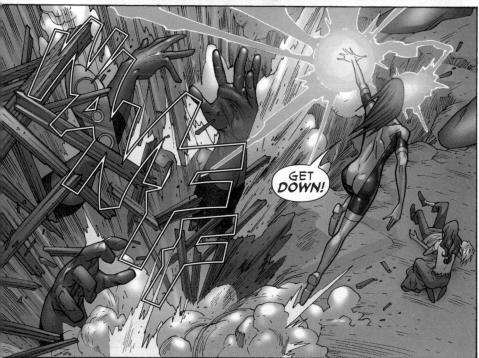

GET *DOWN!*

STOP IT! JUST LEAVE US *ALONE!*

WOW, WANDA!

JUST YOUR REGULAR POWER IS PRETTY AWESOME SOMETIMES!

YEAH, THAT'S GIVING ME SERIOUS CHILLS.

NO...

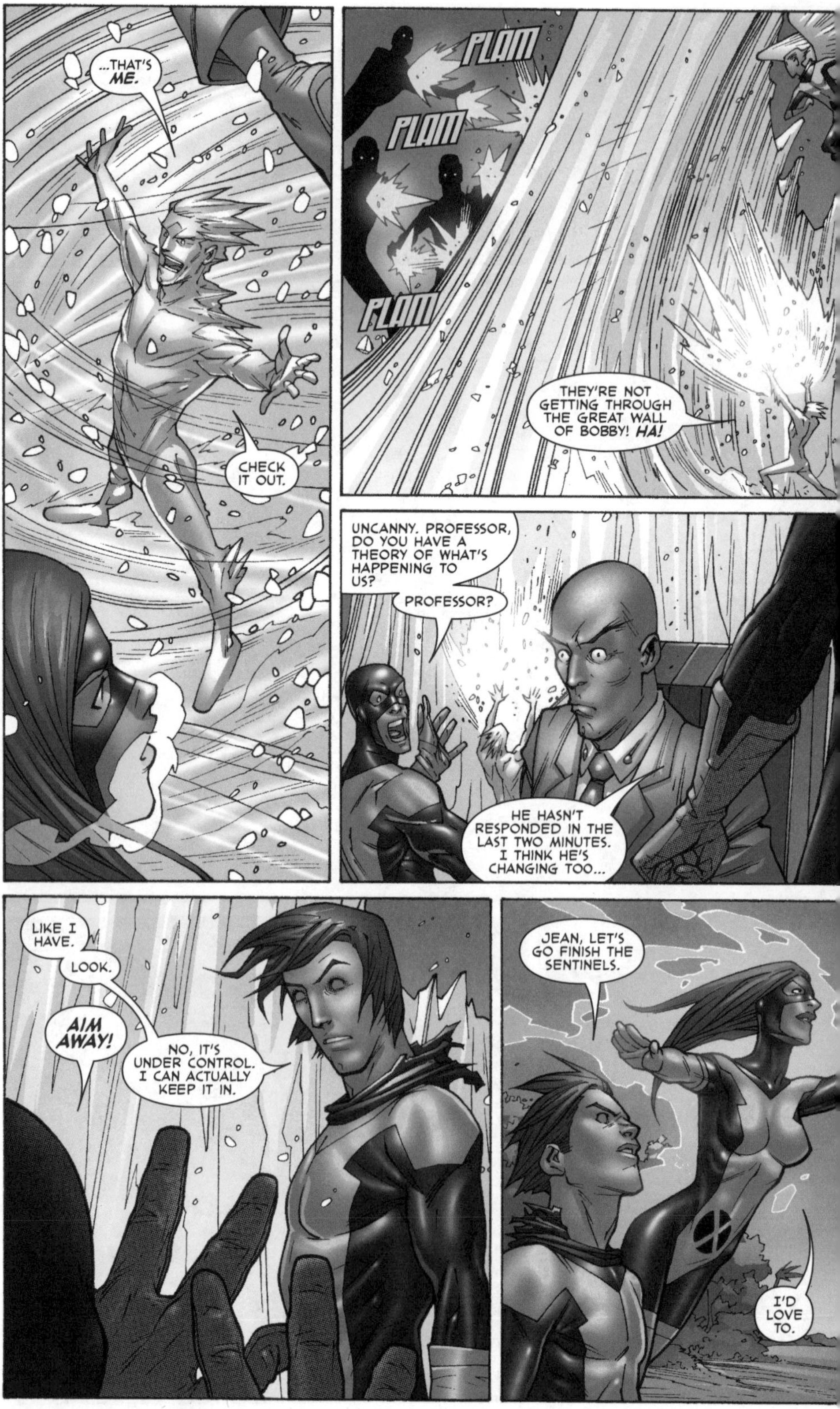

...THAT'S ME.
CHECK IT OUT.
PLAM
PLAM
PLAM
THEY'RE NOT GETTING THROUGH THE GREAT WALL OF BOBBY! HA!
UNCANNY. PROFESSOR, DO YOU HAVE A THEORY OF WHAT'S HAPPENING TO US?
PROFESSOR?
HE HASN'T RESPONDED IN THE LAST TWO MINUTES. I THINK HE'S CHANGING TOO...
LIKE I HAVE.
LOOK.
AIM AWAY!
NO, IT'S UNDER CONTROL. I CAN ACTUALLY KEEP IT IN.
JEAN, LET'S GO FINISH THE SENTINELS.
I'D LOVE TO.

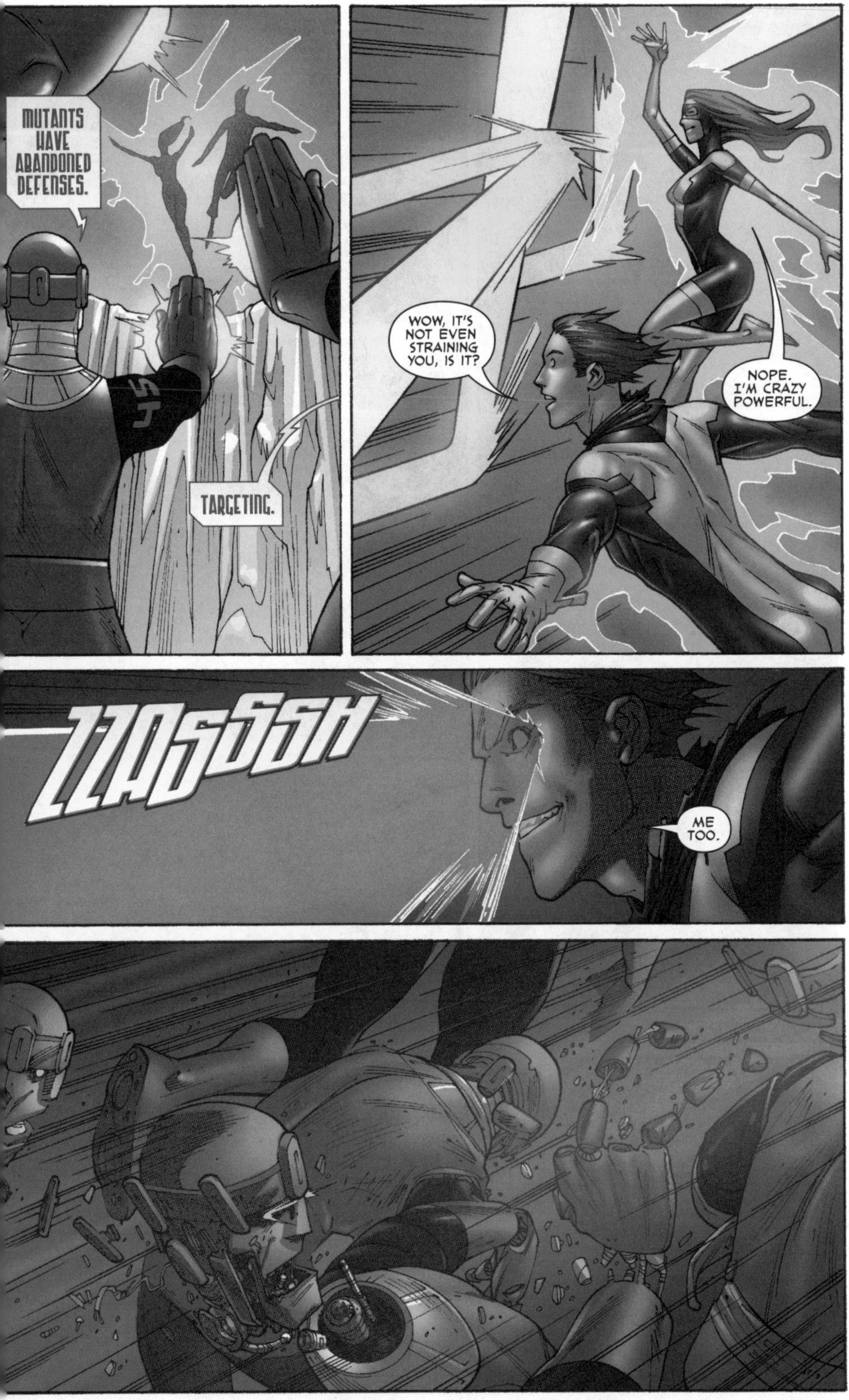
MUTANTS HAVE ABANDONED DEFENSES.
TARGETING.
WOW, IT'S NOT EVEN STRAINING YOU, IS IT?
NOPE. I'M CRAZY POWERFUL.
ZZAOSSSH
ME TOO.

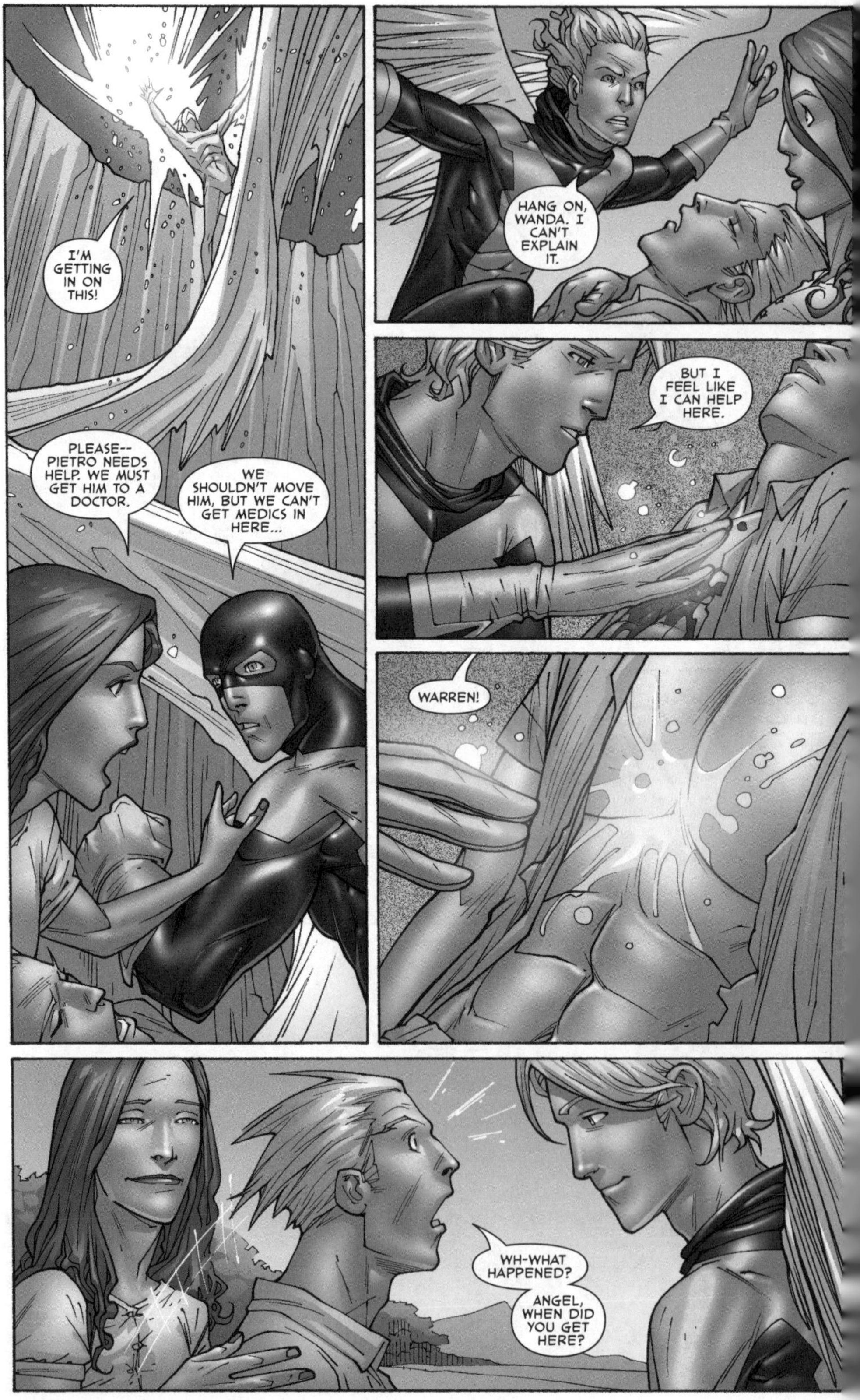
I'M GETTING IN ON THIS!
HANG ON, WANDA. I CAN'T EXPLAIN IT.
BUT I FEEL LIKE I CAN HELP HERE.
PLEASE-- PIETRO NEEDS HELP. WE MUST GET HIM TO A DOCTOR.
WE SHOULDN'T MOVE HIM, BUT WE CAN'T GET MEDICS IN HERE...
WARREN!
WH-WHAT HAPPENED?
ANGEL, WHEN DID YOU GET HERE?

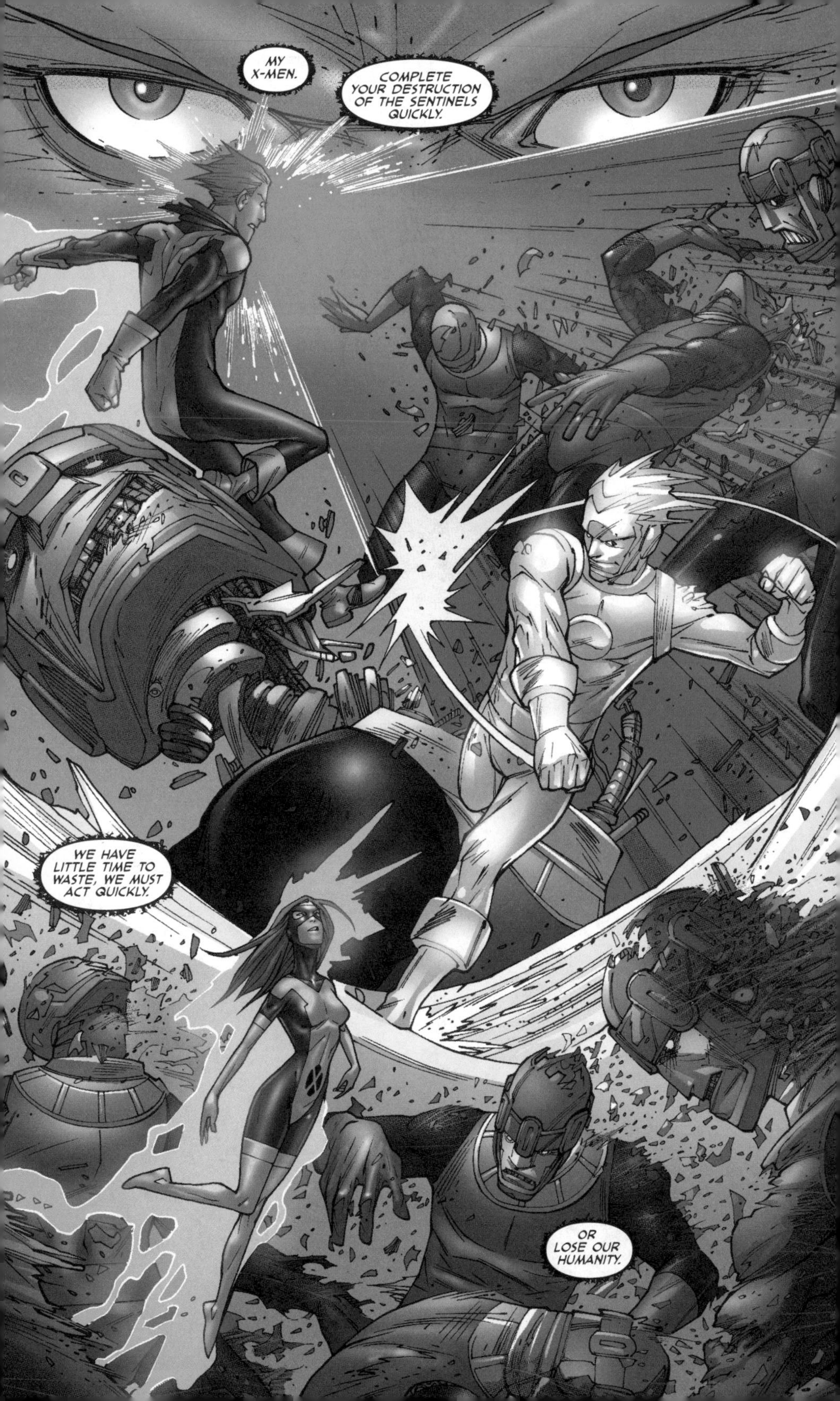
MY X-MEN.
COMPLETE YOUR DESTRUCTION OF THE SENTINELS QUICKLY.
WE HAVE LITTLE TIME TO WASTE, WE MUST ACT QUICKLY.
OR LOSE OUR HUMANITY.

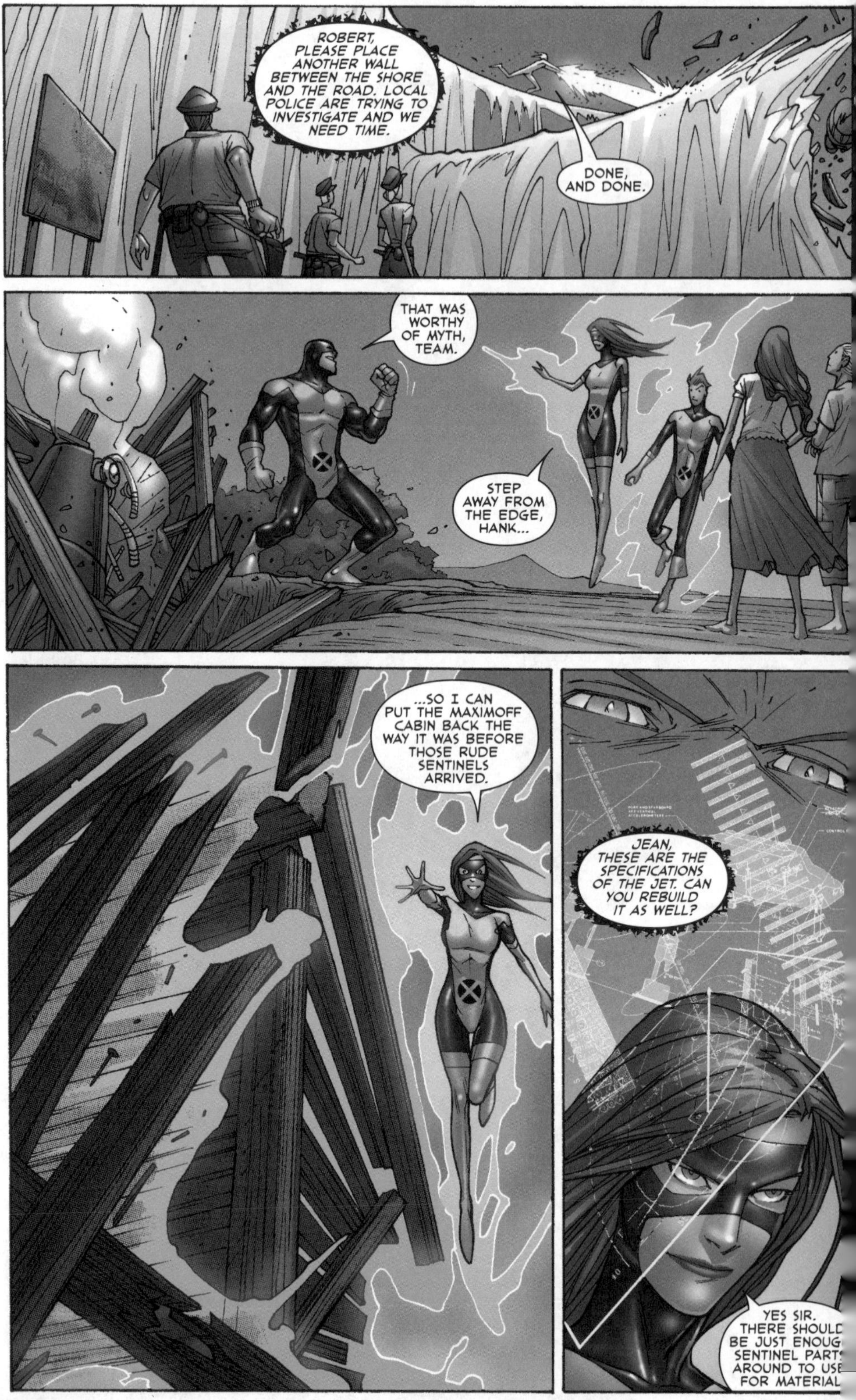
ROBERT, PLEASE PLACE ANOTHER WALL BETWEEN THE SHORE AND THE ROAD. LOCAL POLICE ARE TRYING TO INVESTIGATE AND WE NEED TIME.
DONE, AND DONE.
THAT WAS WORTHY OF MYTH, TEAM.
STEP AWAY FROM THE EDGE, HANK...
...SO I CAN PUT THE MAXIMOFF CABIN BACK THE WAY IT WAS BEFORE THOSE RUDE SENTINELS ARRIVED.
JEAN, THESE ARE THE SPECIFICATIONS OF THE JET. CAN YOU REBUILD IT AS WELL?
YES SIR. THERE SHOULD BE JUST ENOUG SENTINEL PART AROUND TO USE FOR MATERIAL

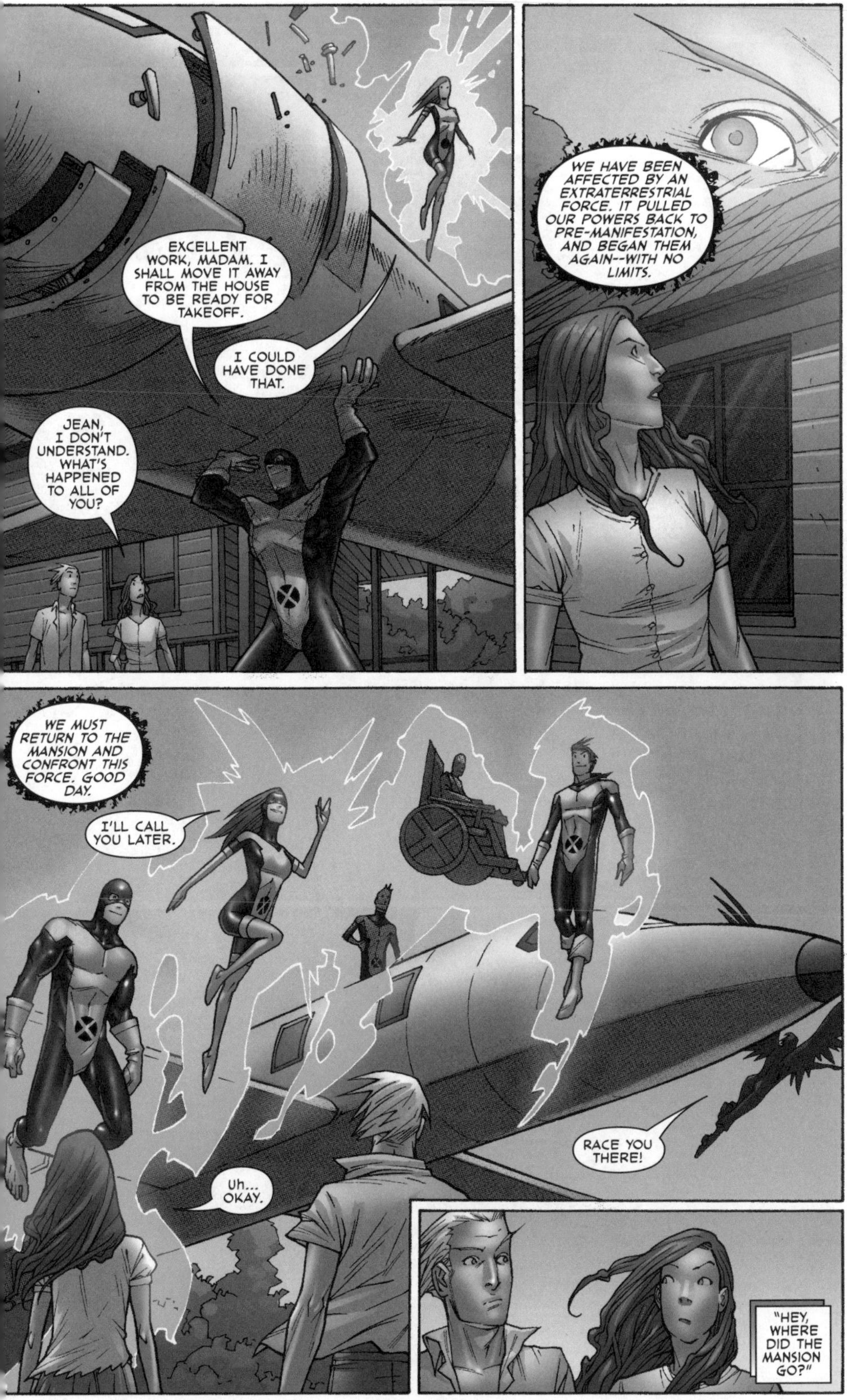
EXCELLENT WORK, MADAM. I SHALL MOVE IT AWAY FROM THE HOUSE TO BE READY FOR TAKEOFF.
I COULD HAVE DONE THAT.
JEAN, I DON'T UNDERSTAND. WHAT'S HAPPENED TO ALL OF YOU?
WE HAVE BEEN AFFECTED BY AN EXTRATERRESTRIAL FORCE. IT PULLED OUR POWERS BACK TO PRE-MANIFESTATION, AND BEGAN THEM AGAIN--WITH NO LIMITS.
WE MUST RETURN TO THE MANSION AND CONFRONT THIS FORCE. GOOD DAY.
I'LL CALL YOU LATER.
Uh... OKAY.
RACE YOU THERE!
"HEY, WHERE DID THE MANSION GO?"

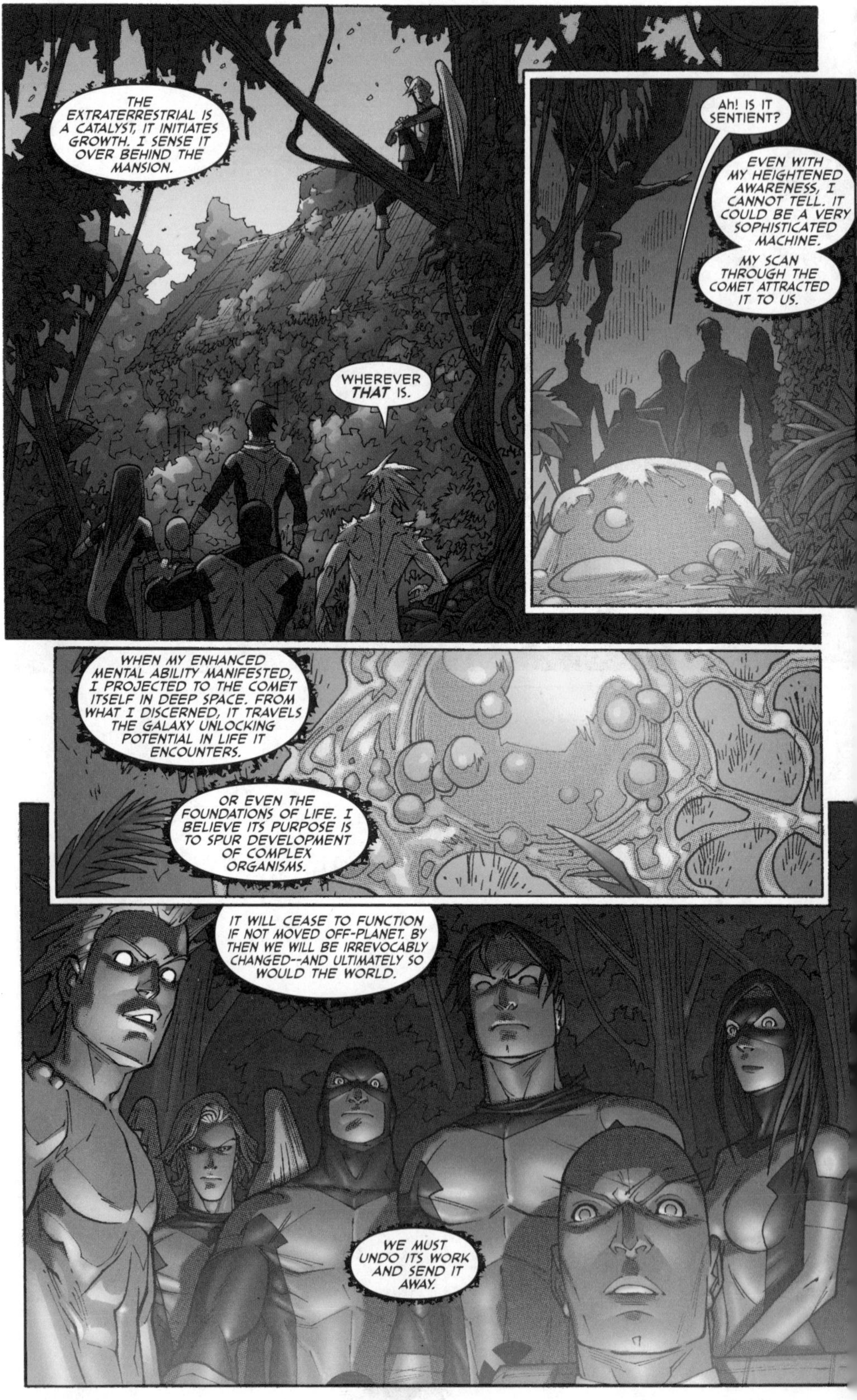
THE EXTRATERRESTRIAL IS A CATALYST, IT INITIATES GROWTH. I SENSE IT OVER BEHIND THE MANSION.
WHEREVER THAT IS.
Ah! IS IT SENTIENT?
EVEN WITH MY HEIGHTENED AWARENESS, I CANNOT TELL. IT COULD BE A VERY SOPHISTICATED MACHINE.
MY SCAN THROUGH THE COMET ATTRACTED IT TO US.
WHEN MY ENHANCED MENTAL ABILITY MANIFESTED, I PROJECTED TO THE COMET ITSELF IN DEEP SPACE. FROM WHAT I DISCERNED, IT TRAVELS THE GALAXY UNLOCKING POTENTIAL IN LIFE IT ENCOUNTERS.
OR EVEN THE FOUNDATIONS OF LIFE. I BELIEVE ITS PURPOSE IS TO SPUR DEVELOPMENT OF COMPLEX ORGANISMS.
IT WILL CEASE TO FUNCTION IF NOT MOVED OFF-PLANET. BY THEN WE WILL BE IRREVOCABLY CHANGED--AND ULTIMATELY SO WOULD THE WORLD.
WE MUST UNDO ITS WORK AND SEND IT AWAY.

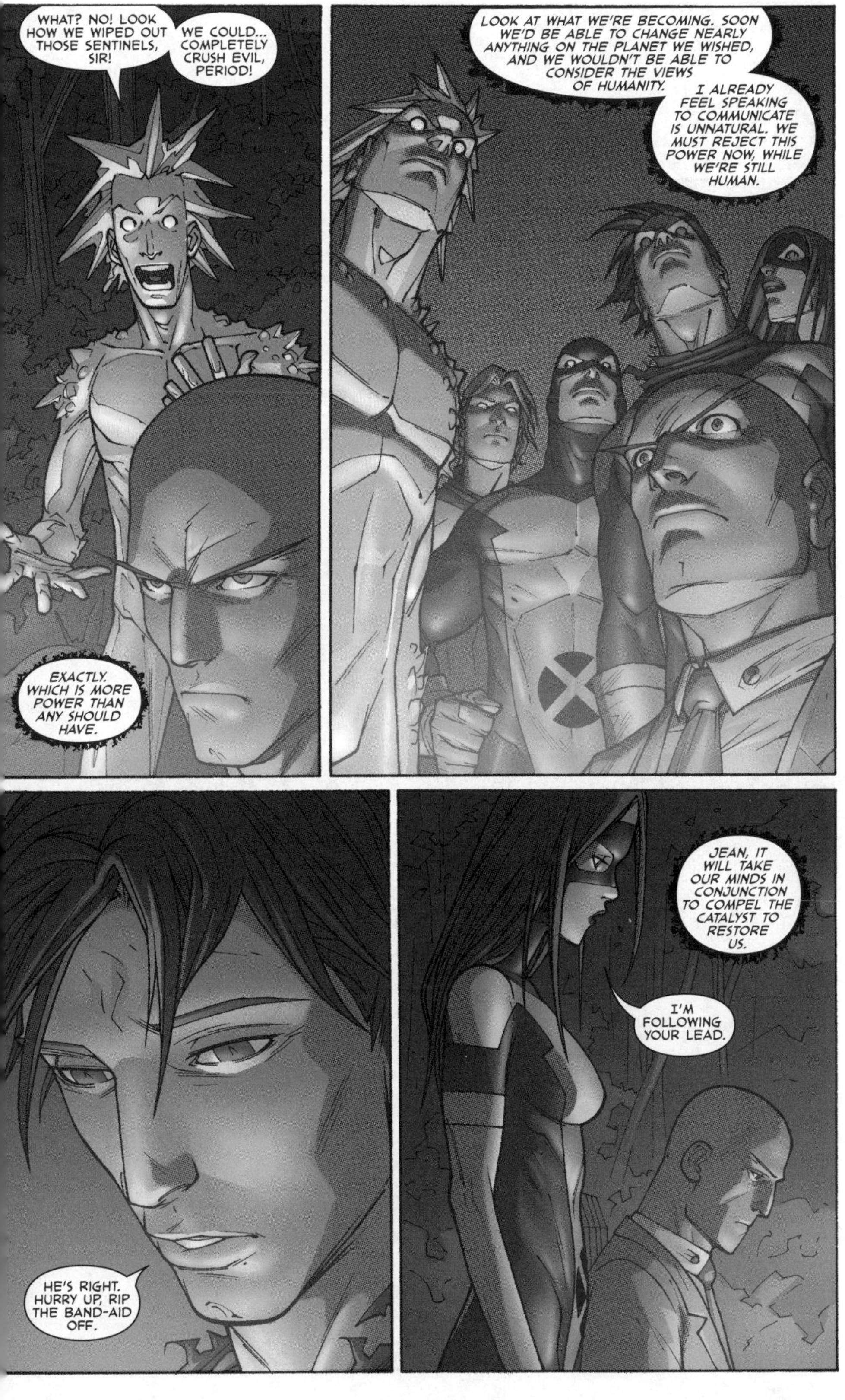
WHAT? NO! LOOK HOW WE WIPED OUT THOSE SENTINELS, SIR!
WE COULD... COMPLETELY CRUSH EVIL, PERIOD!
EXACTLY. WHICH IS MORE POWER THAN ANY SHOULD HAVE.
LOOK AT WHAT WE'RE BECOMING. SOON WE'D BE ABLE TO CHANGE NEARLY ANYTHING ON THE PLANET WE WISHED, AND WE WOULDN'T BE ABLE TO CONSIDER THE VIEWS OF HUMANITY.
I ALREADY FEEL SPEAKING TO COMMUNICATE IS UNNATURAL. WE MUST REJECT THIS POWER NOW, WHILE WE'RE STILL HUMAN.
HE'S RIGHT. HURRY UP, RIP THE BAND-AID OFF.
JEAN, IT WILL TAKE OUR MINDS IN CONJUNCTION TO COMPEL THE CATALYST TO RESTORE US.
I'M FOLLOWING YOUR LEAD.

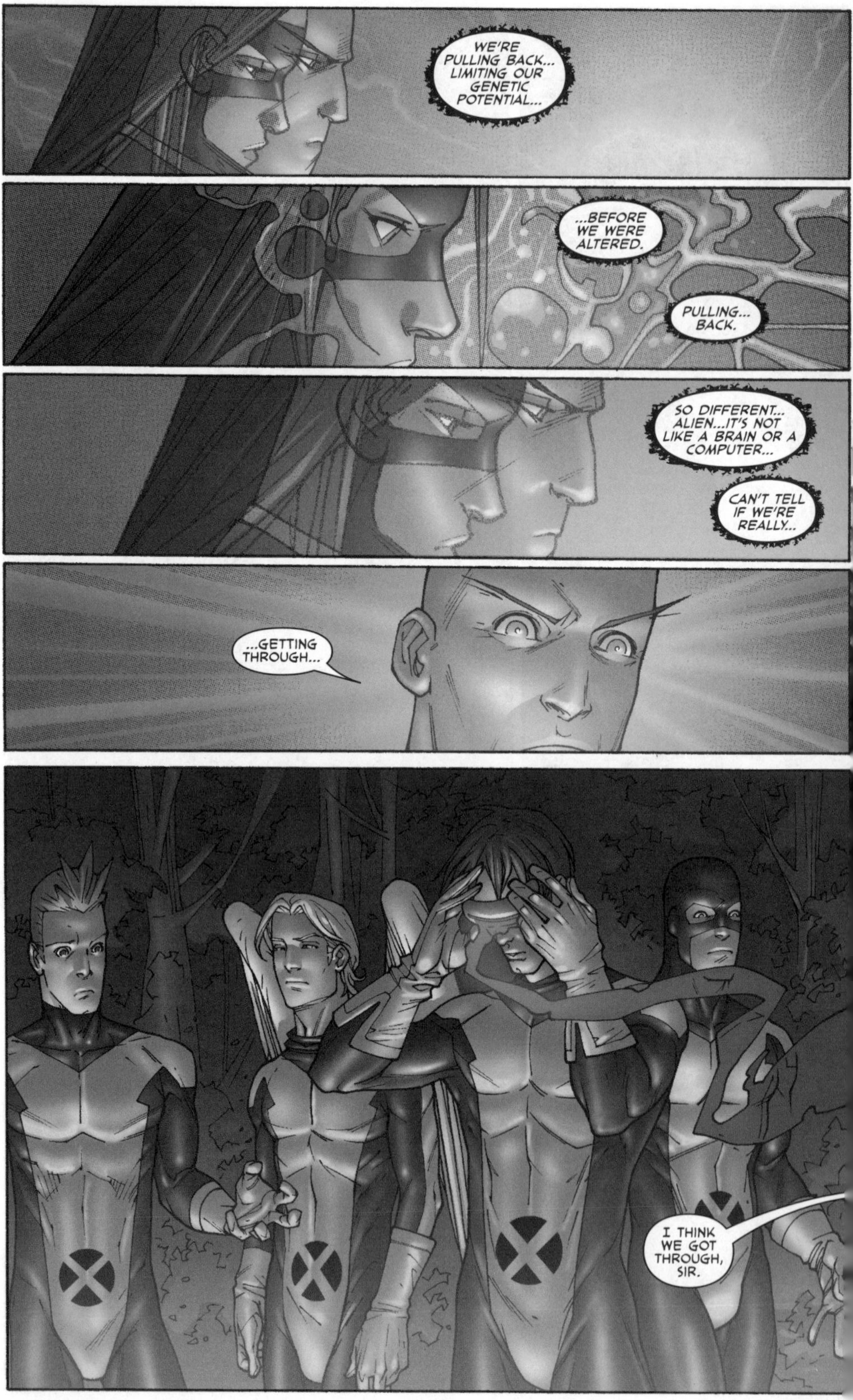
WE'RE PULLING BACK... LIMITING OUR GENETIC POTENTIAL...
...BEFORE WE WERE ALTERED.
PULLING... BACK.
SO DIFFERENT... ALIEN...IT'S NOT LIKE A BRAIN OR A COMPUTER...
CAN'T TELL IF WE'RE REALLY...
...GETTING THROUGH...
I THINK WE GOT THROUGH, SIR.

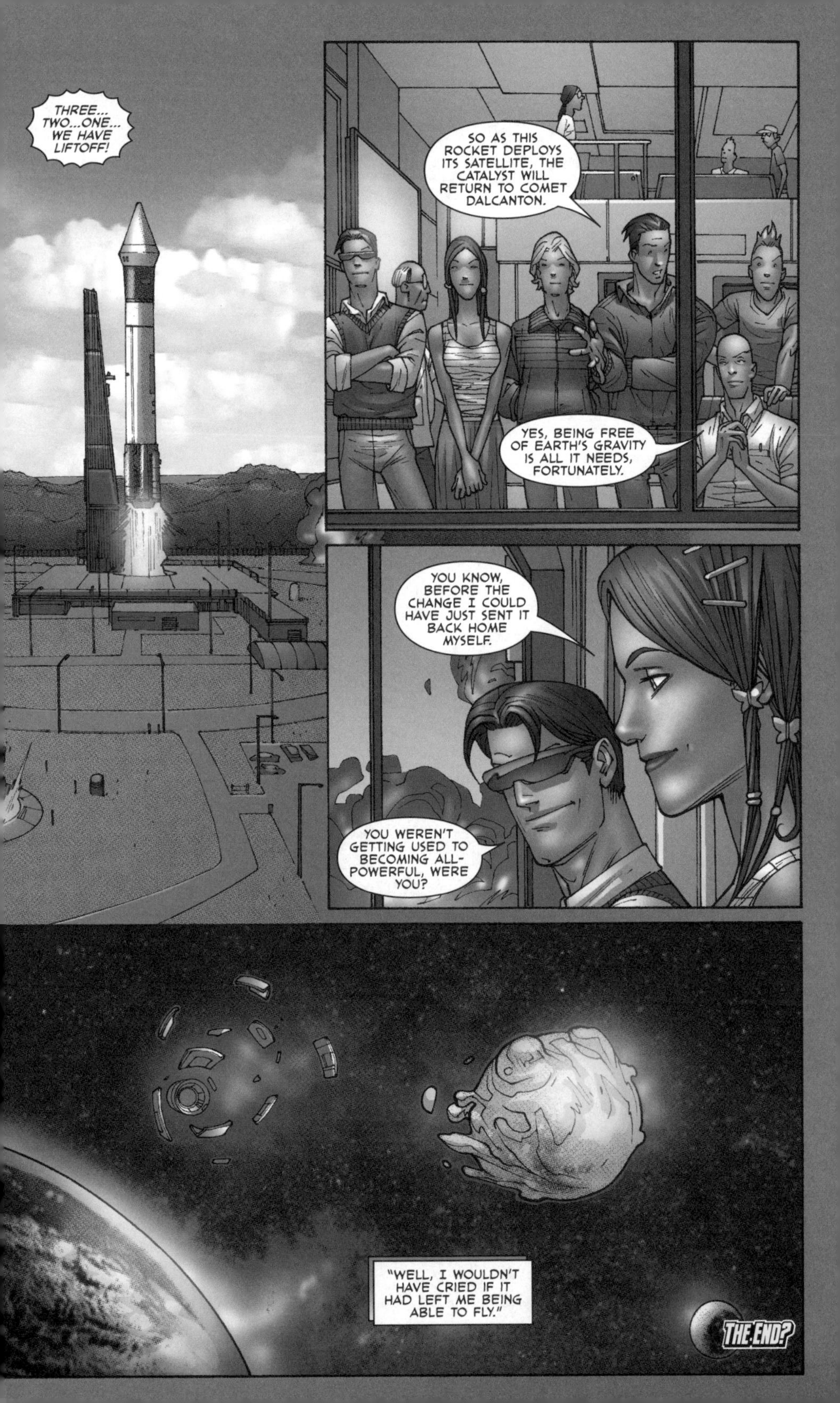
THREE... TWO...ONE... WE HAVE LIFTOFF!
SO AS THIS ROCKET DEPLOYS ITS SATELLITE, THE CATALYST WILL RETURN TO COMET DALCANTON.
YES, BEING FREE OF EARTH'S GRAVITY IS ALL IT NEEDS, FORTUNATELY.
YOU KNOW, BEFORE THE CHANGE I COULD HAVE JUST SENT IT BACK HOME MYSELF.
YOU WEREN'T GETTING USED TO BECOMING ALL-POWERFUL, WERE YOU?
"WELL, I WOULDN'T HAVE CRIED IF IT HAD LEFT ME BEING ABLE TO FLY."
THE END?

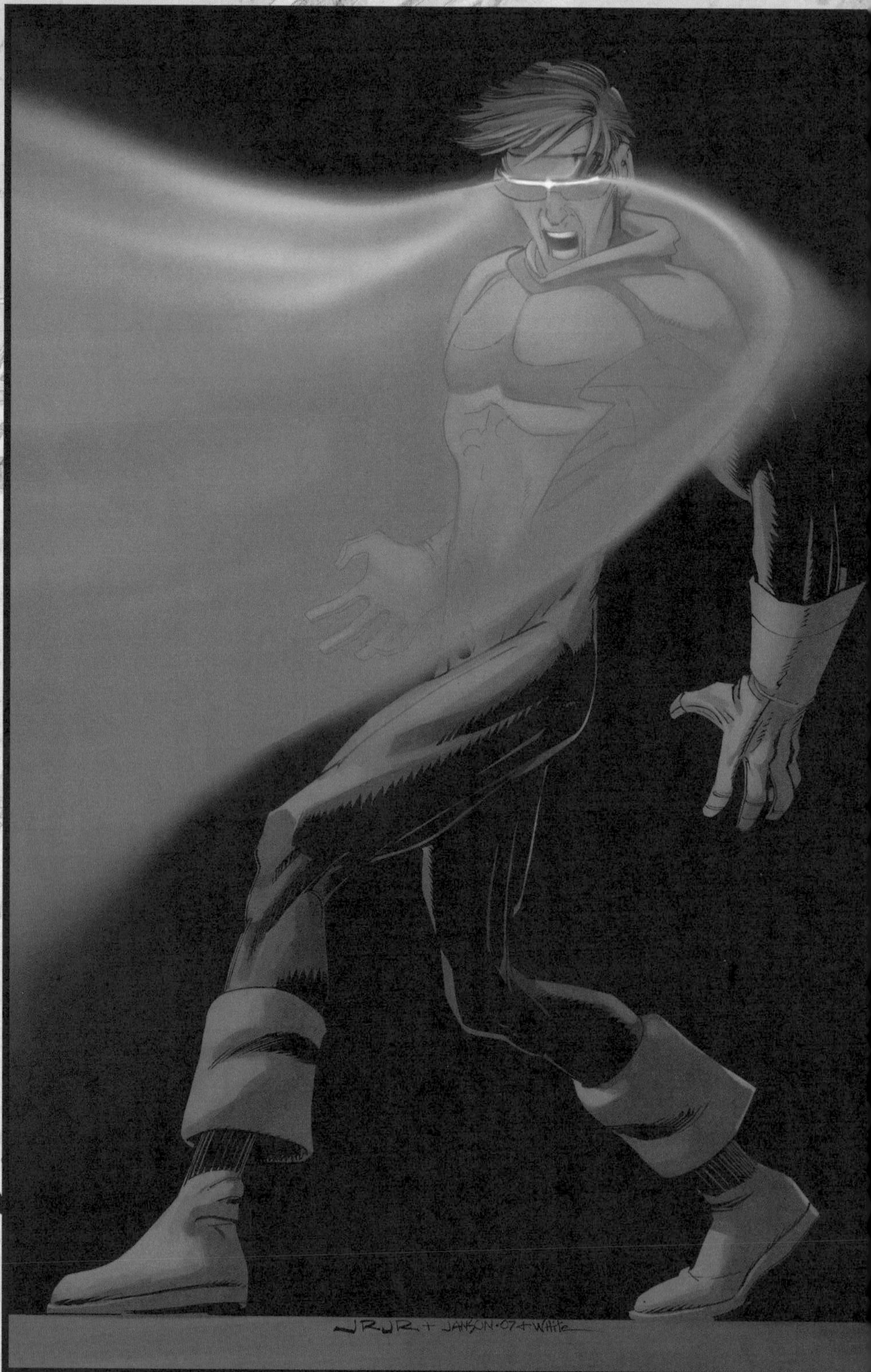
JRJR + JANSON·07 + White

X-Men: First Class (2007) **#10**

Hey! I might be Iceman, a member of a totally rad group of college kid mutant fighter heroes run by a bald dude, but I've also got mad joke game! Check these out!

# BOBBY SNAPS!

What happened to the piece of wood when Cyclops talked to it?

It got board.

HIT ME!

## BOMP!

(I love having a backing band)

Hey! What's the difference between Cyclops and a recreation of Cyclops' body made out of wax?

I don't know.

HIT ME!

## BOMP!

What's got four arms, twenty toes, and one personality?

Cyclops and ANYbody else.

HIT ME TWO TIMES!

## BOMP!

## BOMP!

Knock-knock.

Who's there?

Cyclops.

Cyclops who?

No. Seriously. It's just Cyclops.

Wait..I don't feel so good...

Oh PLEASE, MAKE IT STOP...

FLSSHHHHH

JEAN, WHAT ARE YOU DOING... OUT OF YOUR ROOM?

I MADE SOME... CALMING TEA.

GOTTA GO!

TEA WON'T WORK!

NOTHING WORKS!

Ah, WELL...

...IT'S OVER FOR ME. OBVIOUSLY MY MORE ROBUST PHYSIQUE HAS DEALT WITH THE UNWANTED BACTERIA.

FLSSHH

SPOKE TOO SOON!

WHERE'S SCOTT, IS HE TOTALLY WIPED OUT?

THE PROFESSOR SENT HIM ON A MISSION.

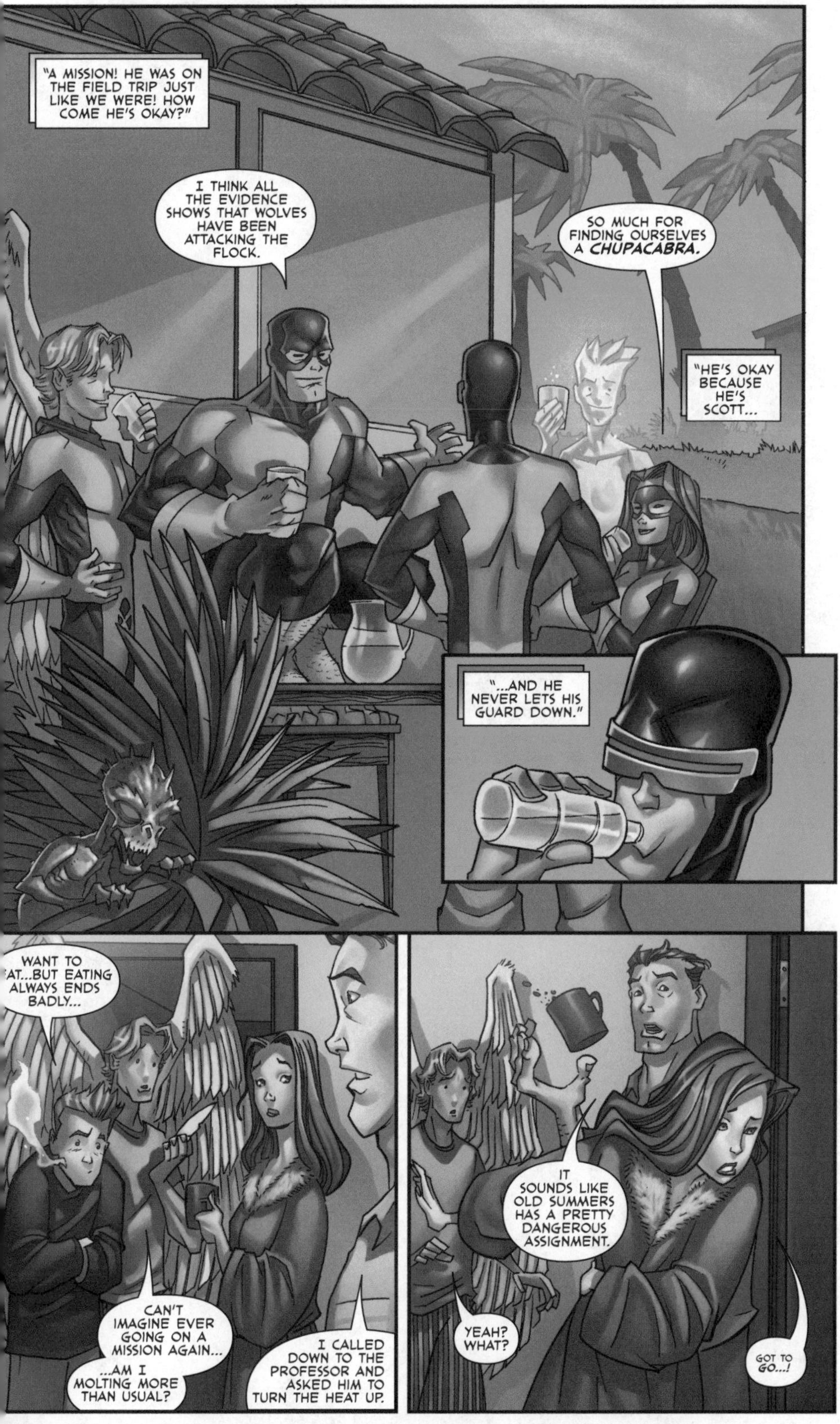

"A MISSION! HE WAS ON THE FIELD TRIP JUST LIKE WE WERE! HOW COME HE'S OKAY?"
I THINK ALL THE EVIDENCE SHOWS THAT WOLVES HAVE BEEN ATTACKING THE FLOCK.
SO MUCH FOR FINDING OURSELVES A *CHUPACABRA.*
"HE'S OKAY BECAUSE HE'S SCOTT...
"...AND HE NEVER LETS HIS GUARD DOWN."
WANT TO EAT...BUT EATING ALWAYS ENDS BADLY...
CAN'T IMAGINE EVER GOING ON A MISSION AGAIN...
...AM I MOLTING MORE THAN USUAL?
I CALLED DOWN TO THE PROFESSOR AND ASKED HIM TO TURN THE HEAT UP.
IT SOUNDS LIKE OLD SUMMERS HAS A PRETTY DANGEROUS ASSIGNMENT.
YEAH? WHAT?
GOT TO *GO...!*

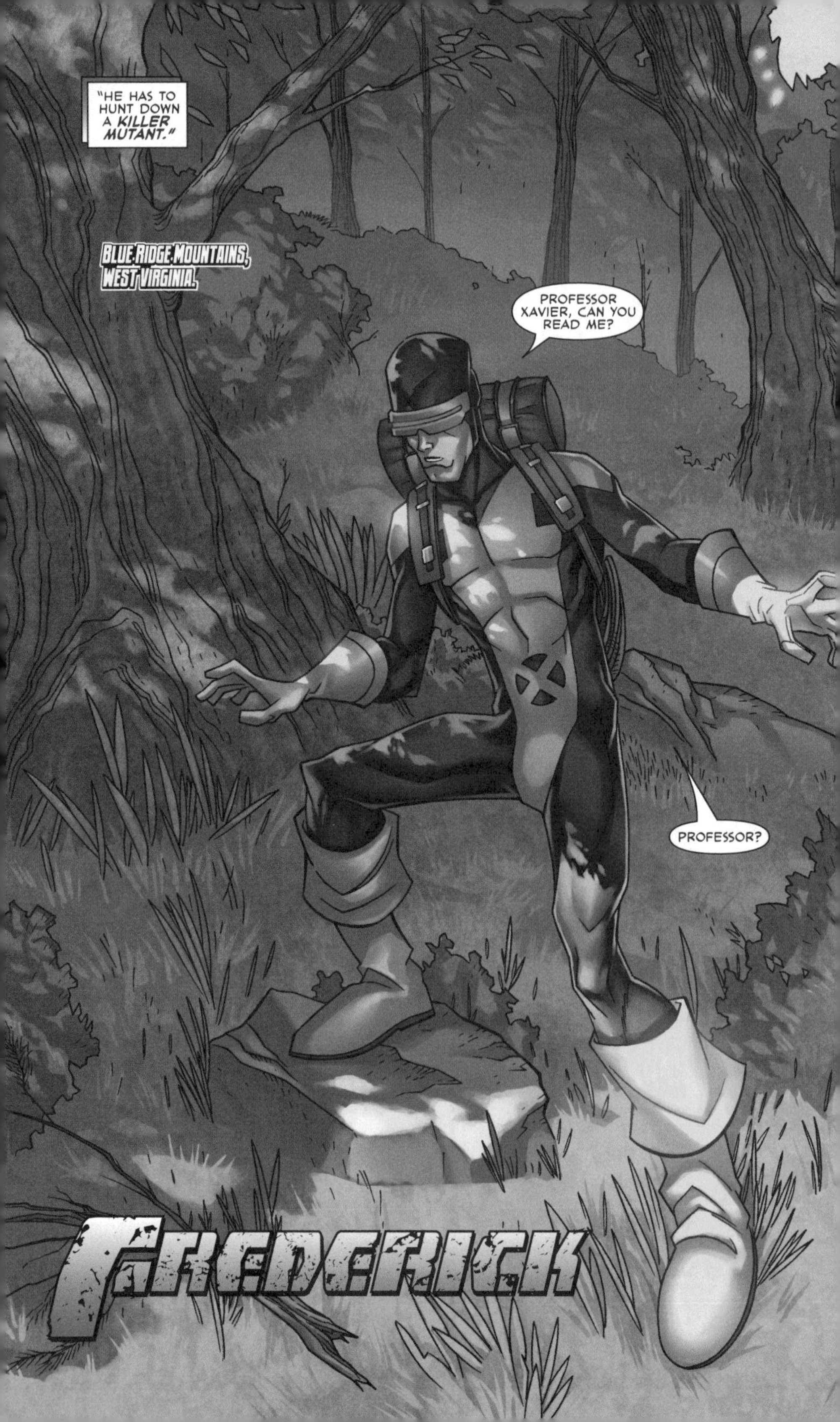
"HE HAS TO HUNT DOWN A *KILLER MUTANT.*"
BLUE RIDGE MOUNTAINS, WEST VIRGINIA.
PROFESSOR XAVIER, CAN YOU READ ME?
PROFESSOR?
FREDERICK

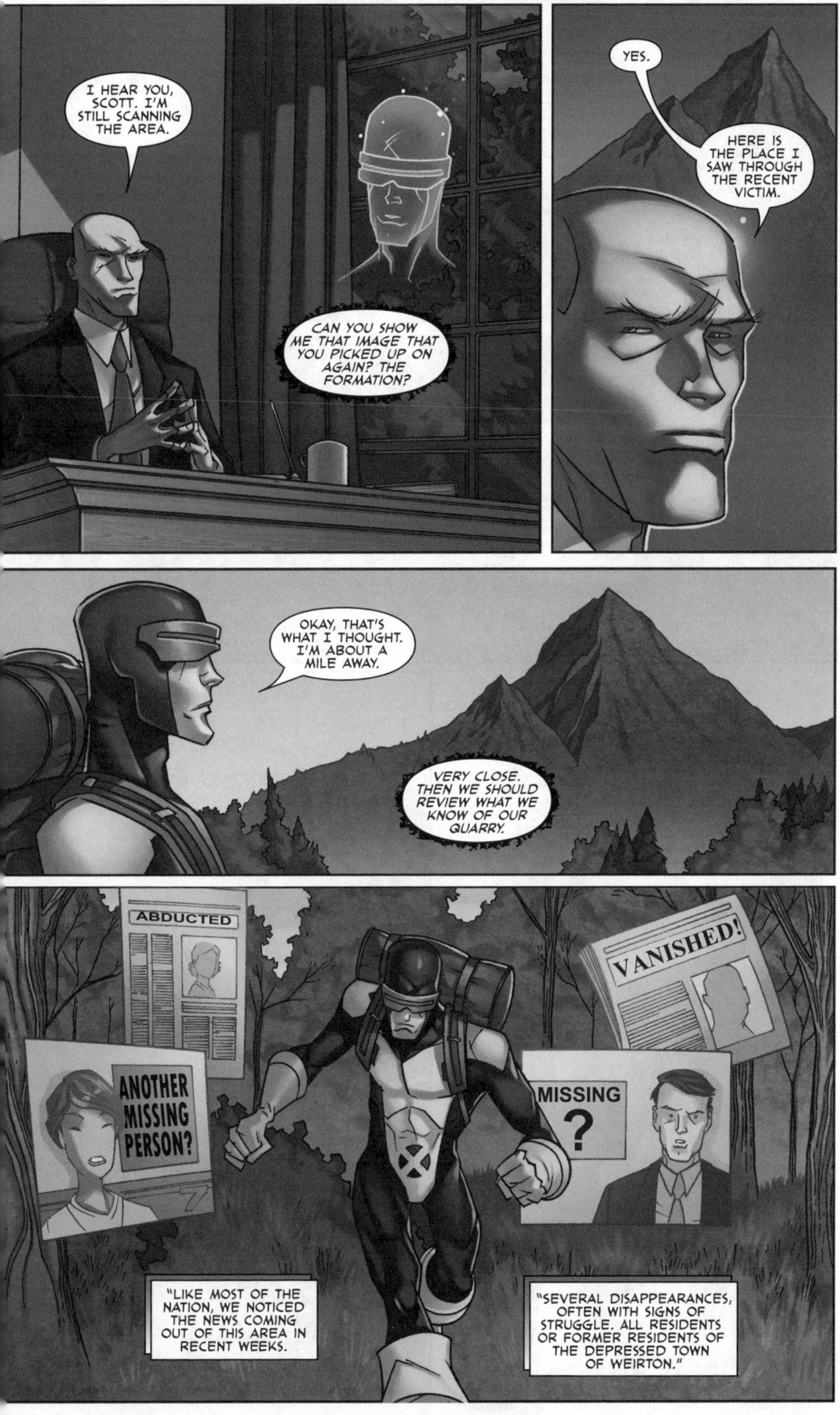

I HEAR YOU, SCOTT. I'M STILL SCANNING THE AREA.
CAN YOU SHOW ME THAT IMAGE THAT YOU PICKED UP ON AGAIN? THE FORMATION?
YES.
HERE IS THE PLACE I SAW THROUGH THE RECENT VICTIM.
OKAY, THAT'S WHAT I THOUGHT. I'M ABOUT A MILE AWAY.
VERY CLOSE. THEN WE SHOULD REVIEW WHAT WE KNOW OF OUR QUARRY.
ABDUCTED
VANISHED!
ANOTHER MISSING PERSON?
MISSING
?
"LIKE MOST OF THE NATION, WE NOTICED THE NEWS COMING OUT OF THIS AREA IN RECENT WEEKS.
"SEVERAL DISAPPEARANCES, OFTEN WITH SIGNS OF STRUGGLE. ALL RESIDENTS OR FORMER RESIDENTS OF THE DEPRESSED TOWN OF WEIRTON."

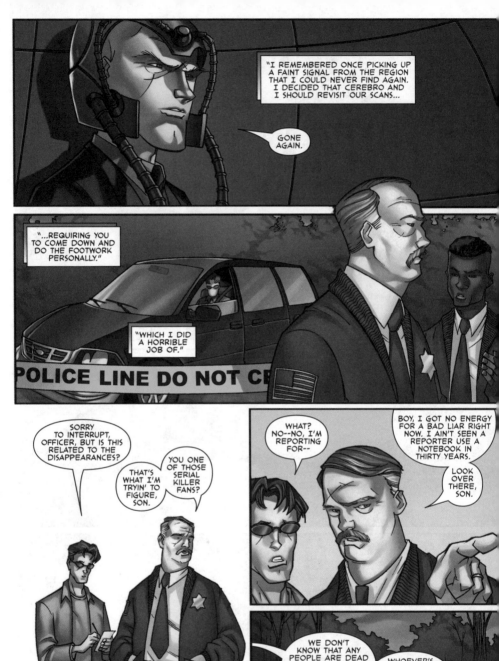

"I REMEMBERED ONCE PICKING UP A FAINT SIGNAL FROM THE REGION THAT I COULD NEVER FIND AGAIN. I DECIDED THAT CEREBRO AND I SHOULD REVISIT OUR SCANS...

GONE AGAIN.

"...REQUIRING YOU TO COME DOWN AND DO THE FOOTWORK PERSONALLY."

"WHICH I DID A HORRIBLE JOB OF."

POLICE LINE DO NOT CR

SORRY TO INTERRUPT, OFFICER, BUT IS THIS RELATED TO THE DISAPPEARANCES?

THAT'S WHAT I'M TRYIN' TO FIGURE, SON.

YOU ONE OF THOSE SERIAL KILLER FANS?

WHAT? NO--NO, I'M REPORTING FOR--

BOY, I GOT NO ENERGY FOR A BAD LIAR RIGHT NOW. I AIN'T SEEN A REPORTER USE A NOTEBOOK IN THIRTY YEARS.

LOOK OVER THERE, SON.

WE DON'T KNOW THAT ANY PEOPLE ARE DEAD YET, BUT THOSE GUARD DOGS WON'T BE BARKING AT US ANYTIME SOON.

WHOEVER'S BEHIND ALL THIS DON'T HAVE A PROBLEM WITH KILLING THINGS IN HIS WAY. SO GET OUT OF IT.

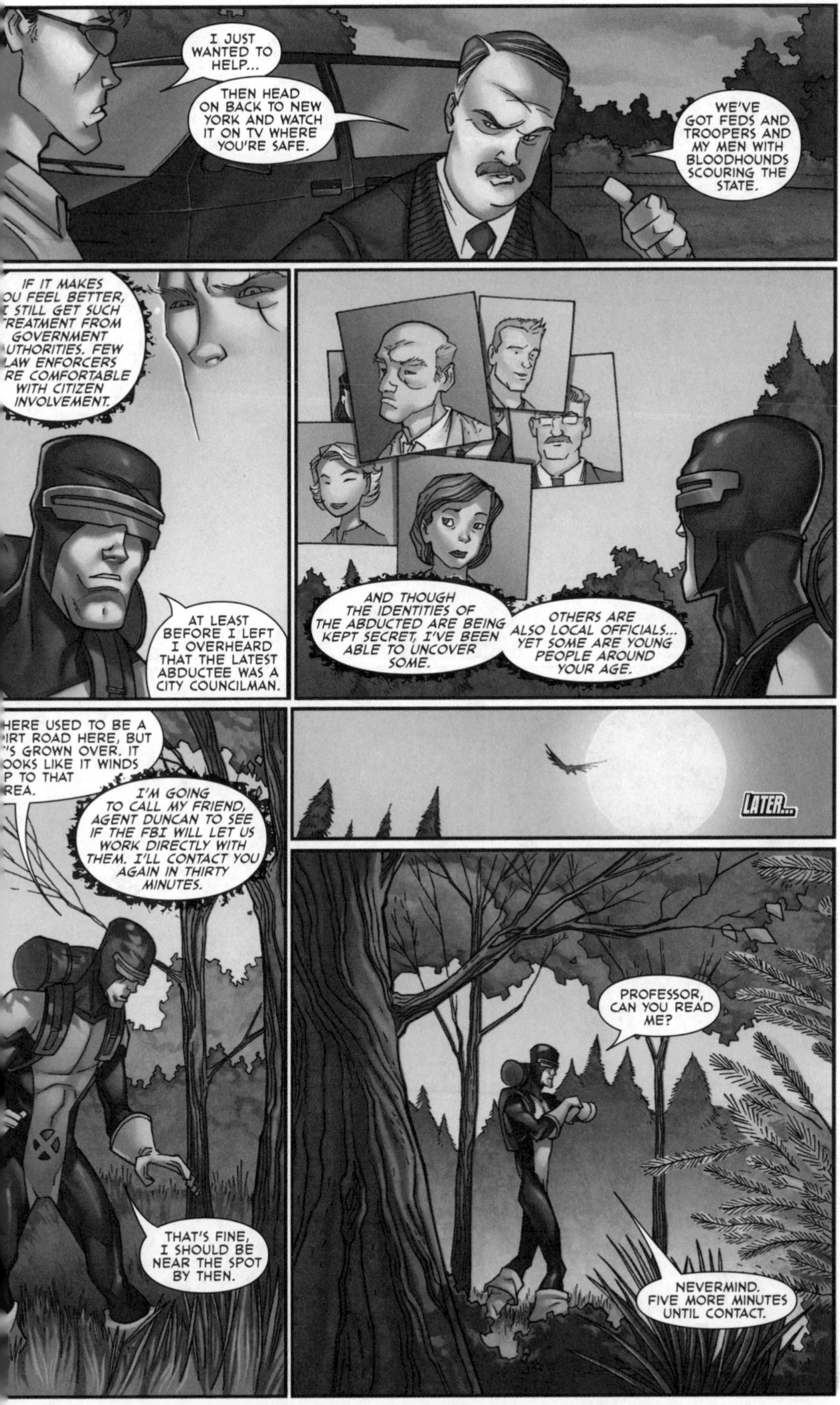
I JUST WANTED TO HELP...
THEN HEAD ON BACK TO NEW YORK AND WATCH IT ON TV WHERE YOU'RE SAFE.
WE'VE GOT FEDS AND TROOPERS AND MY MEN WITH BLOODHOUNDS SCOURING THE STATE.
IF IT MAKES OU FEEL BETTER, I STILL GET SUCH TREATMENT FROM GOVERNMENT UTHORITIES. FEW LAW ENFORCERS RE COMFORTABLE WITH CITIZEN INVOLVEMENT.
AT LEAST BEFORE I LEFT I OVERHEARD THAT THE LATEST ABDUCTEE WAS A CITY COUNCILMAN.
AND THOUGH THE IDENTITIES OF THE ABDUCTED ARE BEING KEPT SECRET, I'VE BEEN ABLE TO UNCOVER SOME.
OTHERS ARE ALSO LOCAL OFFICIALS... YET SOME ARE YOUNG PEOPLE AROUND YOUR AGE.
HERE USED TO BE A IRT ROAD HERE, BUT 'S GROWN OVER. IT OOKS LIKE IT WINDS P TO THAT REA.
I'M GOING TO CALL MY FRIEND, AGENT DUNCAN TO SEE IF THE FBI WILL LET US WORK DIRECTLY WITH THEM. I'LL CONTACT YOU AGAIN IN THIRTY MINUTES.
THAT'S FINE, I SHOULD BE NEAR THE SPOT BY THEN.
LATER...
PROFESSOR, CAN YOU READ ME?
NEVERMIND. FIVE MORE MINUTES UNTIL CONTACT.

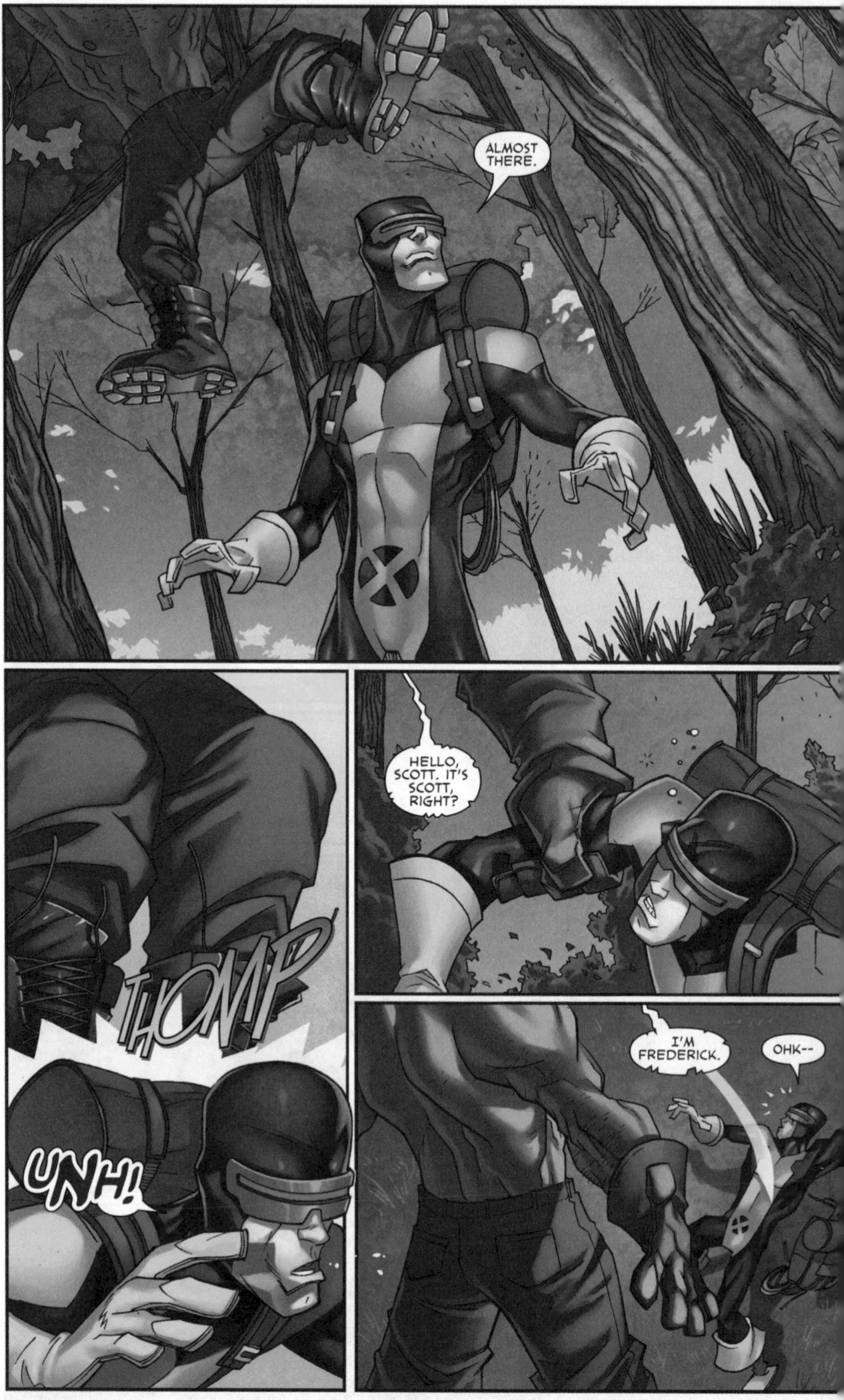

ALMOST THERE.
THOMP
UNH!
HELLO, SCOTT. IT'S SCOTT, RIGHT?
I'M FREDERICK.
OHK--

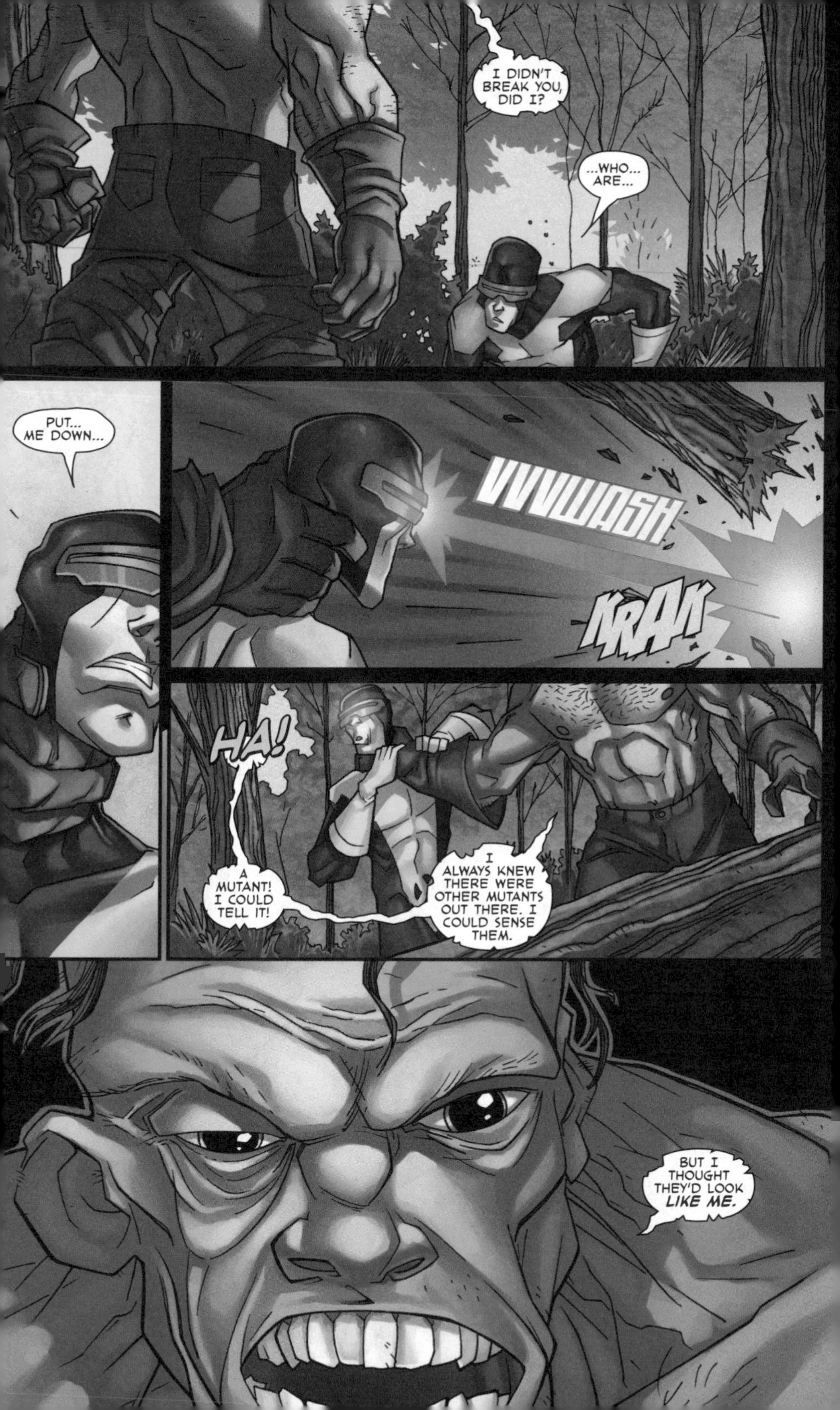

I DIDN'T BREAK YOU, DID I?
...WHO... ARE...
PUT... ME DOWN...
VVVWASH
KRAK
HA!
A MUTANT! I COULD TELL IT!
I ALWAYS KNEW THERE WERE OTHER MUTANTS OUT THERE. I COULD SENSE THEM.
BUT I THOUGHT THEY'D LOOK *LIKE ME.*

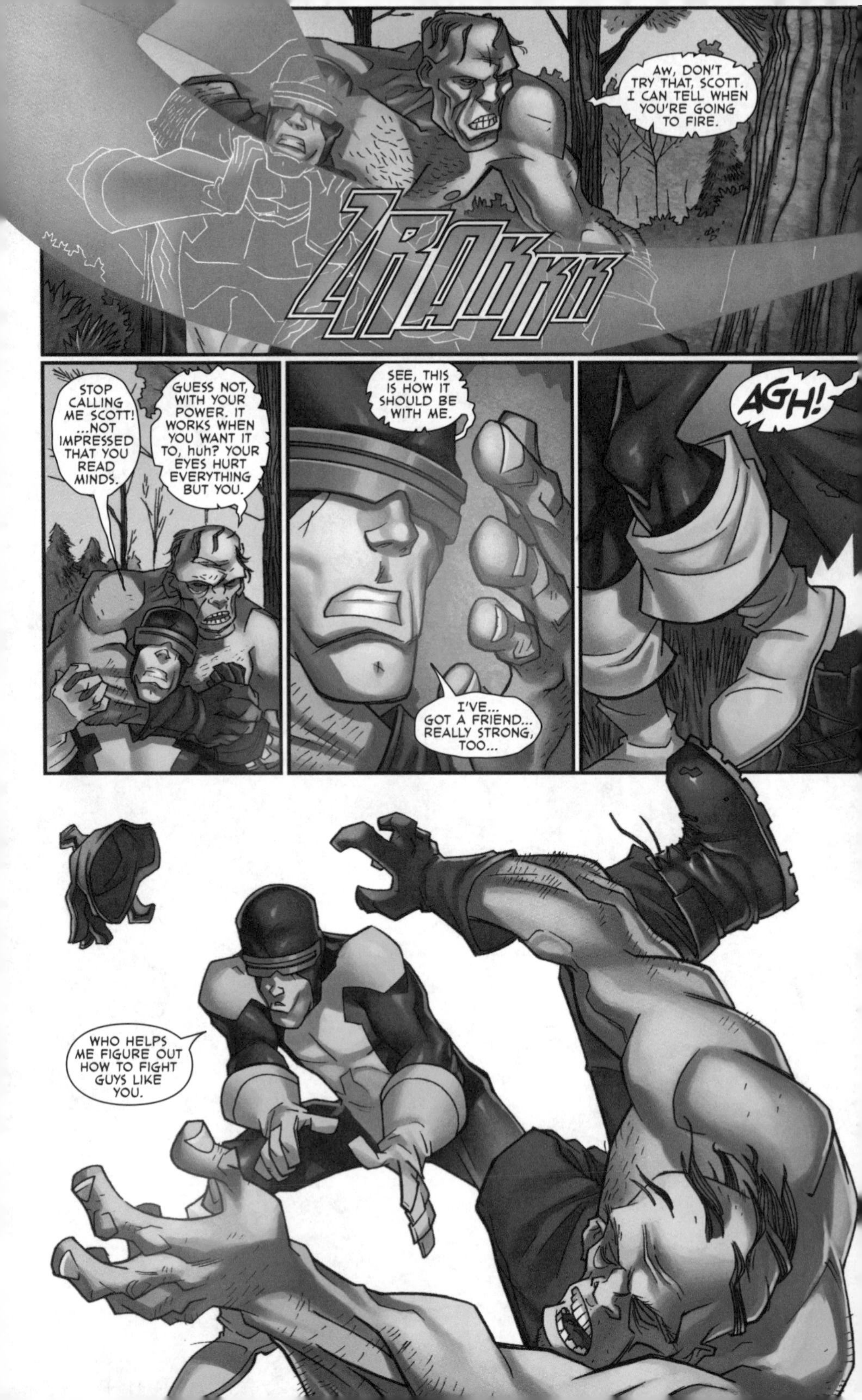
AW, DON'T TRY THAT, SCOTT. I CAN TELL WHEN YOU'RE GOING TO FIRE.
ZRAKKK
STOP CALLING ME SCOTT! ...NOT IMPRESSED THAT YOU READ MINDS.
GUESS NOT, WITH YOUR POWER. IT WORKS WHEN YOU WANT IT TO, huh? YOUR EYES HURT EVERYTHING BUT YOU.
SEE, THIS IS HOW IT SHOULD BE WITH ME.
I'VE... GOT A FRIEND... REALLY STRONG, TOO...
AGH!
WHO HELPS ME FIGURE OUT HOW TO FIGHT GUYS LIKE YOU.

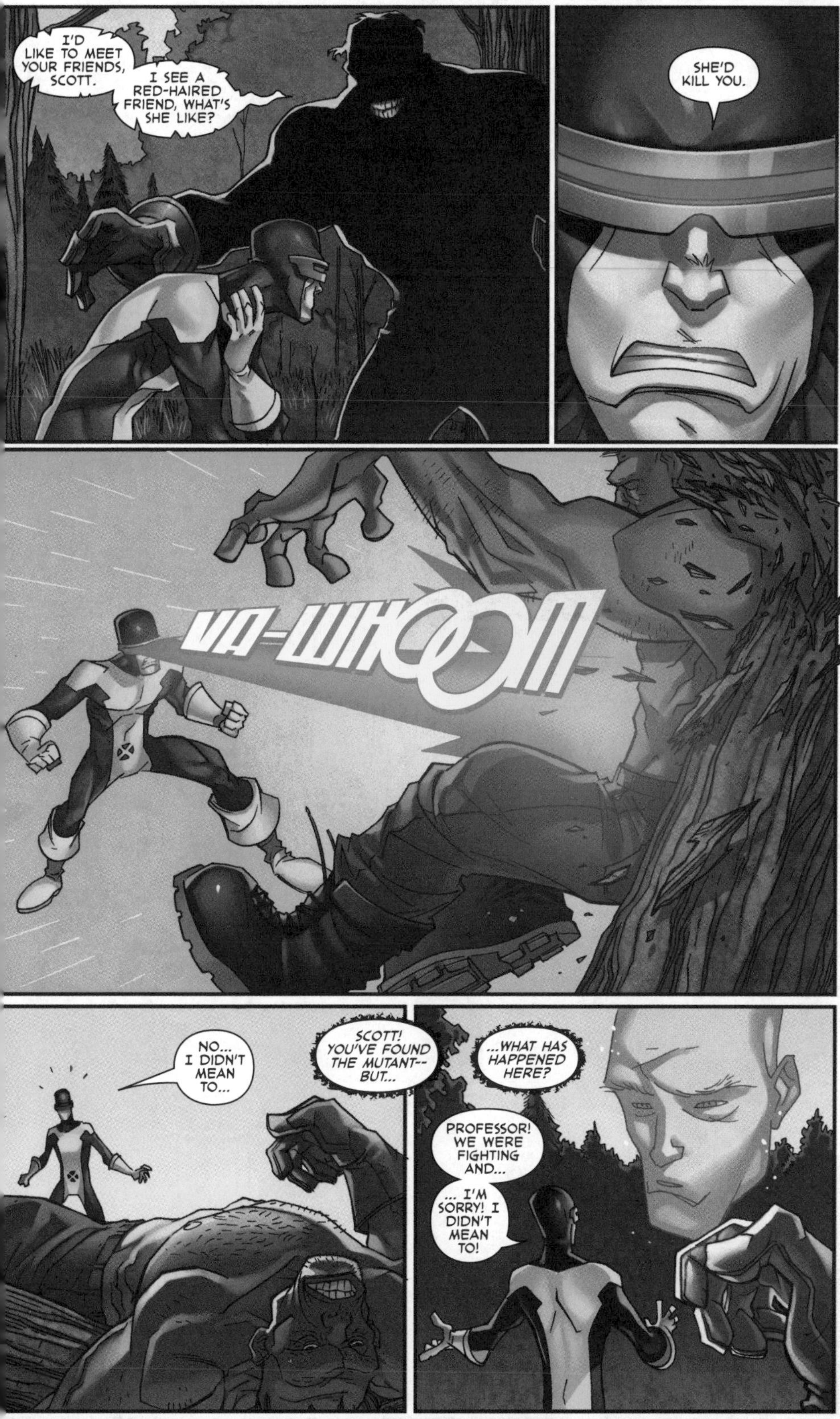
I'D LIKE TO MEET YOUR FRIENDS, SCOTT.
I SEE A RED-HAIRED FRIEND, WHAT'S SHE LIKE?
SHE'D KILL YOU.
VA-WHOOM
NO... I DIDN'T MEAN TO...
SCOTT! YOU'VE FOUND THE MUTANT-- BUT...
...WHAT HAS HAPPENED HERE?
PROFESSOR! WE WERE FIGHTING AND...
... I'M SORRY! I DIDN'T MEAN TO!

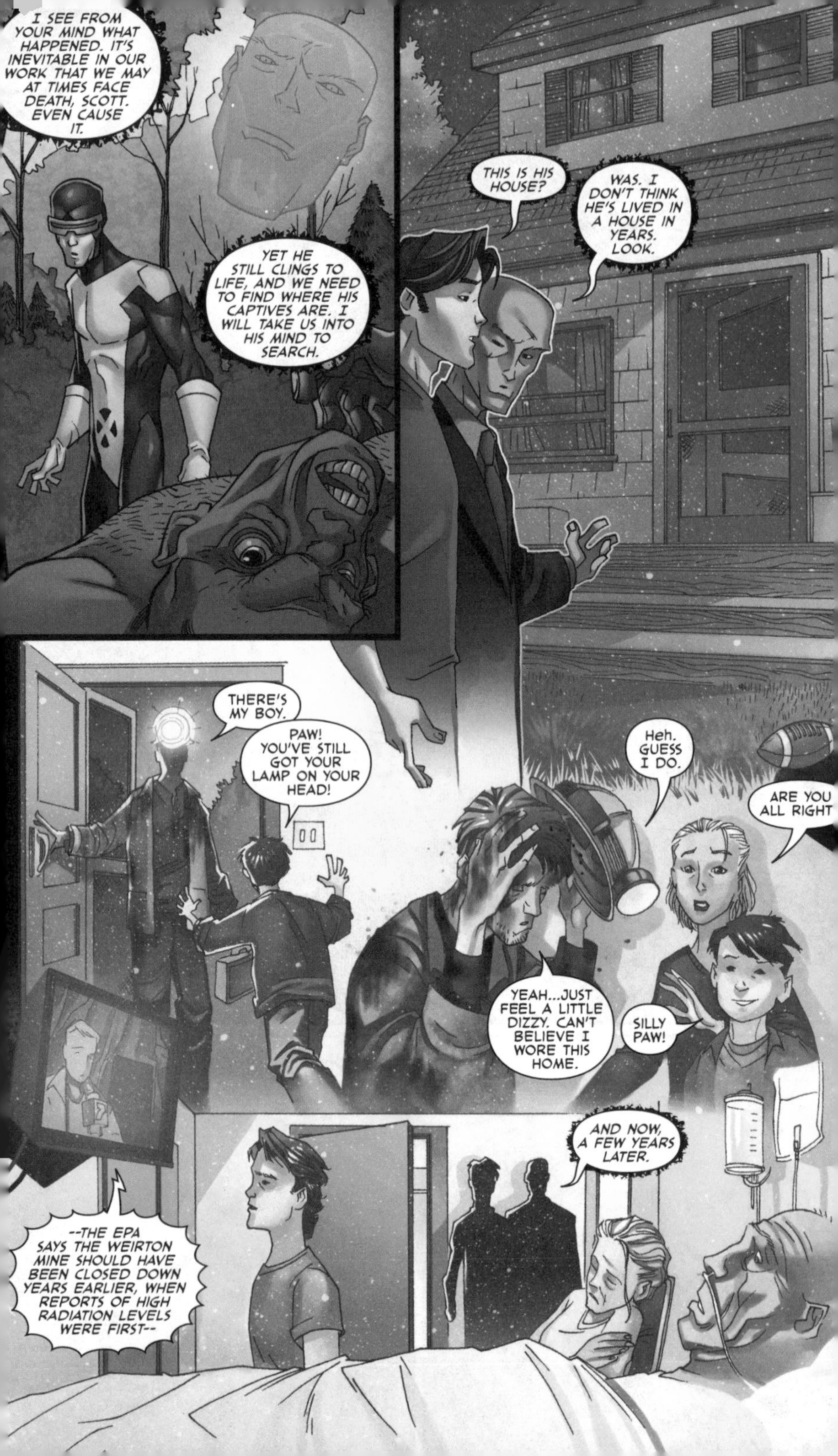

I SEE FROM YOUR MIND WHAT HAPPENED. IT'S INEVITABLE IN OUR WORK THAT WE MAY AT TIMES FACE DEATH, SCOTT. EVEN CAUSE IT.
YET HE STILL CLINGS TO LIFE, AND WE NEED TO FIND WHERE HIS CAPTIVES ARE. I WILL TAKE US INTO HIS MIND TO SEARCH.
THIS IS HIS HOUSE?
WAS. I DON'T THINK HE'S LIVED IN A HOUSE IN YEARS. LOOK.
THERE'S MY BOY.
PAW! YOU'VE STILL GOT YOUR LAMP ON YOUR HEAD!
Heh. GUESS I DO.
ARE YOU ALL RIGHT
YEAH...JUST FEEL A LITTLE DIZZY. CAN'T BELIEVE I WORE THIS HOME.
SILLY PAW!
--THE EPA SAYS THE WEIRTON MINE SHOULD HAVE BEEN CLOSED DOWN YEARS EARLIER, WHEN REPORTS OF HIGH RADIATION LEVELS WERE FIRST--
AND NOW, A FEW YEARS LATER.

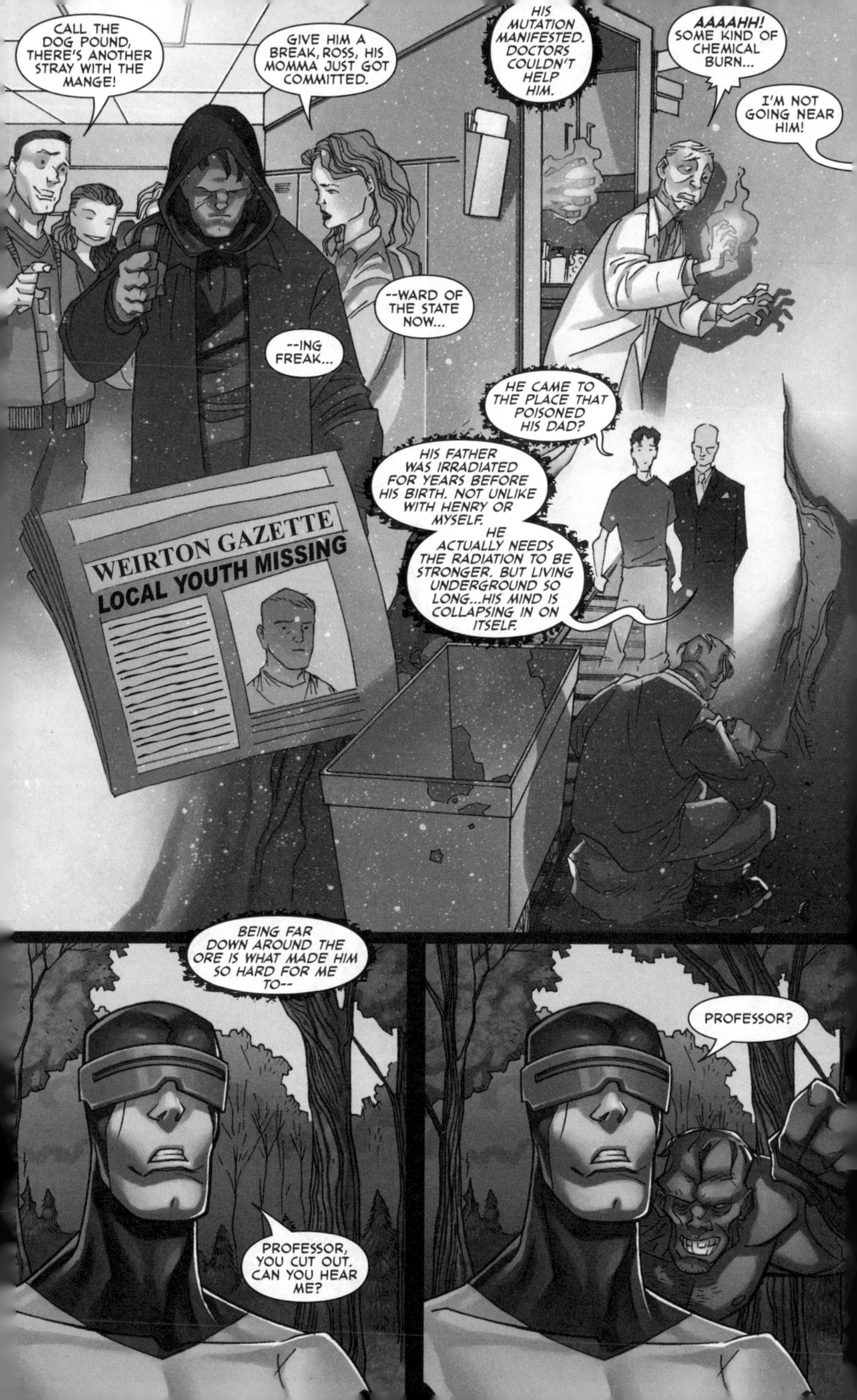
CALL THE DOG POUND, THERE'S ANOTHER STRAY WITH THE MANGE!
GIVE HIM A BREAK, ROSS, HIS MOMMA JUST GOT COMMITTED.
--WARD OF THE STATE NOW...
--ING FREAK...
HIS MUTATION MANIFESTED. DOCTORS COULDN'T HELP HIM.
AAAAHH! SOME KIND OF CHEMICAL BURN...
I'M NOT GOING NEAR HIM!
WEIRTON GAZETTE
LOCAL YOUTH MISSING
HE CAME TO THE PLACE THAT POISONED HIS DAD?
HIS FATHER WAS IRRADIATED FOR YEARS BEFORE HIS BIRTH. NOT UNLIKE WITH HENRY OR MYSELF.
HE ACTUALLY NEEDS THE RADIATION TO BE STRONGER. BUT LIVING UNDERGROUND SO LONG...HIS MIND IS COLLAPSING IN ON ITSELF.
BEING FAR DOWN AROUND THE ORE IS WHAT MADE HIM SO HARD FOR ME TO--
PROFESSOR, YOU CUT OUT. CAN YOU HEAR ME?
PROFESSOR?

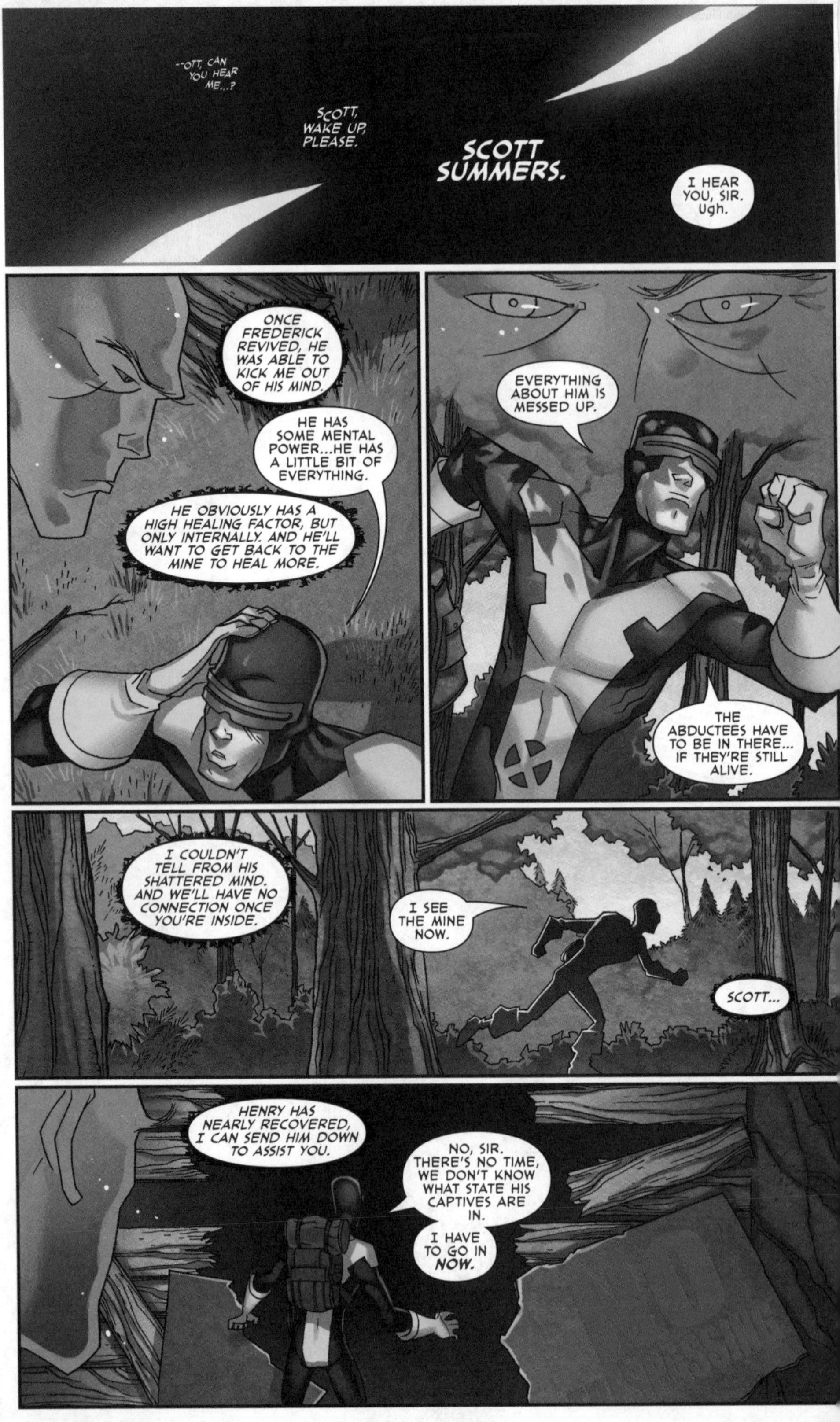
--OTT, CAN YOU HEAR ME...?
SCOTT, WAKE UP, PLEASE.
SCOTT SUMMERS.
I HEAR YOU, SIR. Ugh.
ONCE FREDERICK REVIVED, HE WAS ABLE TO KICK ME OUT OF HIS MIND.
HE HAS SOME MENTAL POWER...HE HAS A LITTLE BIT OF EVERYTHING.
HE OBVIOUSLY HAS A HIGH HEALING FACTOR, BUT ONLY INTERNALLY. AND HE'LL WANT TO GET BACK TO THE MINE TO HEAL MORE.
EVERYTHING ABOUT HIM IS MESSED UP.
THE ABDUCTEES HAVE TO BE IN THERE... IF THEY'RE STILL ALIVE.
I COULDN'T TELL FROM HIS SHATTERED MIND. AND WE'LL HAVE NO CONNECTION ONCE YOU'RE INSIDE.
I SEE THE MINE NOW.
SCOTT...
HENRY HAS NEARLY RECOVERED, I CAN SEND HIM DOWN TO ASSIST YOU.
NO, SIR. THERE'S NO TIME, WE DON'T KNOW WHAT STATE HIS CAPTIVES ARE IN.
I HAVE TO GO IN NOW.

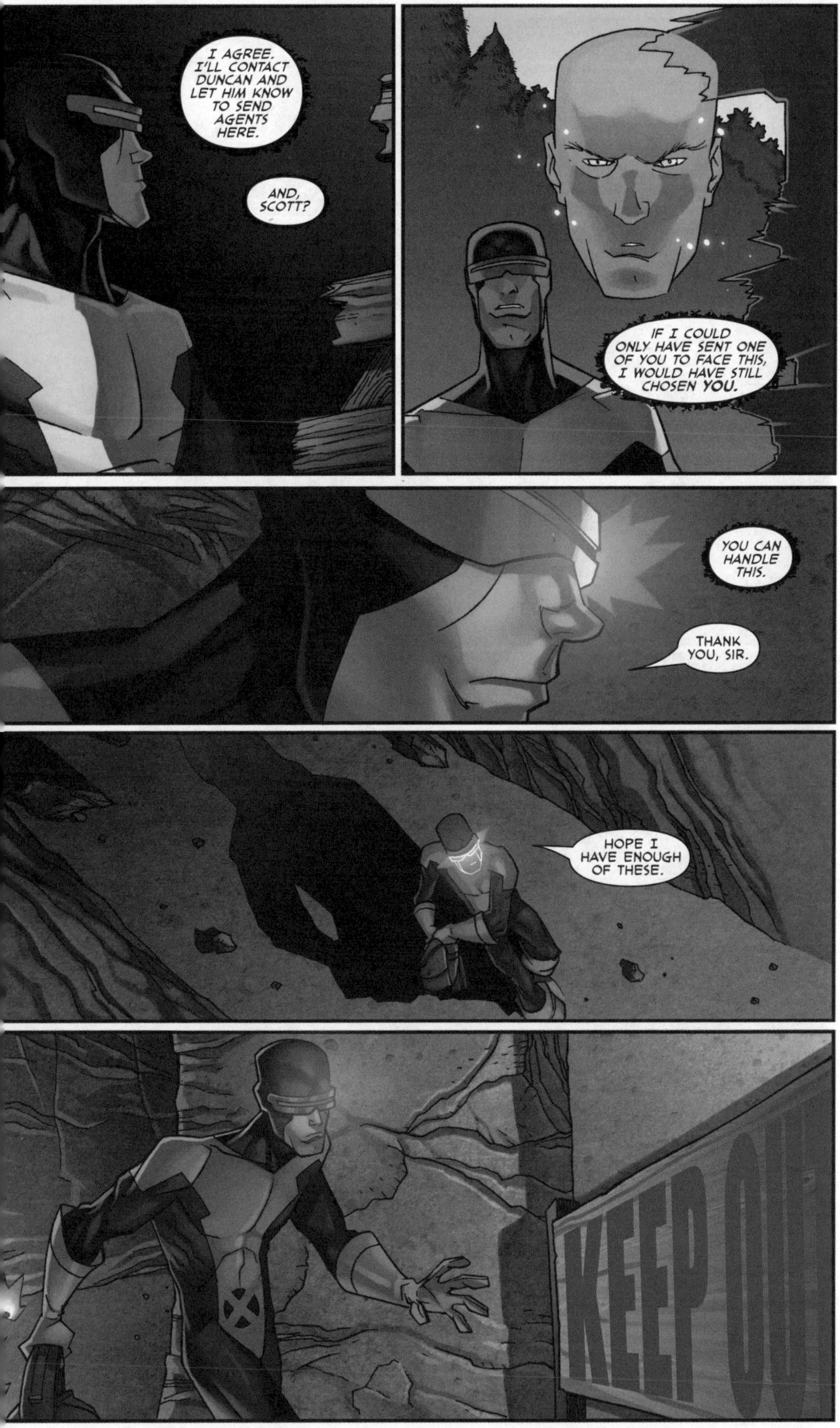

I AGREE. I'LL CONTACT DUNCAN AND LET HIM KNOW TO SEND AGENTS HERE.
AND, SCOTT?
IF I COULD ONLY HAVE SENT ONE OF YOU TO FACE THIS, I WOULD HAVE STILL CHOSEN YOU.
YOU CAN HANDLE THIS.
THANK YOU, SIR.
HOPE I HAVE ENOUGH OF THESE.
KEEP OU

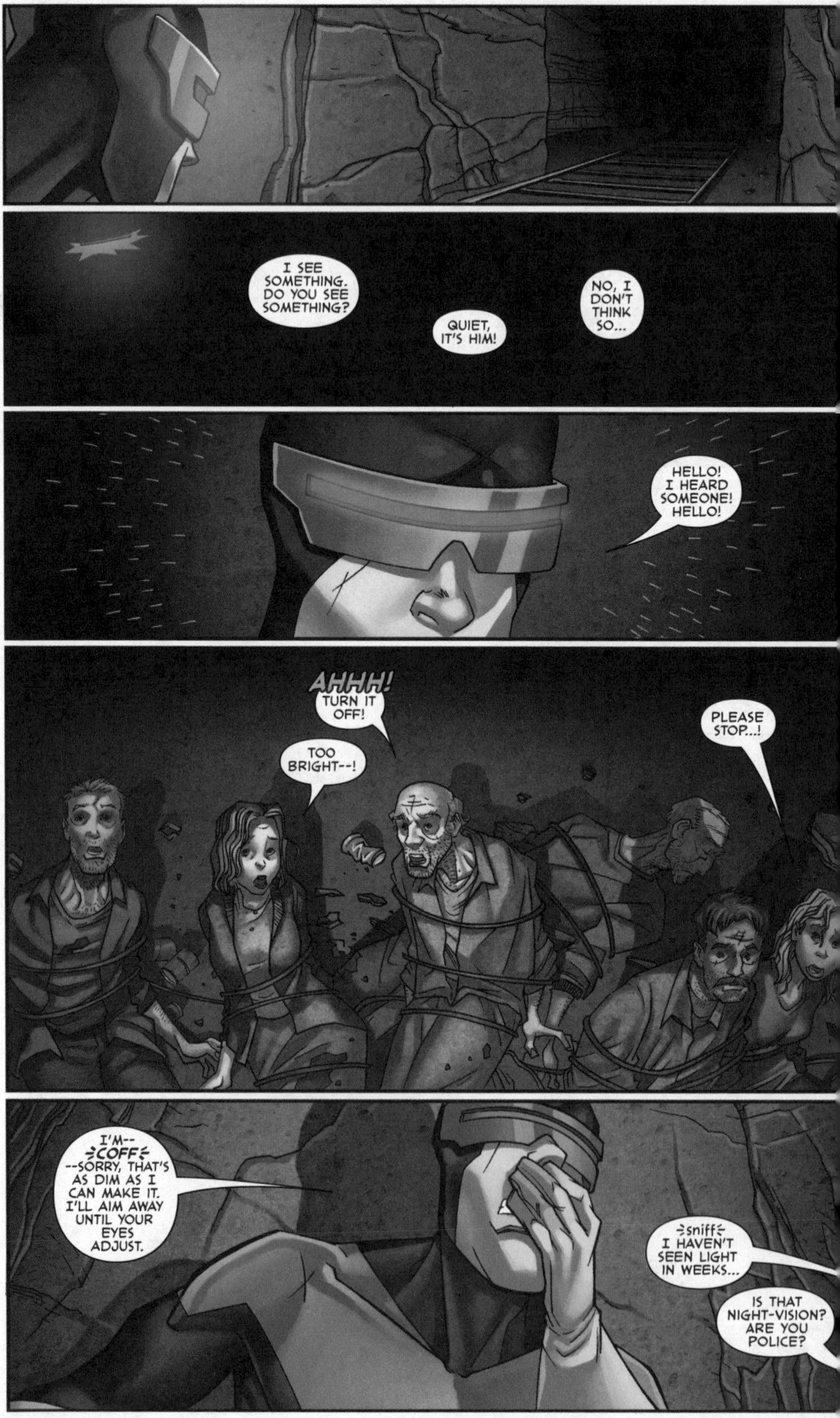
I SEE SOMETHING. DO YOU SEE SOMETHING?
QUIET, IT'S HIM!
NO, I DON'T THINK SO...
HELLO! I HEARD SOMEONE! HELLO!
AHHH! TURN IT OFF!
TOO BRIGHT--!
PLEASE STOP...!
I'M-- COFF --SORRY, THAT'S AS DIM AS I CAN MAKE IT. I'LL AIM AWAY UNTIL YOUR EYES ADJUST.
sniff I HAVEN'T SEEN LIGHT IN WEEKS...
IS THAT NIGHT-VISION? ARE YOU POLICE?

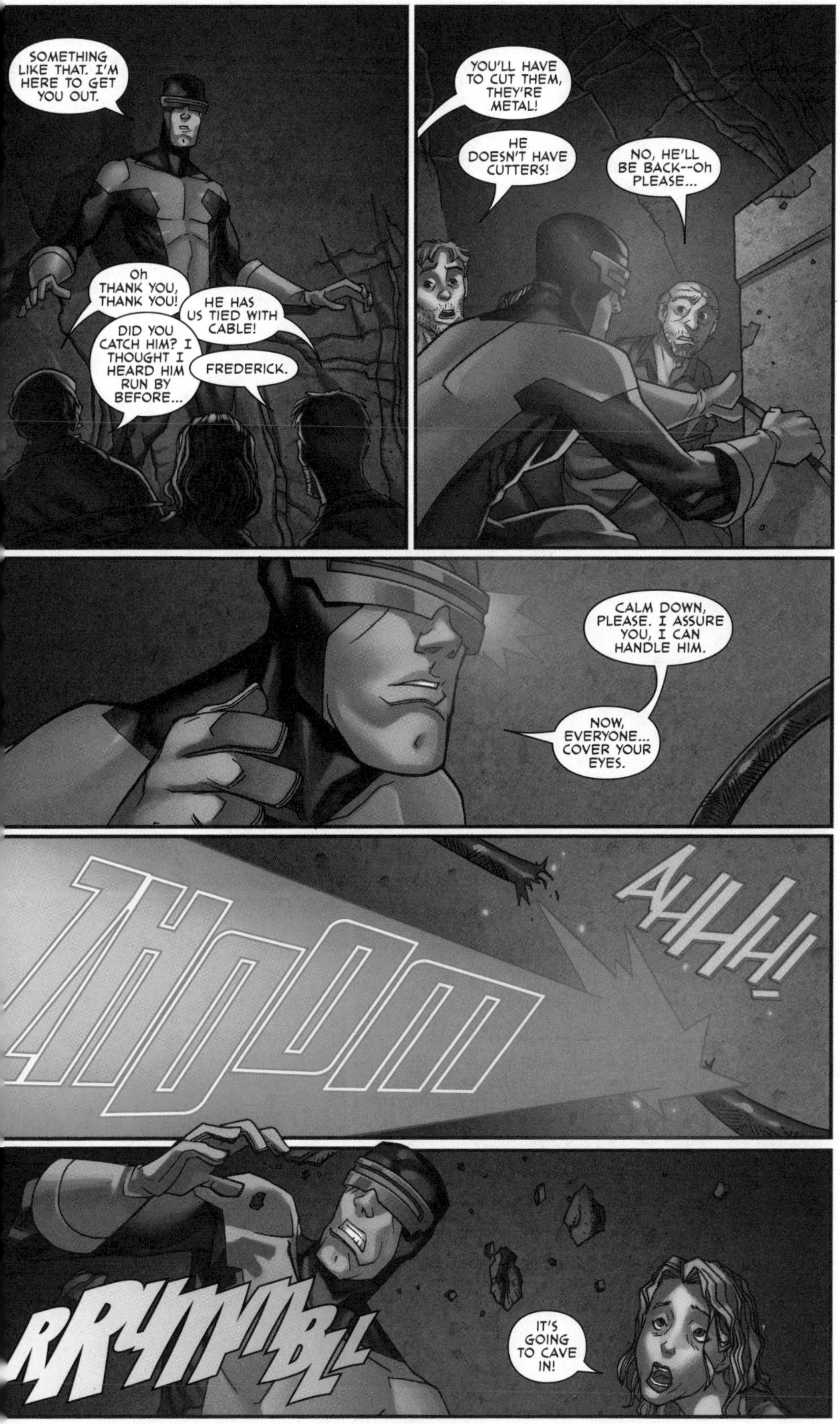
SOMETHING LIKE THAT. I'M HERE TO GET YOU OUT.
Oh THANK YOU, THANK YOU!
HE HAS US TIED WITH CABLE!
DID YOU CATCH HIM? I THOUGHT I HEARD HIM RUN BY BEFORE...
FREDERICK.
YOU'LL HAVE TO CUT THEM, THEY'RE METAL!
HE DOESN'T HAVE CUTTERS!
NO, HE'LL BE BACK--Oh PLEASE...
CALM DOWN, PLEASE. I ASSURE YOU, I CAN HANDLE HIM.
NOW, EVERYONE... COVER YOUR EYES.
ZHOOM
AHHH!
RRUMBL
IT'S GOING TO CAVE IN!

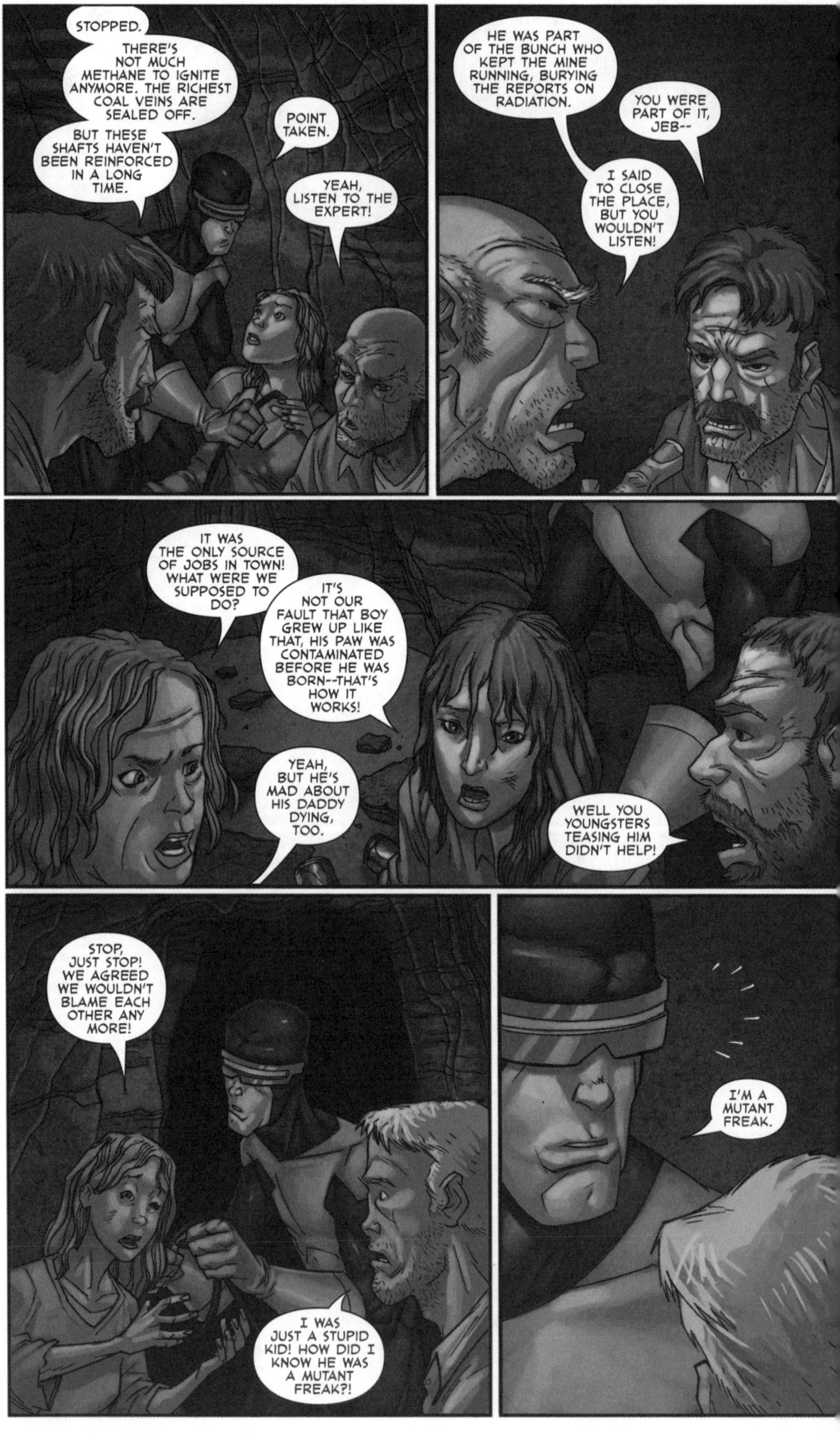
STOPPED.
THERE'S NOT MUCH METHANE TO IGNITE ANYMORE. THE RICHEST COAL VEINS ARE SEALED OFF.
BUT THESE SHAFTS HAVEN'T BEEN REINFORCED IN A LONG TIME.
POINT TAKEN.
YEAH, LISTEN TO THE EXPERT!
HE WAS PART OF THE BUNCH WHO KEPT THE MINE RUNNING, BURYING THE REPORTS ON RADIATION.
YOU WERE PART OF IT, JEB--
I SAID TO CLOSE THE PLACE, BUT YOU WOULDN'T LISTEN!
IT WAS THE ONLY SOURCE OF JOBS IN TOWN! WHAT WERE WE SUPPOSED TO DO?
IT'S NOT OUR FAULT THAT BOY GREW UP LIKE THAT, HIS PAW WAS CONTAMINATED BEFORE HE WAS BORN--THAT'S HOW IT WORKS!
YEAH, BUT HE'S MAD ABOUT HIS DADDY DYING, TOO.
WELL YOU YOUNGSTERS TEASING HIM DIDN'T HELP!
STOP, JUST STOP! WE AGREED WE WOULDN'T BLAME EACH OTHER ANY MORE!
I WAS JUST A STUPID KID! HOW DID I KNOW HE WAS A MUTANT FREAK?!
I'M A MUTANT FREAK.

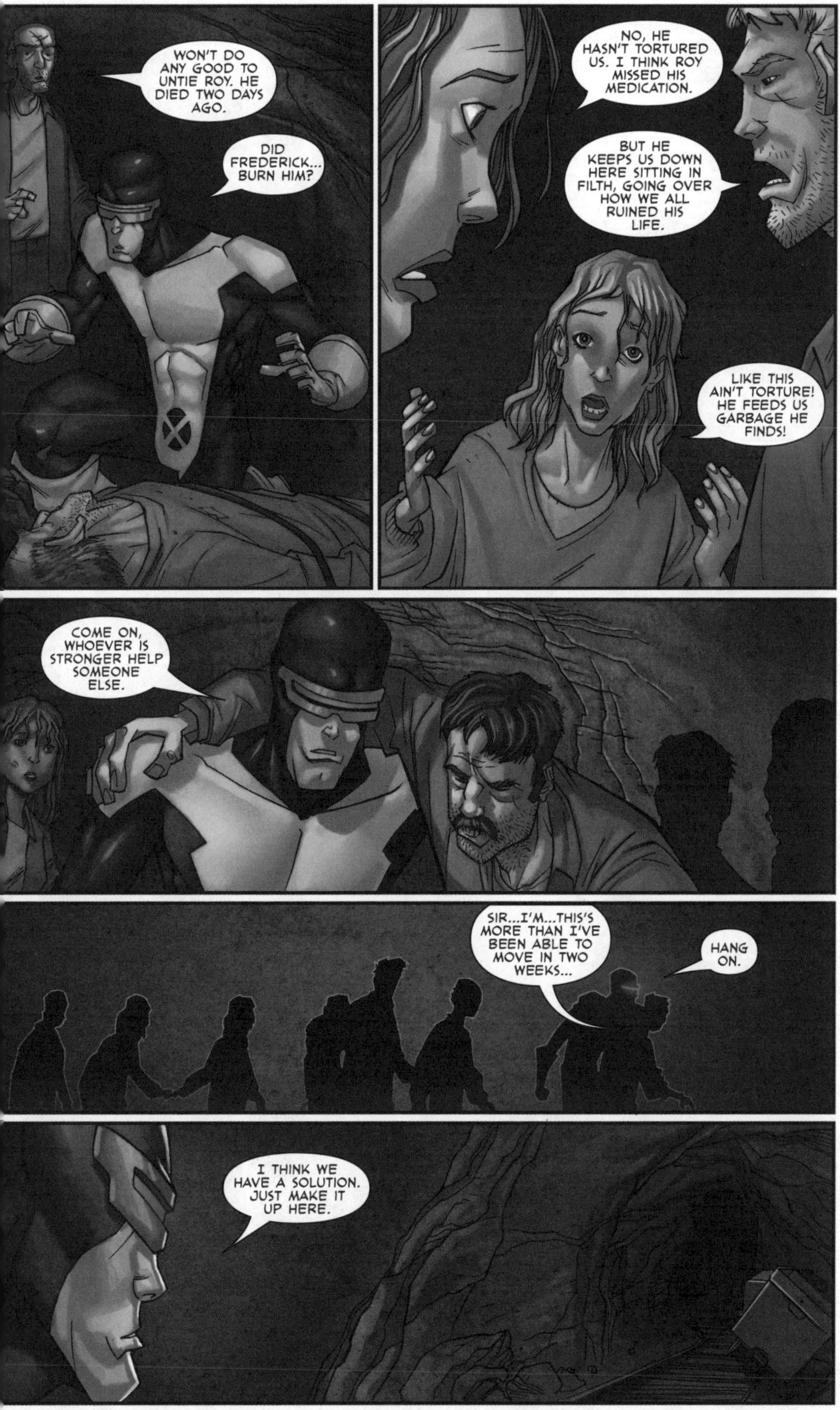
WON'T DO ANY GOOD TO UNTIE ROY. HE DIED TWO DAYS AGO.
DID FREDERICK... BURN HIM?
NO, HE HASN'T TORTURED US. I THINK ROY MISSED HIS MEDICATION.
BUT HE KEEPS US DOWN HERE SITTING IN FILTH, GOING OVER HOW WE ALL RUINED HIS LIFE.
LIKE THIS AIN'T TORTURE! HE FEEDS US GARBAGE HE FINDS!
COME ON, WHOEVER IS STRONGER HELP SOMEONE ELSE.
SIR...I'M...THIS'S MORE THAN I'VE BEEN ABLE TO MOVE IN TWO WEEKS...
HANG ON.
I THINK WE HAVE A SOLUTION. JUST MAKE IT UP HERE.

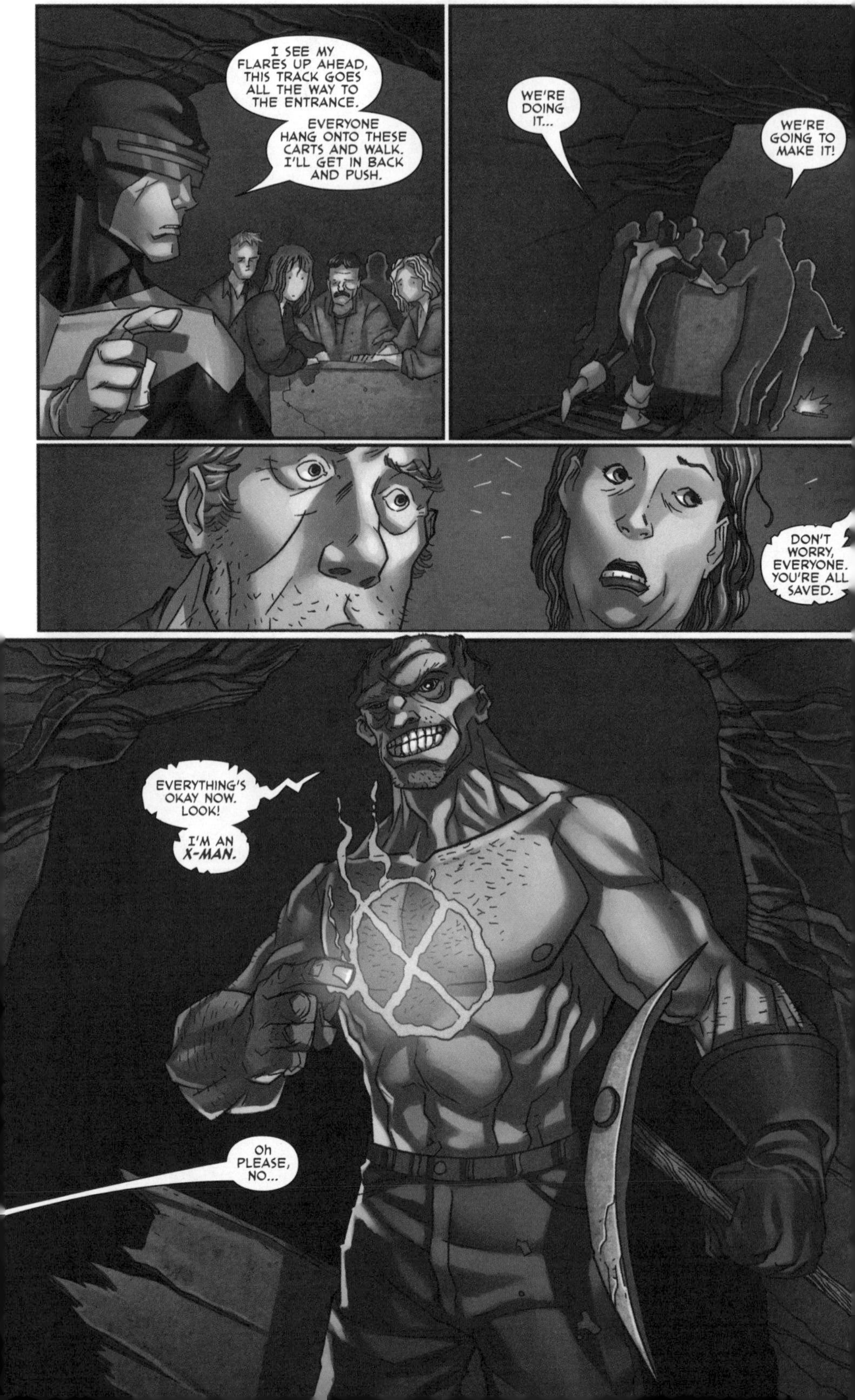

I SEE MY FLARES UP AHEAD, THIS TRACK GOES ALL THE WAY TO THE ENTRANCE.
EVERYONE HANG ONTO THESE CARTS AND WALK. I'LL GET IN BACK AND PUSH.
WE'RE DOING IT...
WE'RE GOING TO MAKE IT!
DON'T WORRY, EVERYONE. YOU'RE ALL SAVED.
EVERYTHING'S OKAY NOW. LOOK!
I'M AN *X-MAN.*
Oh PLEASE, NO...

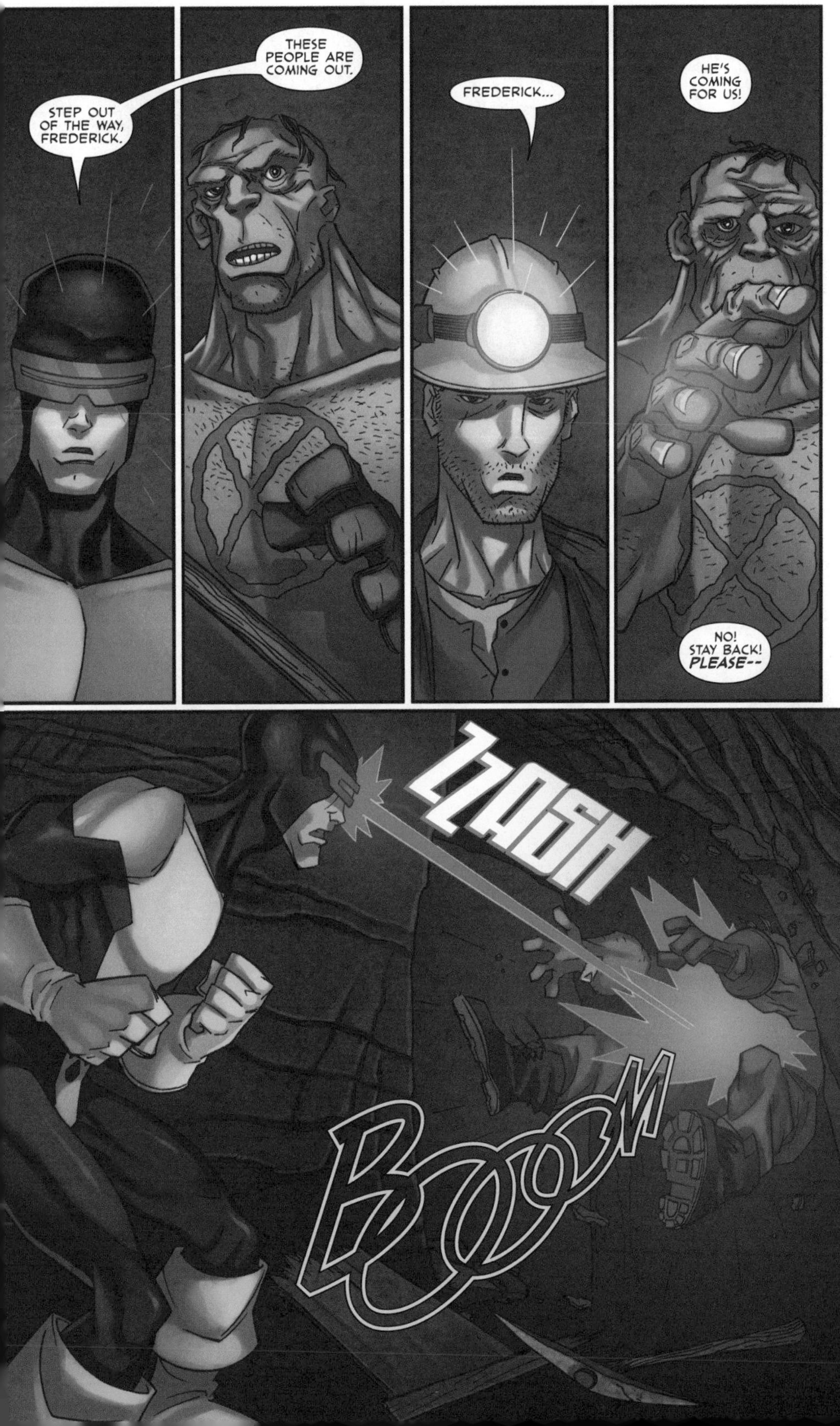

STEP OUT OF THE WAY, FREDERICK.
THESE PEOPLE ARE COMING OUT.
FREDERICK...
HE'S COMING FOR US!
NO! STAY BACK! *PLEASE--*
ZZAOSH
BOOOM

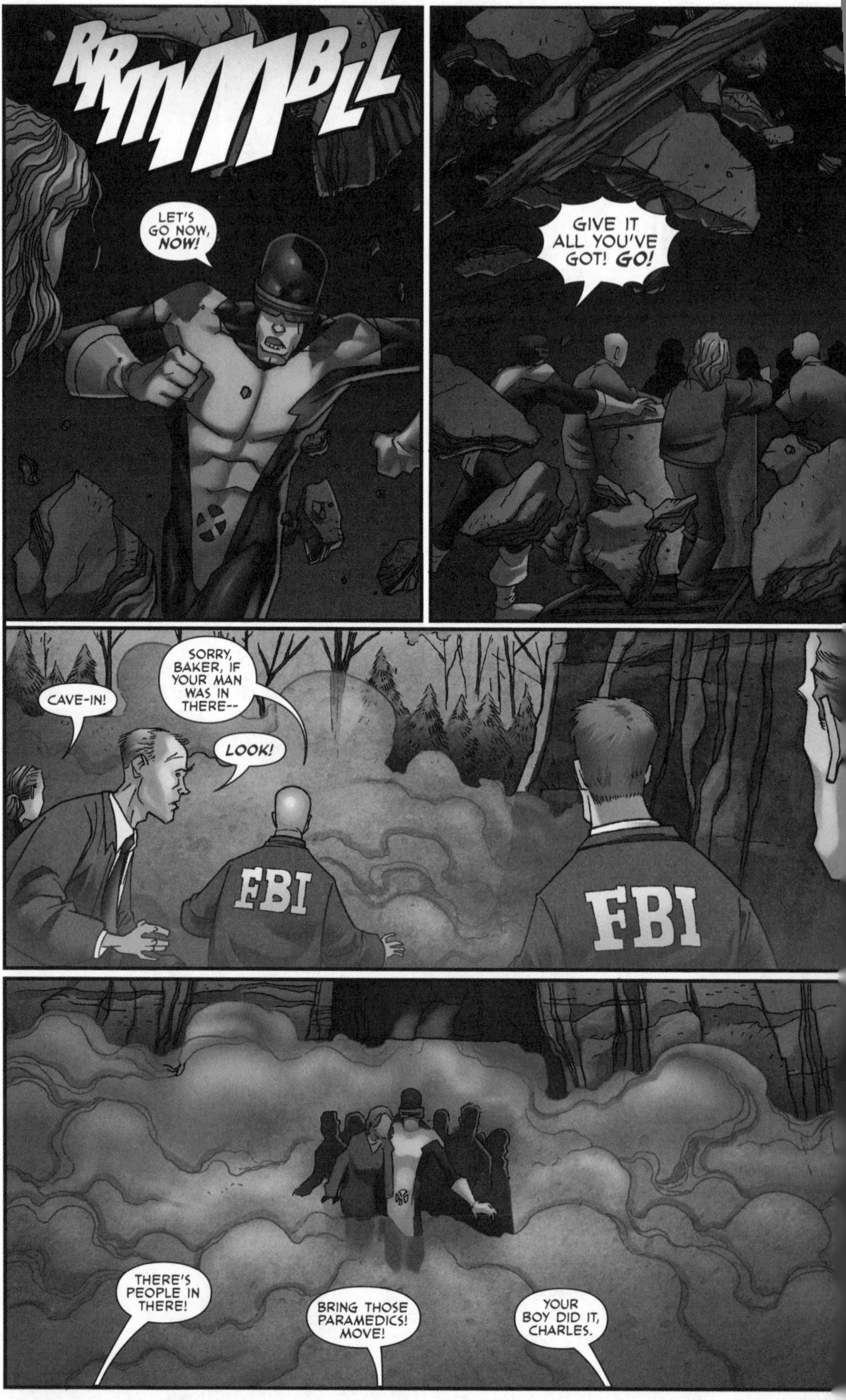
RRMMBLL
LET'S GO NOW, NOW!
GIVE IT ALL YOU'VE GOT! GO!
CAVE-IN!
SORRY, BAKER, IF YOUR MAN WAS IN THERE--
LOOK!
FBI
FBI
THERE'S PEOPLE IN THERE!
BRING THOSE PARAMEDICS! MOVE!
YOUR BOY DID IT, CHARLES.

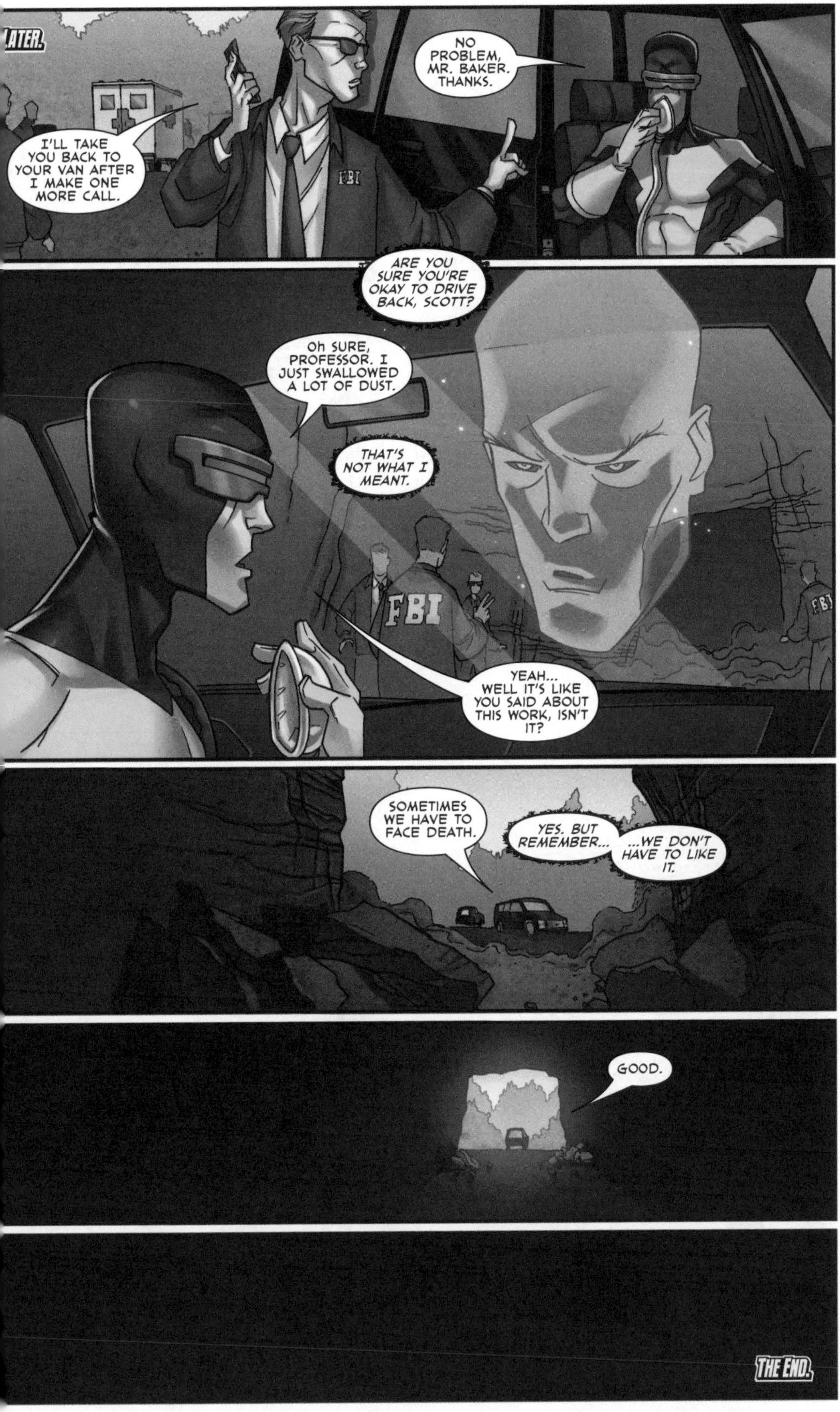
LATER.
I'LL TAKE YOU BACK TO YOUR VAN AFTER I MAKE ONE MORE CALL.
NO PROBLEM, MR. BAKER. THANKS.
FBI
ARE YOU SURE YOU'RE OKAY TO DRIVE BACK, SCOTT?
Oh SURE, PROFESSOR. I JUST SWALLOWED A LOT OF DUST.
THAT'S NOT WHAT I MEANT.
FBI
YEAH... WELL IT'S LIKE YOU SAID ABOUT THIS WORK, ISN'T IT?
SOMETIMES WE HAVE TO FACE DEATH.
YES. BUT REMEMBER...
...WE DON'T HAVE TO LIKE IT.
GOOD.
THE END.

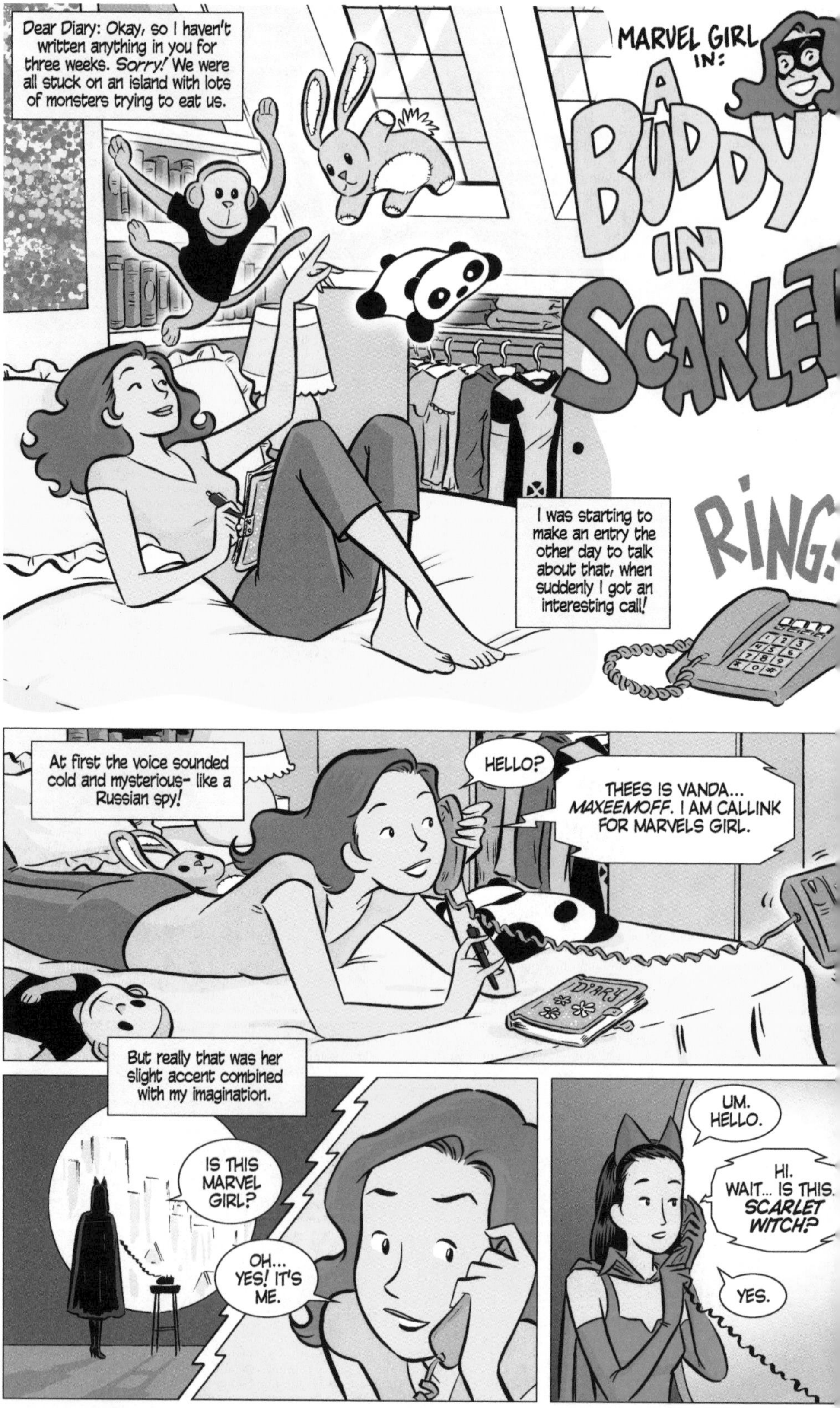

Dear Diary: Okay, so I haven't written anything in you for three weeks. *Sorry!* We were all stuck on an island with lots of monsters trying to eat us.
MARVEL GIRL IN:
A BUDDY IN SCARLET
I was starting to make an entry the other day to talk about that, when suddenly I got an interesting call!
RING!
At first the voice sounded cold and mysterious- like a Russian spy!
HELLO?
THEES IS VANDA... *MAXEEMOFF*. I AM CALLINK FOR MARVELS GIRL.
DIARY
But really that was her slight accent combined with my imagination.
IS THIS MARVEL GIRL?
OH... YES! IT'S ME.
UM. HELLO.
HI. WAIT... IS THIS. *SCARLET WITCH?*
YES.

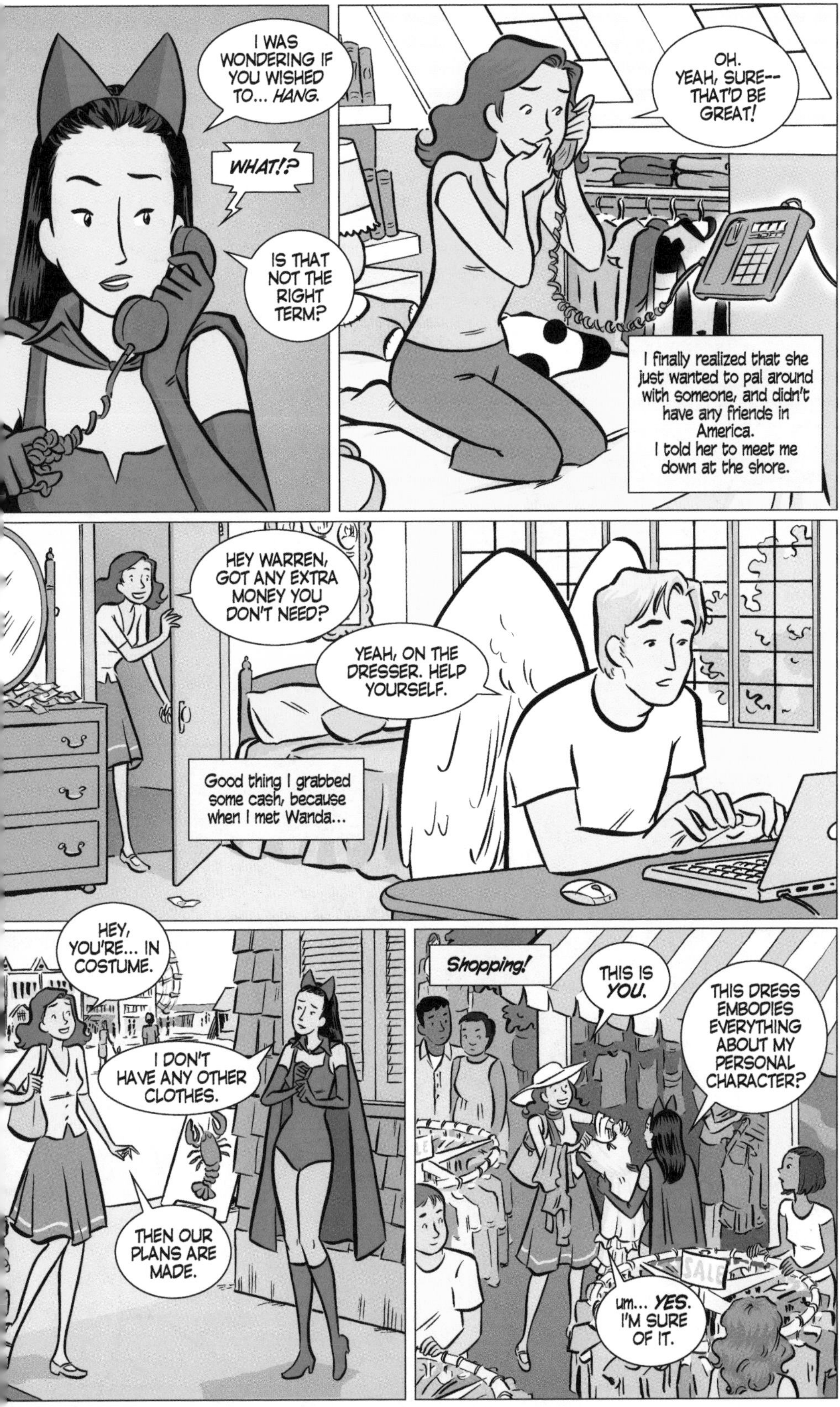

I WAS WONDERING IF YOU WISHED TO... *HANG.*
*WHAT!?*
IS THAT NOT THE RIGHT TERM?
OH. YEAH, SURE-- THAT'D BE GREAT!
I finally realized that she just wanted to pal around with someone, and didn't have any friends in America. I told her to meet me down at the shore.
HEY WARREN, GOT ANY EXTRA MONEY YOU DON'T NEED?
YEAH, ON THE DRESSER. HELP YOURSELF.
Good thing I grabbed some cash, because when I met Wanda...
HEY, YOU'RE... IN COSTUME.
I DON'T HAVE ANY OTHER CLOTHES.
THEN OUR PLANS ARE MADE.
*Shopping!*
THIS IS *YOU.*
THIS DRESS EMBODIES EVERYTHING ABOUT MY PERSONAL CHARACTER?
um... *YES.* I'M SURE OF IT.

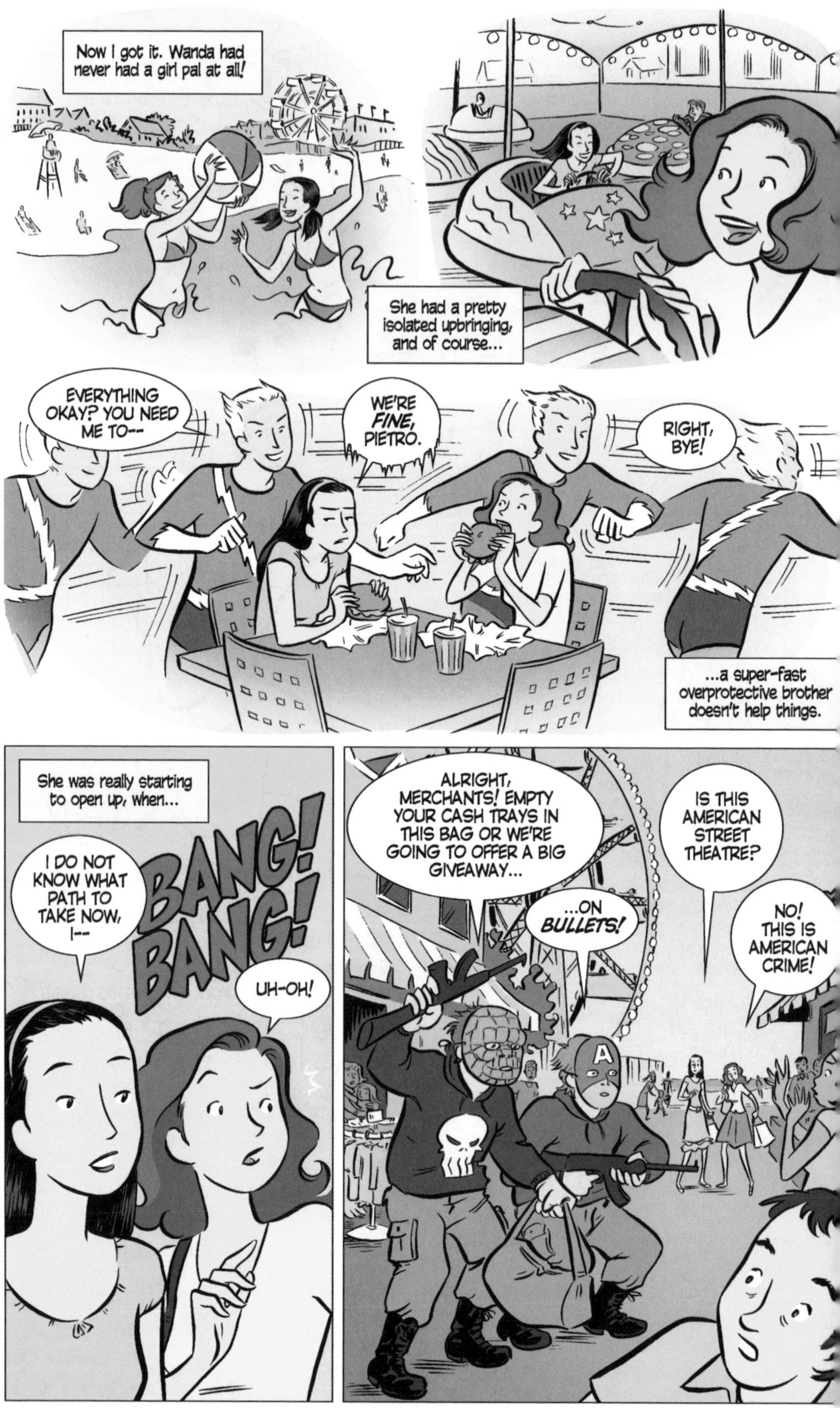

Now I got it. Wanda had never had a girl pal at all!
She had a pretty isolated upbringing, and of course...
EVERYTHING OKAY? YOU NEED ME TO--
WE'RE FINE, PIETRO.
RIGHT, BYE!
...a super-fast overprotective brother doesn't help things.
She was really starting to open up, when...
I DO NOT KNOW WHAT PATH TO TAKE NOW, I--
BANG! BANG!
UH-OH!
ALRIGHT, MERCHANTS! EMPTY YOUR CASH TRAYS IN THIS BAG OR WE'RE GOING TO OFFER A BIG GIVEAWAY...
...ON BULLETS!
IS THIS AMERICAN STREET THEATRE?
NO! THIS IS AMERICAN CRIME!

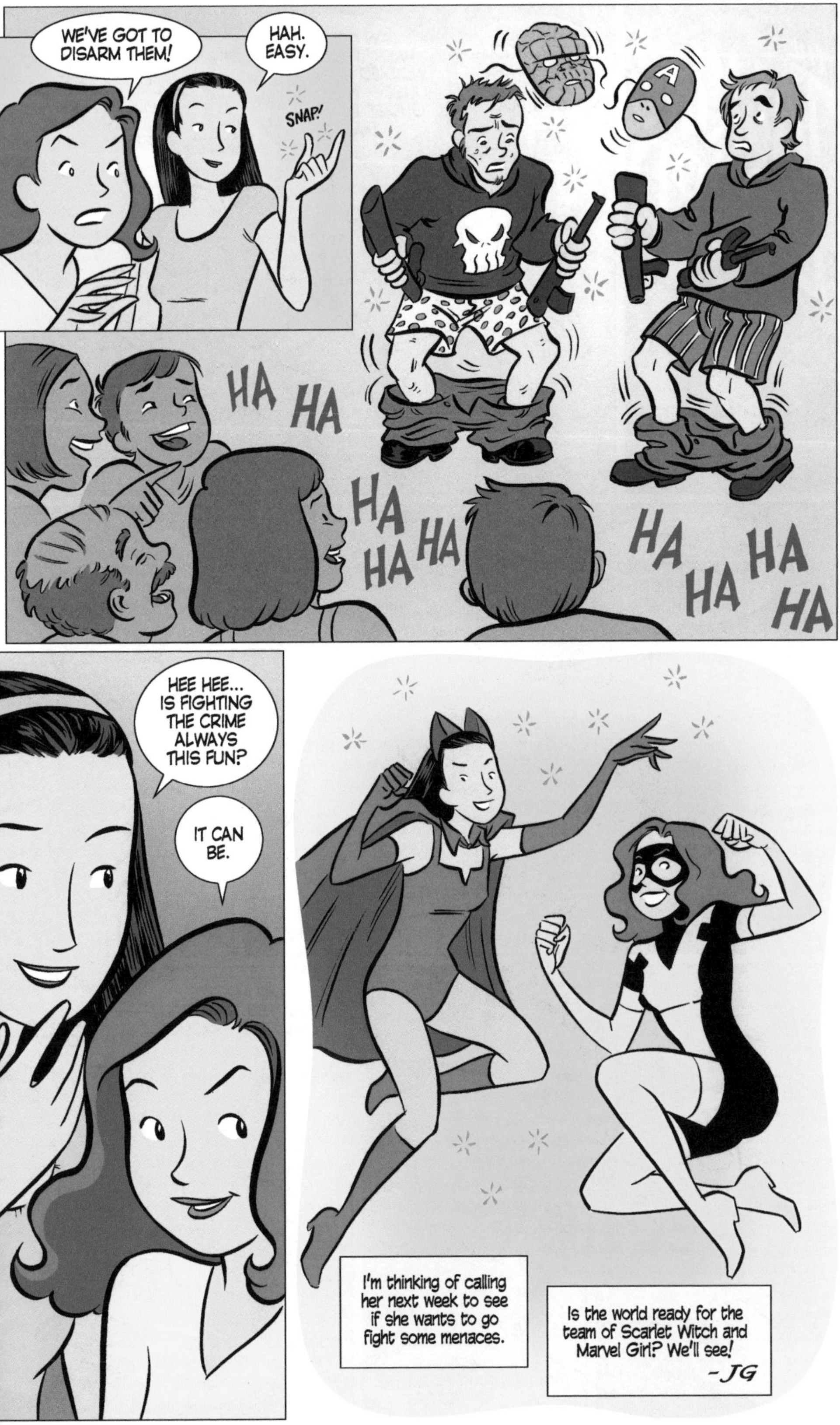

WE'VE GOT TO DISARM THEM!
HAH. EASY.
SNAP!
HA HA
HA HA HA
HA HA HA HA HA
HEE HEE... IS FIGHTING THE CRIME ALWAYS THIS FUN?
IT CAN BE.
I'm thinking of calling her next week to see if she wants to go fight some menaces.
Is the world ready for the team of Scarlet Witch and Marvel Girl? We'll see!
-JG

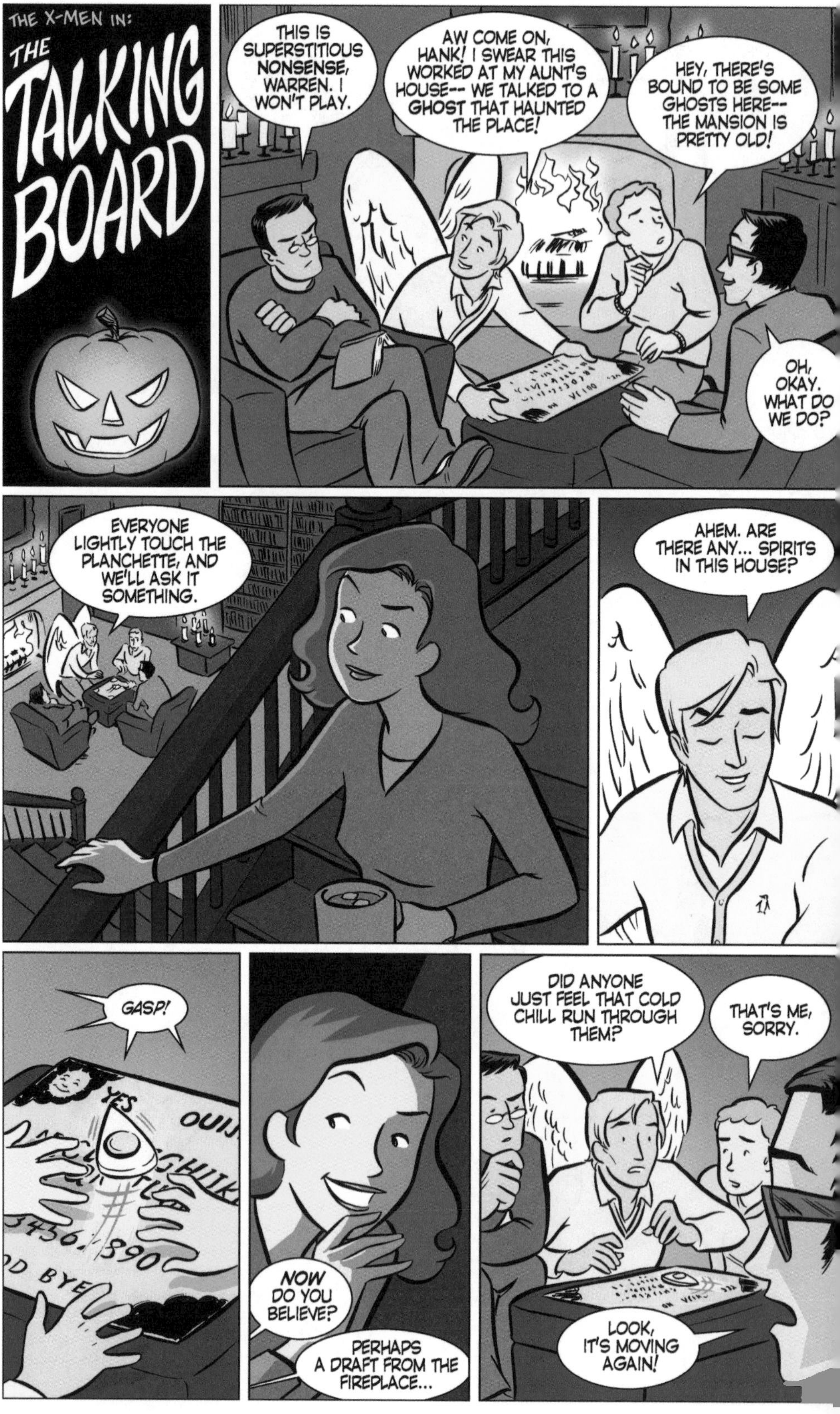
THE X-MEN IN:
THE TALKING BOARD
THIS IS SUPERSTITIOUS NONSENSE, WARREN. I WON'T PLAY.
AW COME ON, HANK! I SWEAR THIS WORKED AT MY AUNT'S HOUSE-- WE TALKED TO A GHOST THAT HAUNTED THE PLACE!
HEY, THERE'S BOUND TO BE SOME GHOSTS HERE-- THE MANSION IS PRETTY OLD!
OH, OKAY. WHAT DO WE DO?
EVERYONE LIGHTLY TOUCH THE PLANCHETTE, AND WE'LL ASK IT SOMETHING.
AHEM. ARE THERE ANY... SPIRITS IN THIS HOUSE?
GASP!
YES
NOW DO YOU BELIEVE?
PERHAPS A DRAFT FROM THE FIREPLACE...
DID ANYONE JUST FEEL THAT COLD CHILL RUN THROUGH THEM?
THAT'S ME, SORRY.
LOOK, IT'S MOVING AGAIN!

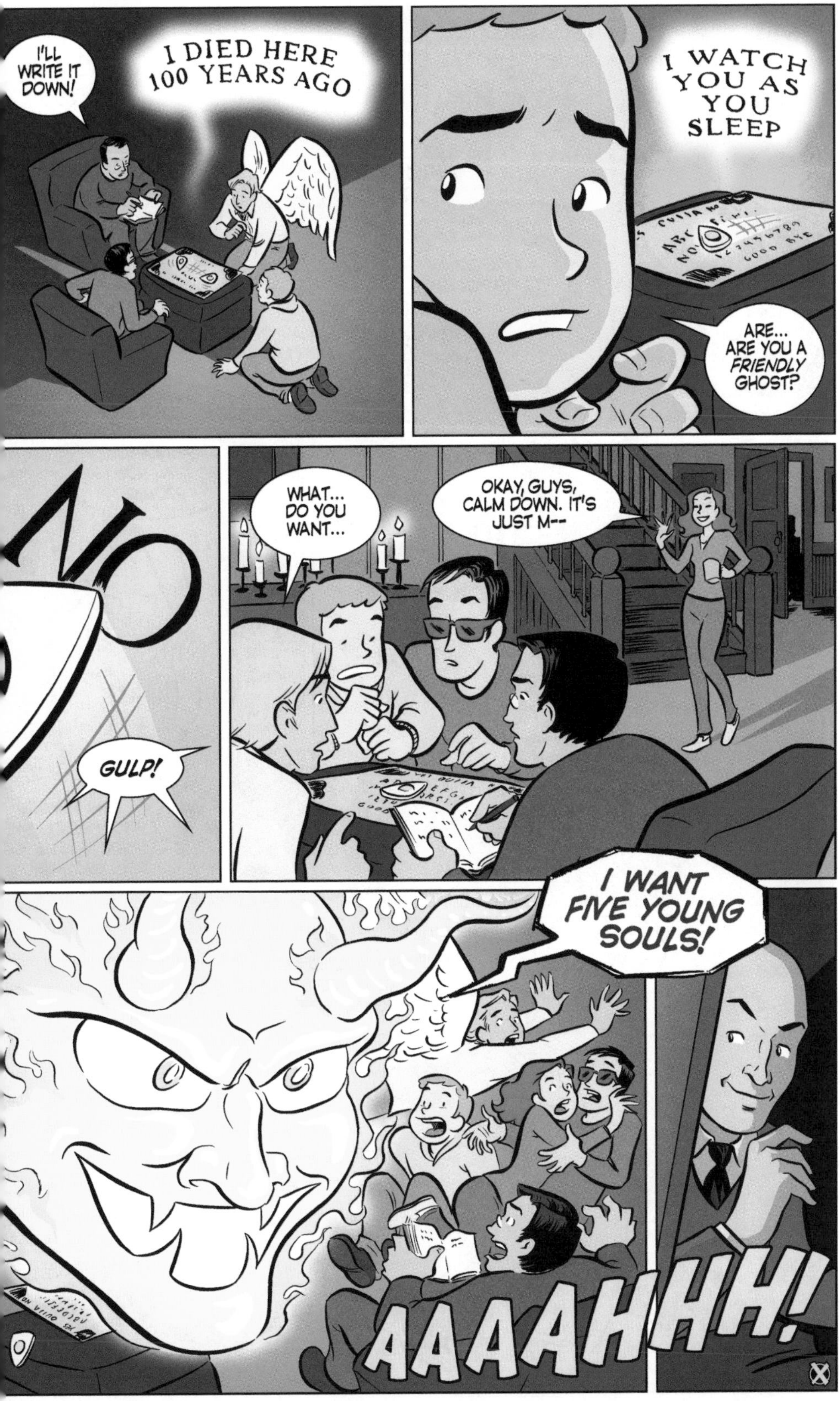
I'LL WRITE IT DOWN!
I DIED HERE 100 YEARS AGO
I WATCH YOU AS YOU SLEEP
ARE... ARE YOU A FRIENDLY GHOST?
NO
GULP!
WHAT... DO YOU WANT...
OKAY, GUYS, CALM DOWN. IT'S JUST M--
I WANT FIVE YOUNG SOULS!
AAAAHHH!

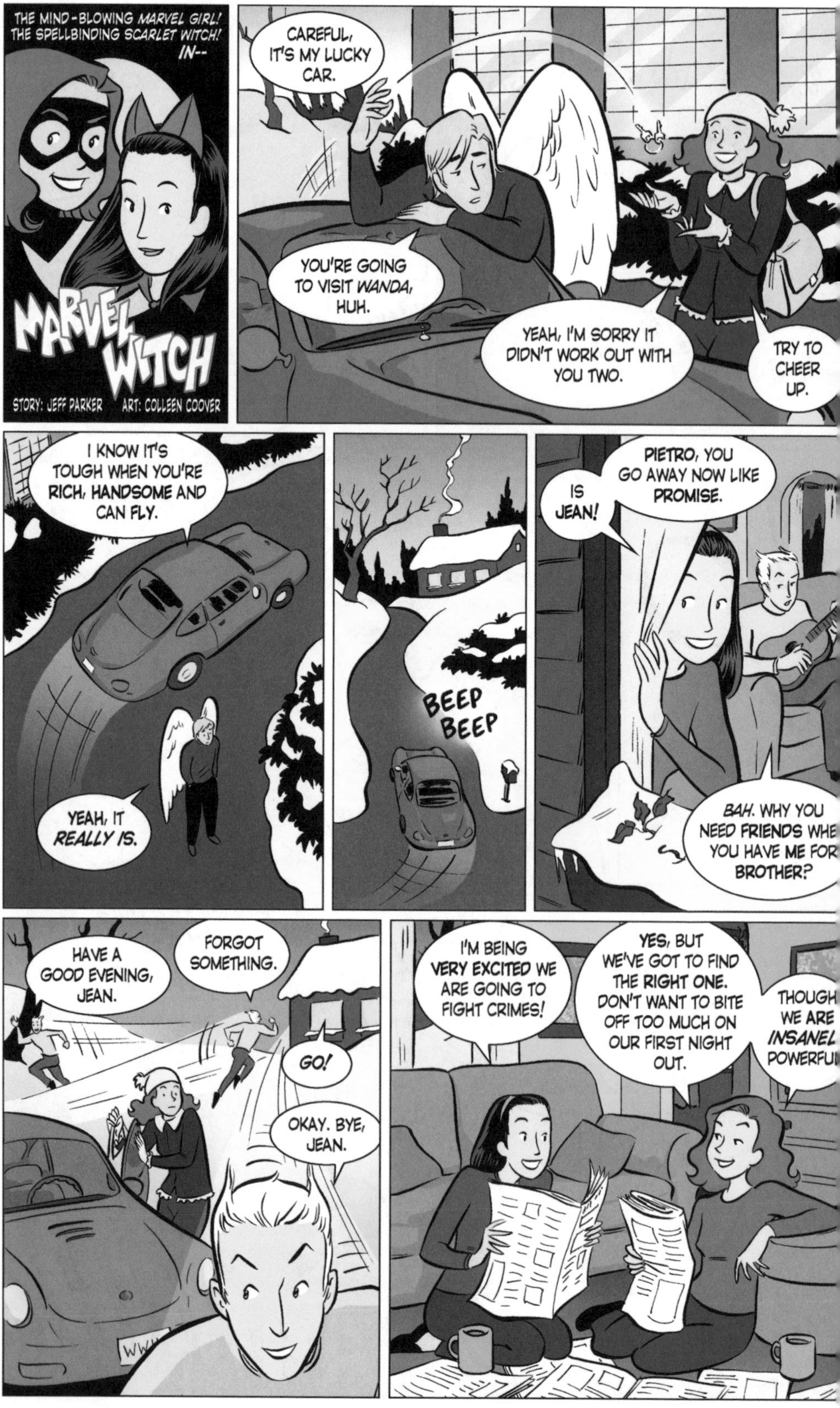

THE MIND-BLOWING MARVEL GIRL! THE SPELLBINDING SCARLET WITCH! IN--
MARVEL WITCH
STORY: JEFF PARKER ART: COLLEEN COOVER
CAREFUL, IT'S MY LUCKY CAR.
YOU'RE GOING TO VISIT WANDA, HUH.
YEAH, I'M SORRY IT DIDN'T WORK OUT WITH YOU TWO.
TRY TO CHEER UP.
I KNOW IT'S TOUGH WHEN YOU'RE RICH, HANDSOME AND CAN FLY.
YEAH, IT REALLY IS.
BEEP BEEP
IS JEAN!
PIETRO, YOU GO AWAY NOW LIKE PROMISE.
BAH. WHY YOU NEED FRIENDS WHE YOU HAVE ME FOR BROTHER?
HAVE A GOOD EVENING, JEAN.
FORGOT SOMETHING.
GO!
OKAY. BYE, JEAN.
I'M BEING VERY EXCITED WE ARE GOING TO FIGHT CRIMES!
YES, BUT WE'VE GOT TO FIND THE RIGHT ONE. DON'T WANT TO BITE OFF TOO MUCH ON OUR FIRST NIGHT OUT.
THOUGH WE ARE INSANEL POWERFU

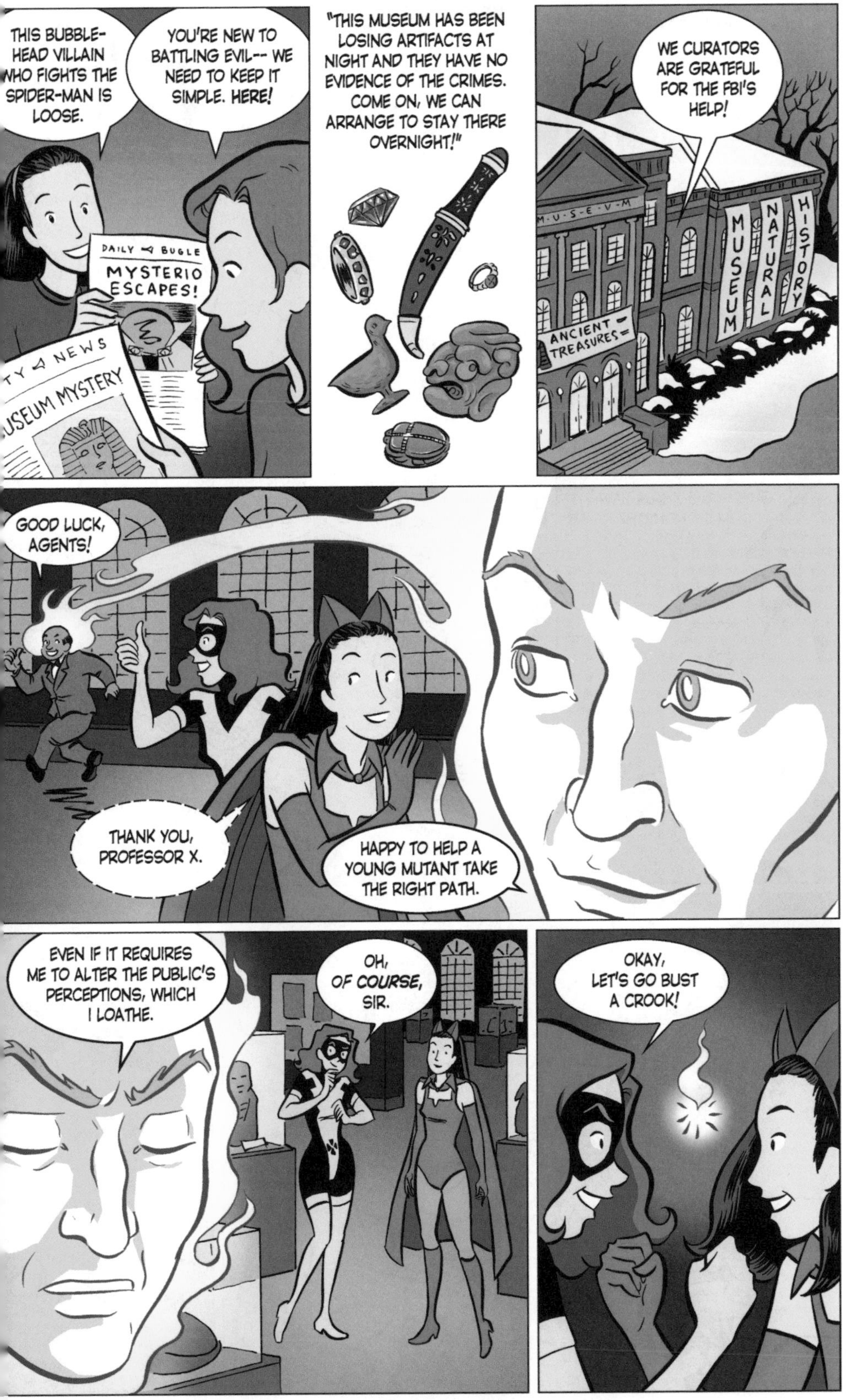
THIS BUBBLE-HEAD VILLAIN WHO FIGHTS THE SPIDER-MAN IS LOOSE.
YOU'RE NEW TO BATTLING EVIL-- WE NEED TO KEEP IT SIMPLE. HERE!
DAILY BUGLE
MYSTERIO ESCAPES!
NEWS
MUSEUM MYSTERY
"THIS MUSEUM HAS BEEN LOSING ARTIFACTS AT NIGHT AND THEY HAVE NO EVIDENCE OF THE CRIMES. COME ON, WE CAN ARRANGE TO STAY THERE OVERNIGHT!"
WE CURATORS ARE GRATEFUL FOR THE FBI'S HELP!
M-U-S-E-V-M
MUSEUM
NATURAL
HISTORY
ANCIENT TREASURES
GOOD LUCK, AGENTS!
THANK YOU, PROFESSOR X.
HAPPY TO HELP A YOUNG MUTANT TAKE THE RIGHT PATH.
EVEN IF IT REQUIRES ME TO ALTER THE PUBLIC'S PERCEPTIONS, WHICH I LOATHE.
OH, OF COURSE, SIR.
OKAY, LET'S GO BUST A CROOK!

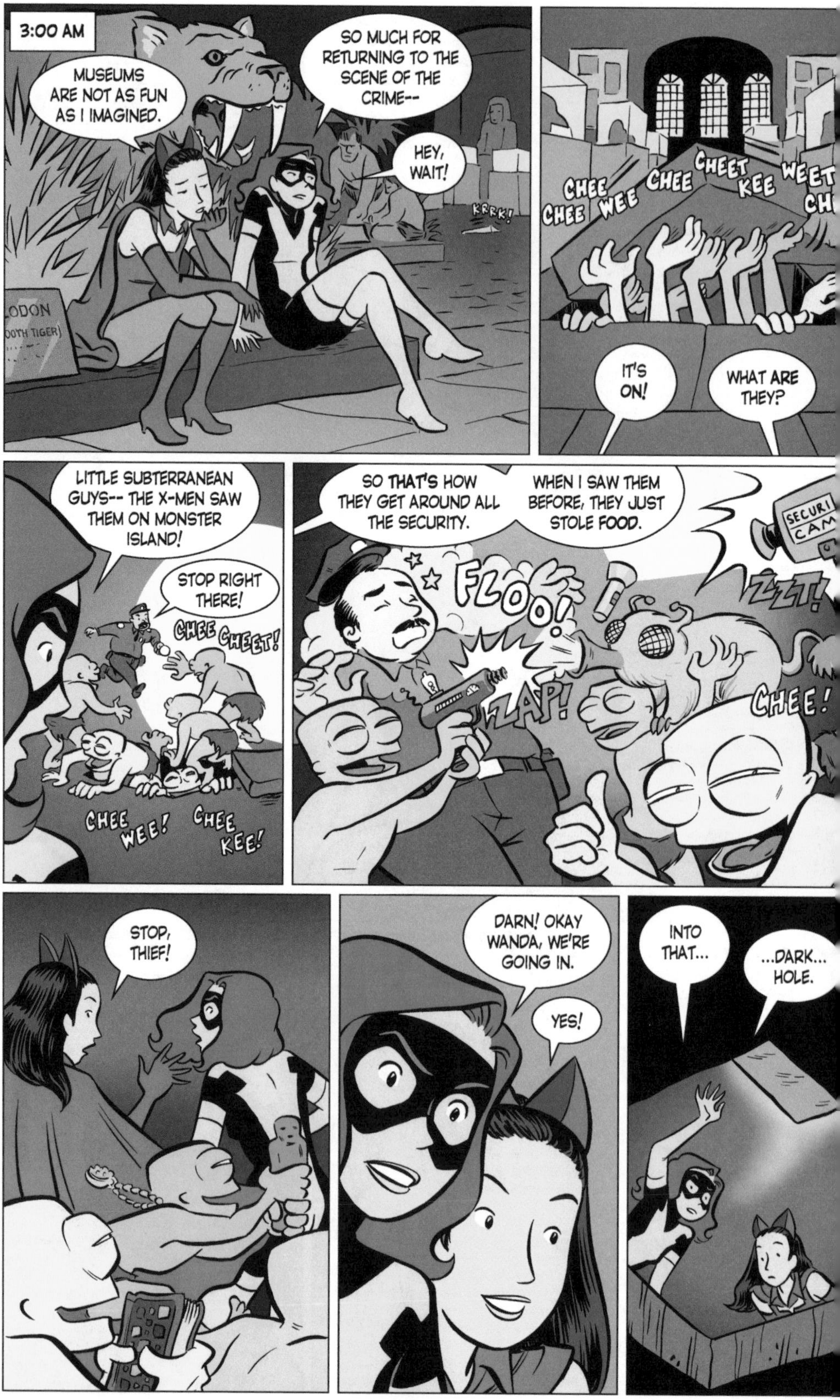
3:00 AM
MUSEUMS ARE NOT AS FUN AS I IMAGINED.
SO MUCH FOR RETURNING TO THE SCENE OF THE CRIME--
HEY, WAIT!
KRRK!
CHEE CHEE WEE CHEE CHEET KEE WEET
IT'S ON!
WHAT ARE THEY?
LITTLE SUBTERRANEAN GUYS-- THE X-MEN SAW THEM ON MONSTER ISLAND!
STOP RIGHT THERE!
CHEE CHEET!
CHEE WEE!
CHEE KEE!
SO THAT'S HOW THEY GET AROUND ALL THE SECURITY.
WHEN I SAW THEM BEFORE, THEY JUST STOLE FOOD.
FLOO!
ZAP!
ZZT!
CHEE!
STOP, THIEF!
DARN! OKAY WANDA, WE'RE GOING IN.
YES!
INTO THAT...
...DARK... HOLE.

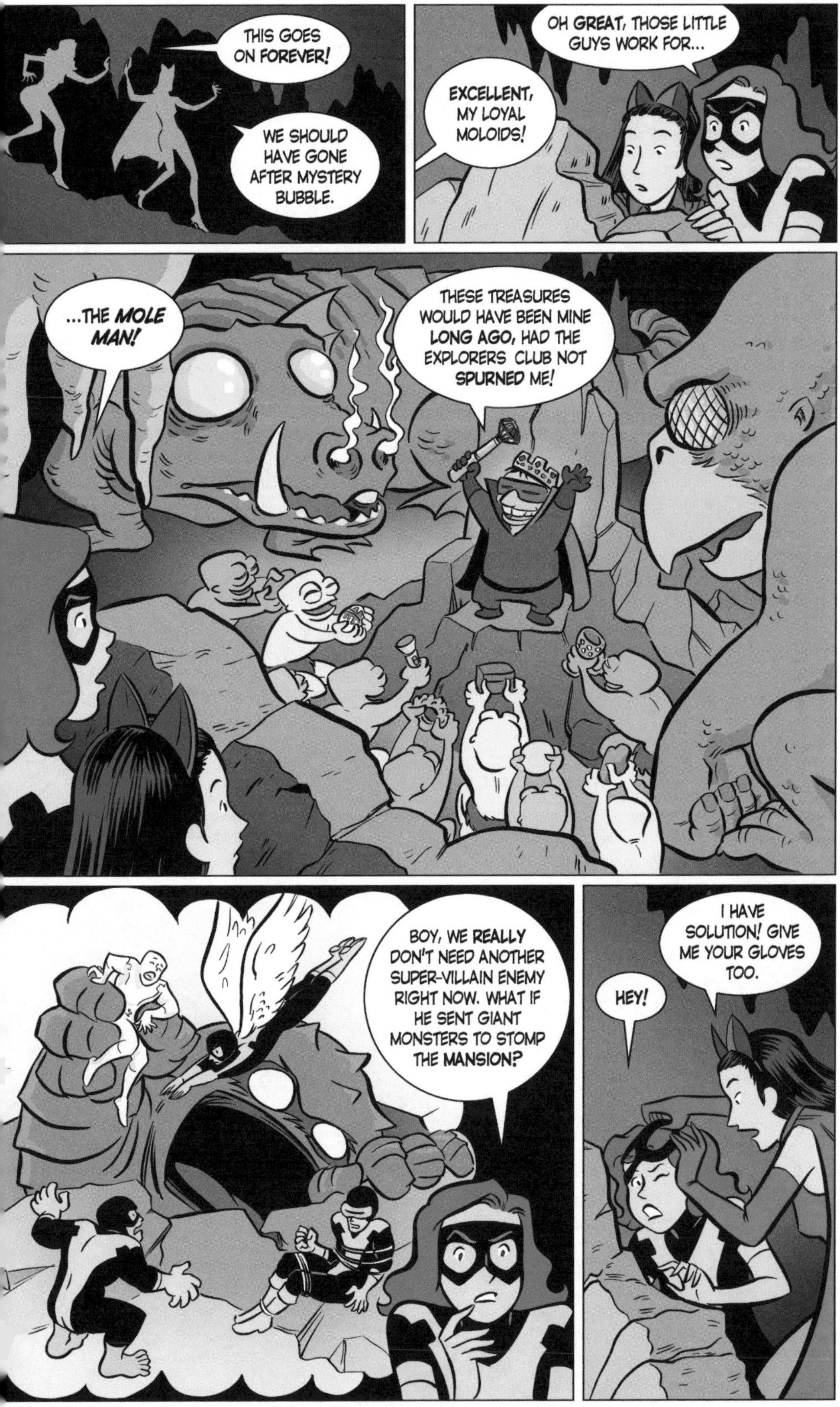
THIS GOES ON FOREVER!
WE SHOULD HAVE GONE AFTER MYSTERY BUBBLE.
OH GREAT, THOSE LITTLE GUYS WORK FOR...
EXCELLENT, MY LOYAL MOLOIDS!
...THE MOLE MAN!
THESE TREASURES WOULD HAVE BEEN MINE LONG AGO, HAD THE EXPLORERS CLUB NOT SPURNED ME!
BOY, WE REALLY DON'T NEED ANOTHER SUPER-VILLAIN ENEMY RIGHT NOW. WHAT IF HE SENT GIANT MONSTERS TO STOMP THE MANSION?
I HAVE SOLUTION! GIVE ME YOUR GLOVES TOO.
HEY!

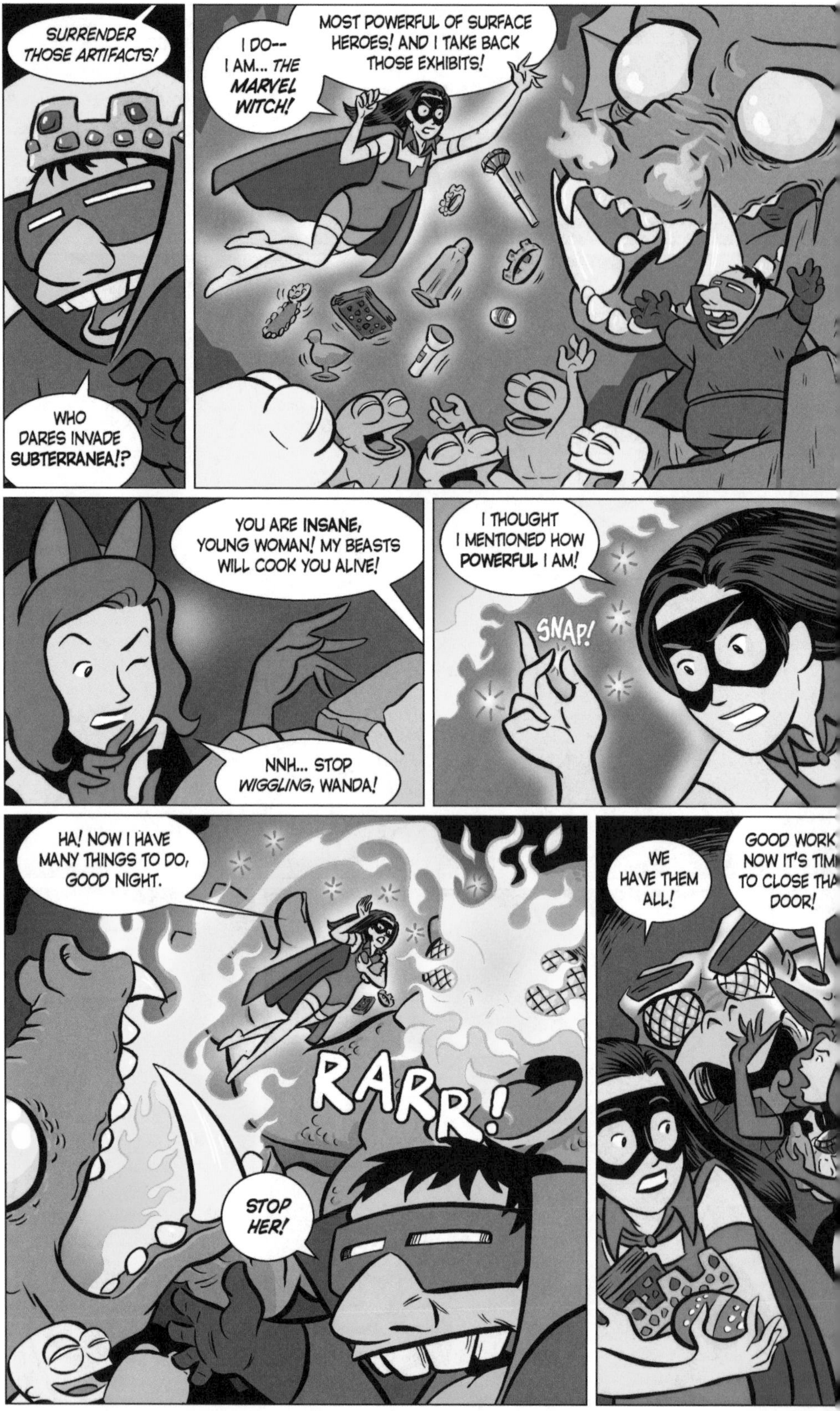

SURRENDER THOSE ARTIFACTS!
WHO DARES INVADE SUBTERRANEA!?
I DO-- I AM... THE MARVEL WITCH!
MOST POWERFUL OF SURFACE HEROES! AND I TAKE BACK THOSE EXHIBITS!
YOU ARE INSANE, YOUNG WOMAN! MY BEASTS WILL COOK YOU ALIVE!
NNH... STOP WIGGLING, WANDA!
I THOUGHT I MENTIONED HOW POWERFUL I AM!
SNAP!
HA! NOW I HAVE MANY THINGS TO DO, GOOD NIGHT.
RARR!
STOP HER!
WE HAVE THEM ALL!

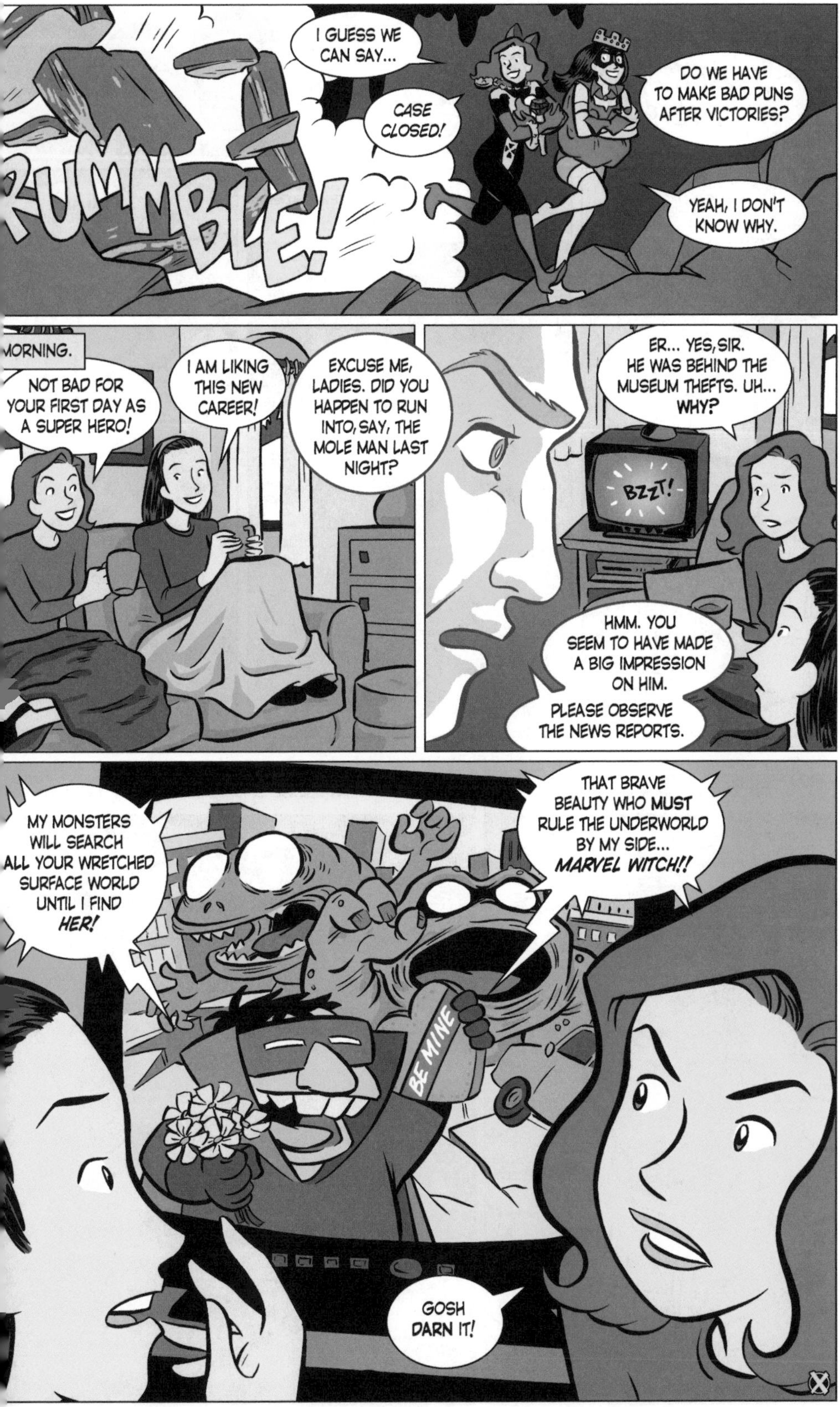

I GUESS WE CAN SAY...
CASE CLOSED!
DO WE HAVE TO MAKE BAD PUNS AFTER VICTORIES?
YEAH, I DON'T KNOW WHY.
RUMMBLE!
MORNING.
NOT BAD FOR YOUR FIRST DAY AS A SUPER HERO!
I AM LIKING THIS NEW CAREER!
EXCUSE ME, LADIES. DID YOU HAPPEN TO RUN INTO, SAY, THE MOLE MAN LAST NIGHT?
ER... YES, SIR. HE WAS BEHIND THE MUSEUM THEFTS. UH... WHY?
BZZT!
HMM. YOU SEEM TO HAVE MADE A BIG IMPRESSION ON HIM.
PLEASE OBSERVE THE NEWS REPORTS.
MY MONSTERS WILL SEARCH ALL YOUR WRETCHED SURFACE WORLD UNTIL I FIND HER!
THAT BRAVE BEAUTY WHO MUST RULE THE UNDERWORLD BY MY SIDE... MARVEL WITCH!!
BE MINE
GOSH DARN IT!

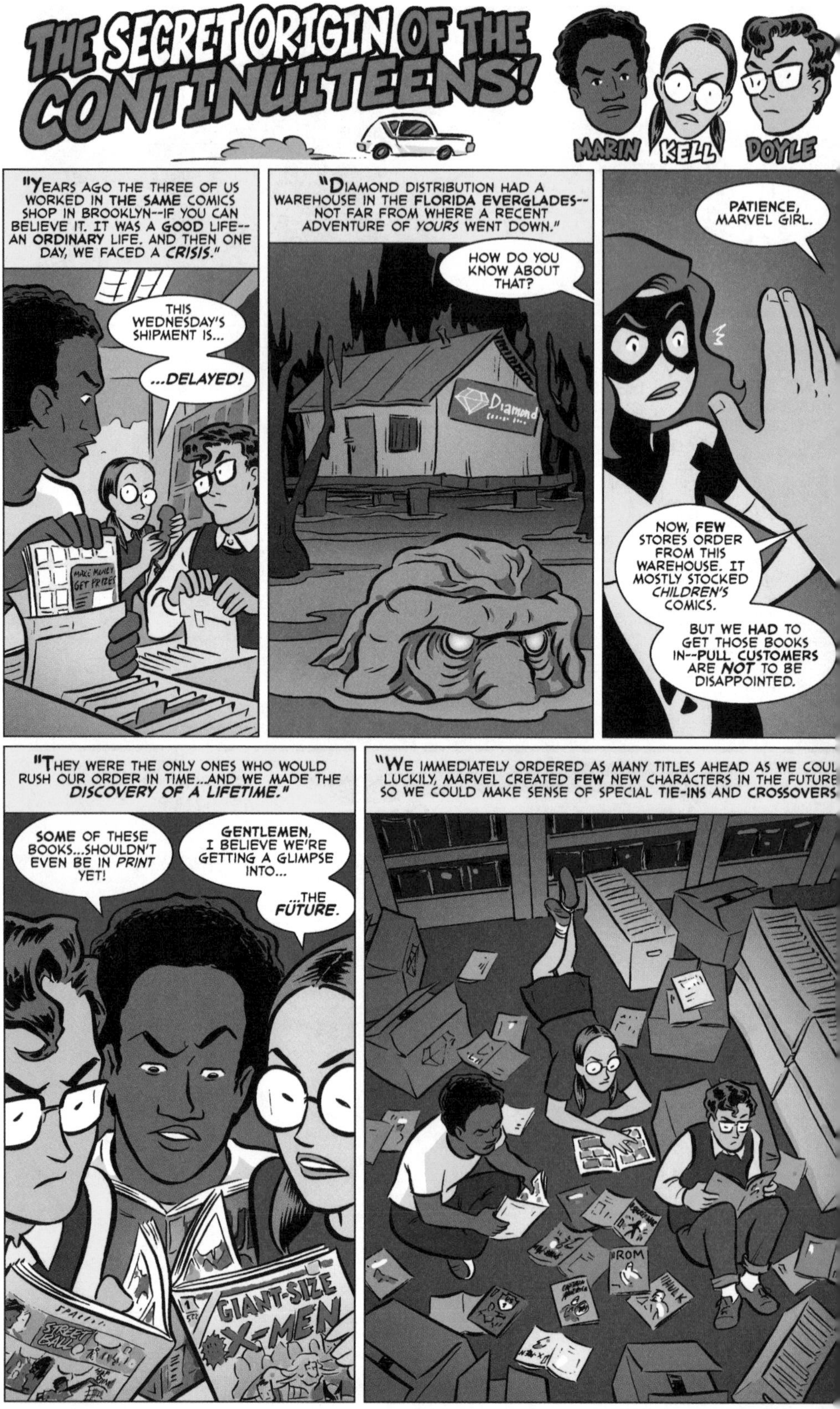
THE SECRET ORIGIN OF THE CONTINUITEENS!
MARIN
KELL
DOYLE
"YEARS AGO THE THREE OF US WORKED IN THE SAME COMICS SHOP IN BROOKLYN--IF YOU CAN BELIEVE IT. IT WAS A GOOD LIFE--AN ORDINARY LIFE. AND THEN ONE DAY, WE FACED A CRISIS."
THIS WEDNESDAY'S SHIPMENT IS...
...DELAYED!
MAKE MONEY GET PRIZES
"DIAMOND DISTRIBUTION HAD A WAREHOUSE IN THE FLORIDA EVERGLADES--NOT FAR FROM WHERE A RECENT ADVENTURE OF YOURS WENT DOWN."
HOW DO YOU KNOW ABOUT THAT?
Diamond
PATIENCE, MARVEL GIRL.
NOW, FEW STORES ORDER FROM THIS WAREHOUSE. IT MOSTLY STOCKED CHILDREN'S COMICS.
BUT WE HAD TO GET THOSE BOOKS IN--PULL CUSTOMERS ARE NOT TO BE DISAPPOINTED.
"THEY WERE THE ONLY ONES WHO WOULD RUSH OUR ORDER IN TIME...AND WE MADE THE DISCOVERY OF A LIFETIME."
SOME OF THESE BOOKS...SHOULDN'T EVEN BE IN PRINT YET!
GENTLEMEN, I BELIEVE WE'RE GETTING A GLIMPSE INTO...
...THE FUTURE.
STREET BALL
GIANT-SIZE X-MEN
"WE IMMEDIATELY ORDERED AS MANY TITLES AHEAD AS WE COUL
LUCKILY, MARVEL CREATED FEW NEW CHARACTERS IN THE FUTURE
SO WE COULD MAKE SENSE OF SPECIAL TIE-INS AND CROSSOVERS
ROM
HULK

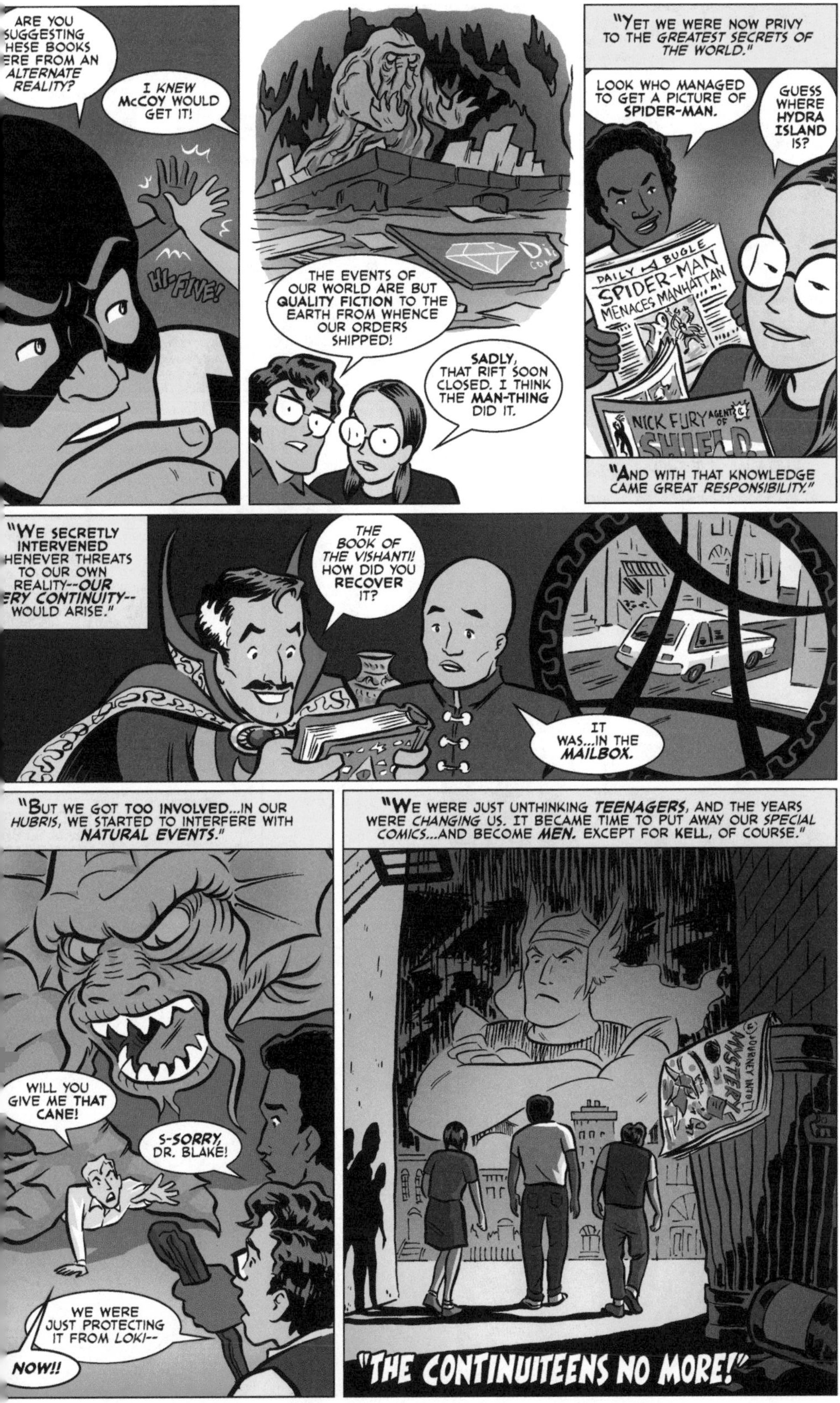

ARE YOU SUGGESTING HESE BOOKS ERE FROM AN ALTERNATE REALITY?
I KNEW McCOY WOULD GET IT!
HI-FIVE!
THE EVENTS OF OUR WORLD ARE BUT QUALITY FICTION TO THE EARTH FROM WHENCE OUR ORDERS SHIPPED!
SADLY, THAT RIFT SOON CLOSED. I THINK THE MAN-THING DID IT.
"YET WE WERE NOW PRIVY TO THE GREATEST SECRETS OF THE WORLD."
LOOK WHO MANAGED TO GET A PICTURE OF SPIDER-MAN.
GUESS WHERE HYDRA ISLAND IS?
DAILY BUGLE
SPIDER-MAN MENACES MANHATTAN
NICK FURY AGENT OF SHIELD
"AND WITH THAT KNOWLEDGE CAME GREAT RESPONSIBILITY."
"WE SECRETLY INTERVENED HENEVER THREATS TO OUR OWN REALITY--OUR ERY CONTINUITY--WOULD ARISE."
THE BOOK OF THE VISHANTI! HOW DID YOU RECOVER IT?
IT WAS...IN THE MAILBOX.
"BUT WE GOT TOO INVOLVED...IN OUR HUBRIS, WE STARTED TO INTERFERE WITH NATURAL EVENTS."
WILL YOU GIVE ME THAT CANE!
S-SORRY, DR. BLAKE!
WE WERE JUST PROTECTING IT FROM LOKI--
NOW!!
"WE WERE JUST UNTHINKING TEENAGERS, AND THE YEARS WERE CHANGING US. IT BECAME TIME TO PUT AWAY OUR SPECIAL COMICS...AND BECOME MEN. EXCEPT FOR KELL, OF COURSE."
JOURNEY INTO MYSTERY
"THE CONTINUITEENS NO MORE!"

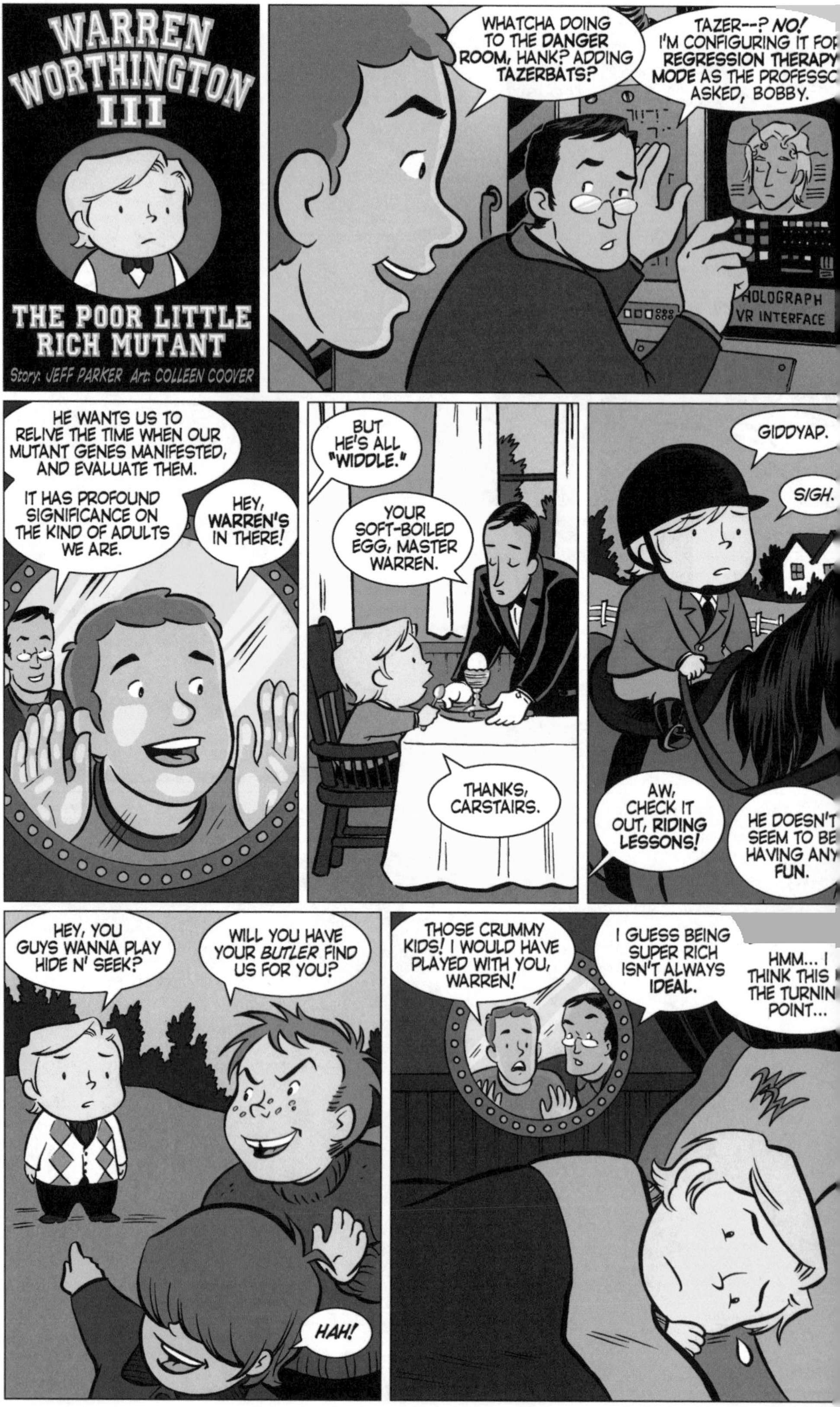

WARREN WORTHINGTON III
THE POOR LITTLE RICH MUTANT
Story: JEFF PARKER Art: COLLEEN COOVER
WHATCHA DOING TO THE DANGER ROOM, HANK? ADDING TAZERBATS?
TAZER--? NO! I'M CONFIGURING IT FOR REGRESSION THERAPY MODE AS THE PROFESSOR ASKED, BOBBY.
HOLOGRAPH VR INTERFACE
HE WANTS US TO RELIVE THE TIME WHEN OUR MUTANT GENES MANIFESTED, AND EVALUATE THEM.
IT HAS PROFOUND SIGNIFICANCE ON THE KIND OF ADULTS WE ARE.
HEY, WARREN'S IN THERE!
BUT HE'S ALL "WIDDLE."
YOUR SOFT-BOILED EGG, MASTER WARREN.
THANKS, CARSTAIRS.
GIDDYAP.
SIGH.
AW, CHECK IT OUT, RIDING LESSONS!
HE DOESN'T SEEM TO BE HAVING ANY FUN.
HEY, YOU GUYS WANNA PLAY HIDE N' SEEK?
WILL YOU HAVE YOUR BUTLER FIND US FOR YOU?
HAH!
THOSE CRUMMY KIDS! I WOULD HAVE PLAYED WITH YOU, WARREN!
I GUESS BEING SUPER RICH ISN'T ALWAYS IDEAL.
HMM... I THINK THIS THE TURNIN POINT...

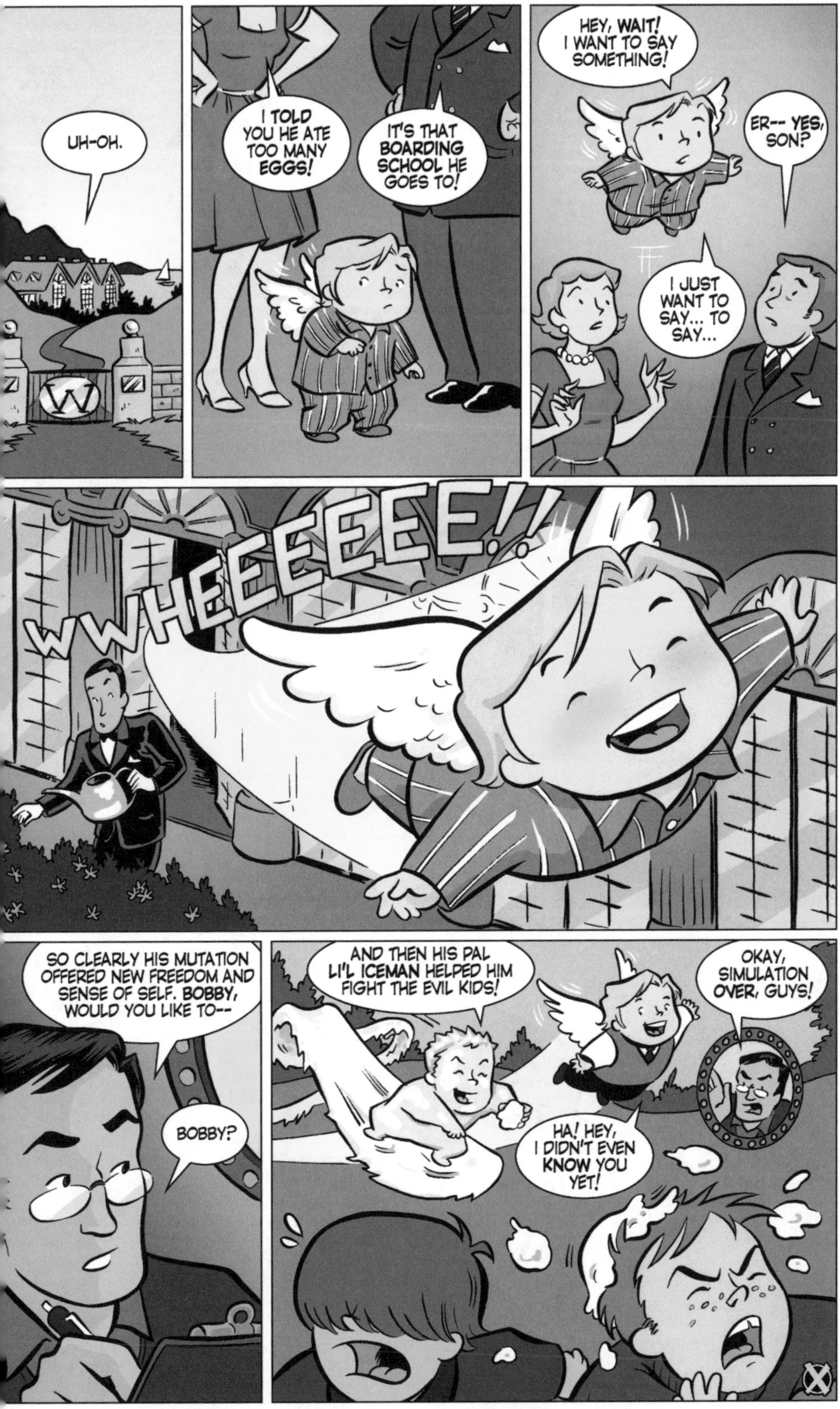
UH-OH.
I TOLD YOU HE ATE TOO MANY EGGS!
IT'S THAT BOARDING SCHOOL HE GOES TO!
HEY, WAIT! I WANT TO SAY SOMETHING!
ER-- YES, SON?
I JUST WANT TO SAY... TO SAY...
WWHEEEEEE!!
SO CLEARLY HIS MUTATION OFFERED NEW FREEDOM AND SENSE OF SELF. BOBBY, WOULD YOU LIKE TO--
BOBBY?
AND THEN HIS PAL LI'L ICEMAN HELPED HIM FIGHT THE EVIL KIDS!
OKAY, SIMULATION OVER, GUYS!
HA! HEY, I DIDN'T EVEN KNOW YOU YET!

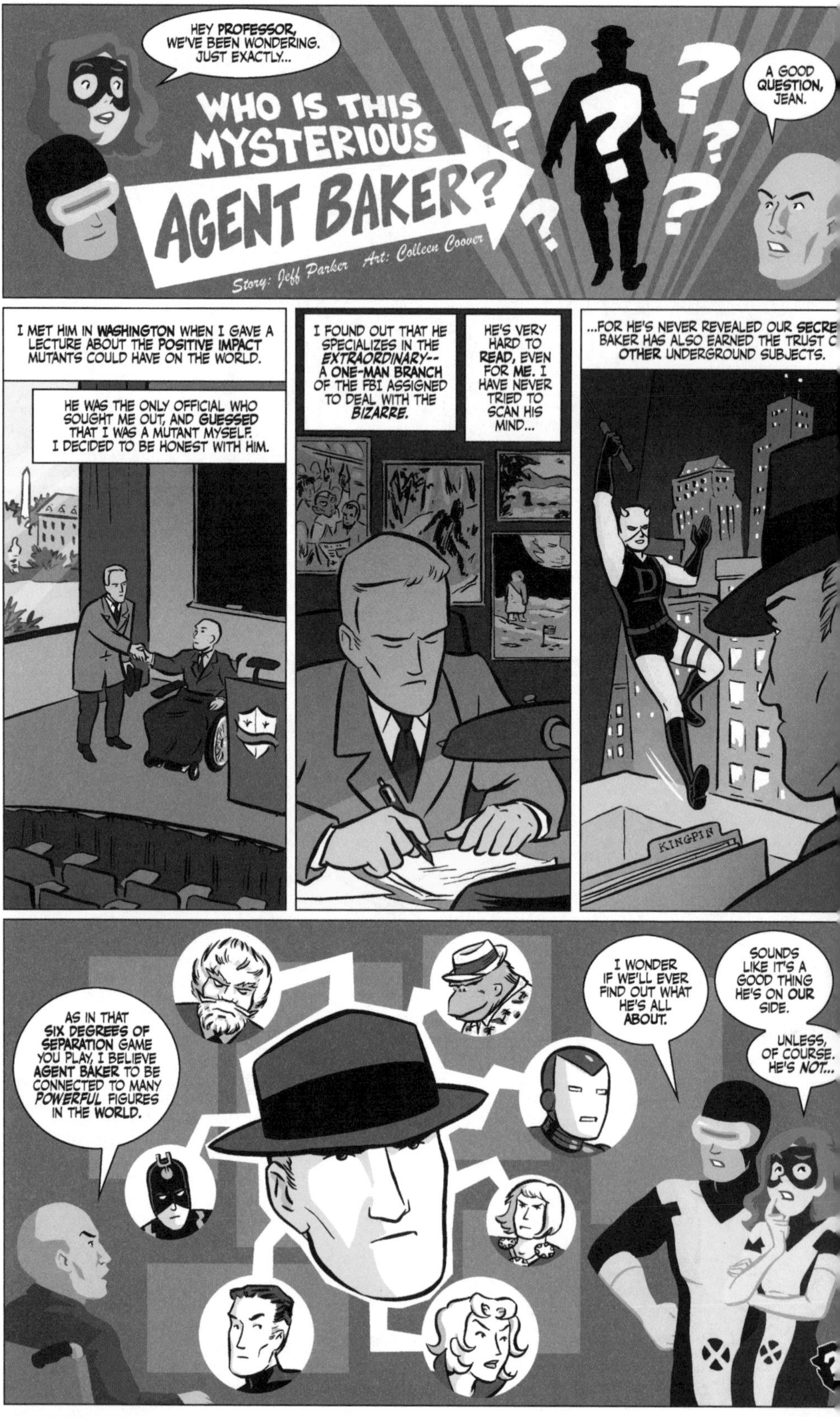

HEY PROFESSOR, WE'VE BEEN WONDERING. JUST EXACTLY...
WHO IS THIS MYSTERIOUS AGENT BAKER?
A GOOD QUESTION, JEAN.
Story: Jeff Parker Art: Colleen Coover
I MET HIM IN WASHINGTON WHEN I GAVE A LECTURE ABOUT THE POSITIVE IMPACT MUTANTS COULD HAVE ON THE WORLD.
HE WAS THE ONLY OFFICIAL WHO SOUGHT ME OUT, AND GUESSED THAT I WAS A MUTANT MYSELF. I DECIDED TO BE HONEST WITH HIM.
I FOUND OUT THAT HE SPECIALIZES IN THE EXTRAORDINARY-- A ONE-MAN BRANCH OF THE FBI ASSIGNED TO DEAL WITH THE BIZARRE.
HE'S VERY HARD TO READ, EVEN FOR ME. I HAVE NEVER TRIED TO SCAN HIS MIND...
...FOR HE'S NEVER REVEALED OUR SECRE BAKER HAS ALSO EARNED THE TRUST O OTHER UNDERGROUND SUBJECTS.
KINGPIN
AS IN THAT SIX DEGREES OF SEPARATION GAME YOU PLAY, I BELIEVE AGENT BAKER TO BE CONNECTED TO MANY POWERFUL FIGURES IN THE WORLD.
I WONDER IF WE'LL EVER FIND OUT WHAT HE'S ALL ABOUT.
SOUNDS LIKE IT'S A GOOD THING HE'S ON OUR SIDE.
UNLESS, OF COURSE. HE'S NOT...

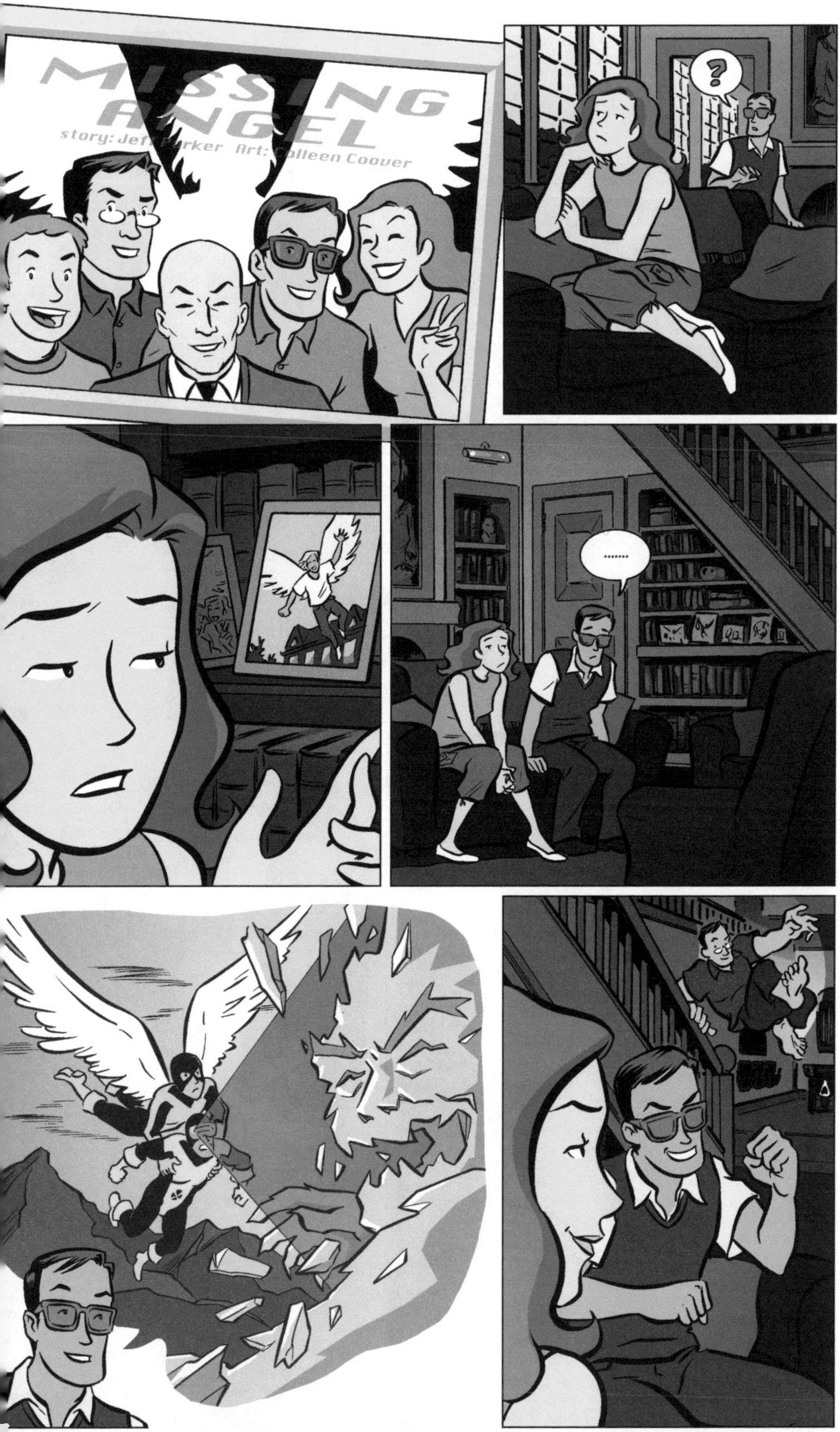
MISSING ANGEL
story: Jef rker Art: olleen Coover
?
.......

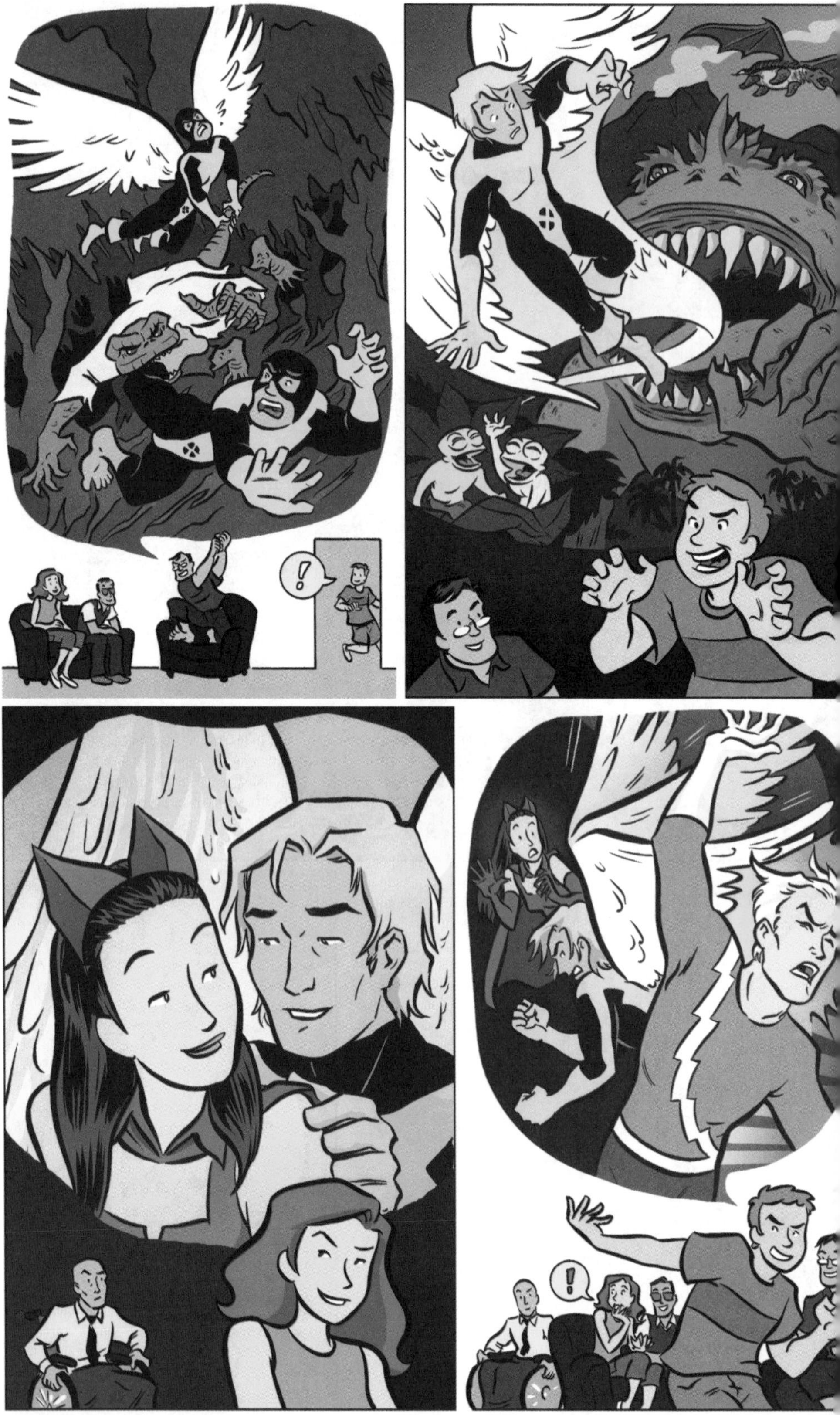

!
!

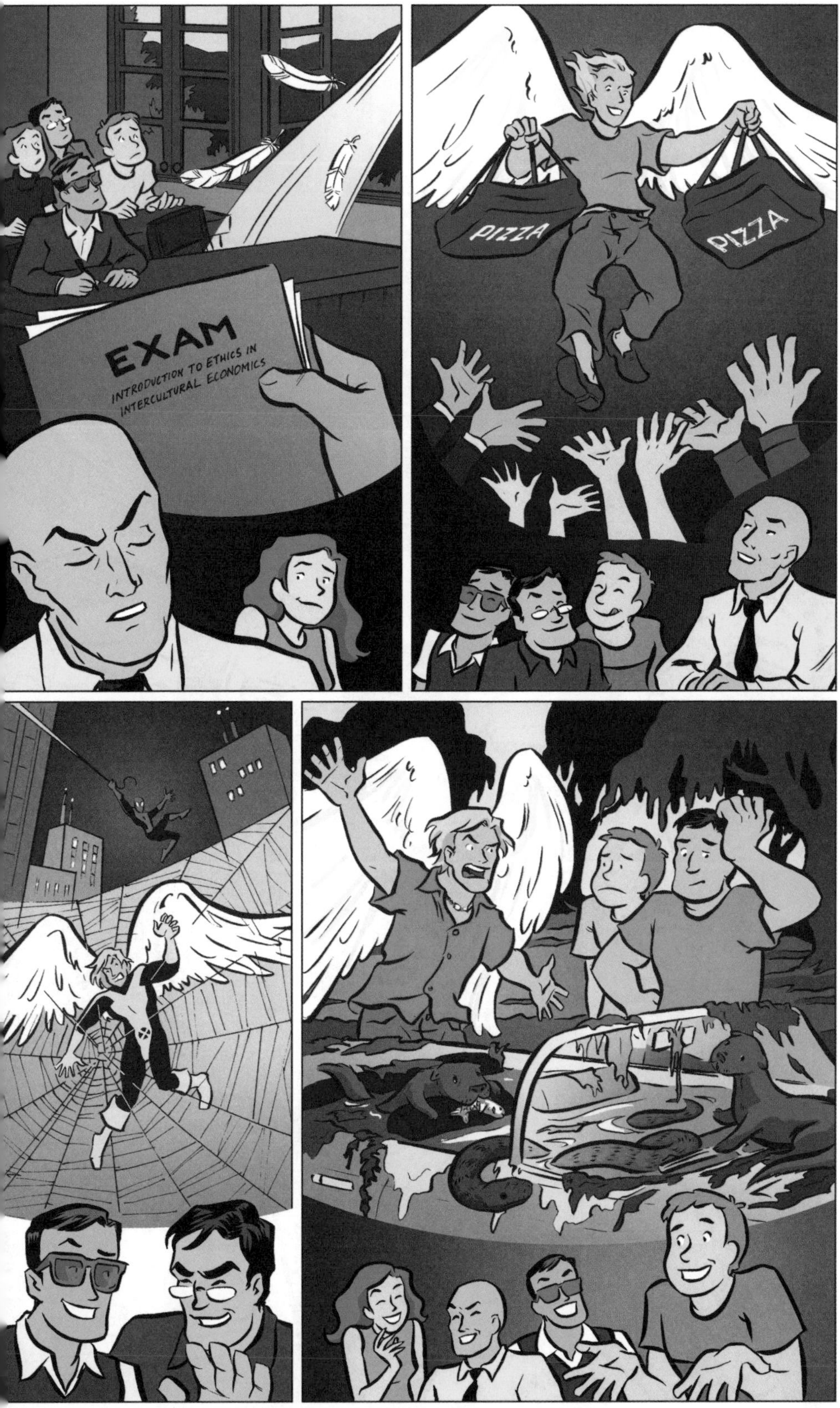
EXAM
INTRODUCTION TO ETHICS IN INTERCULTURAL ECONOMICS
PIZZA
PIZZA

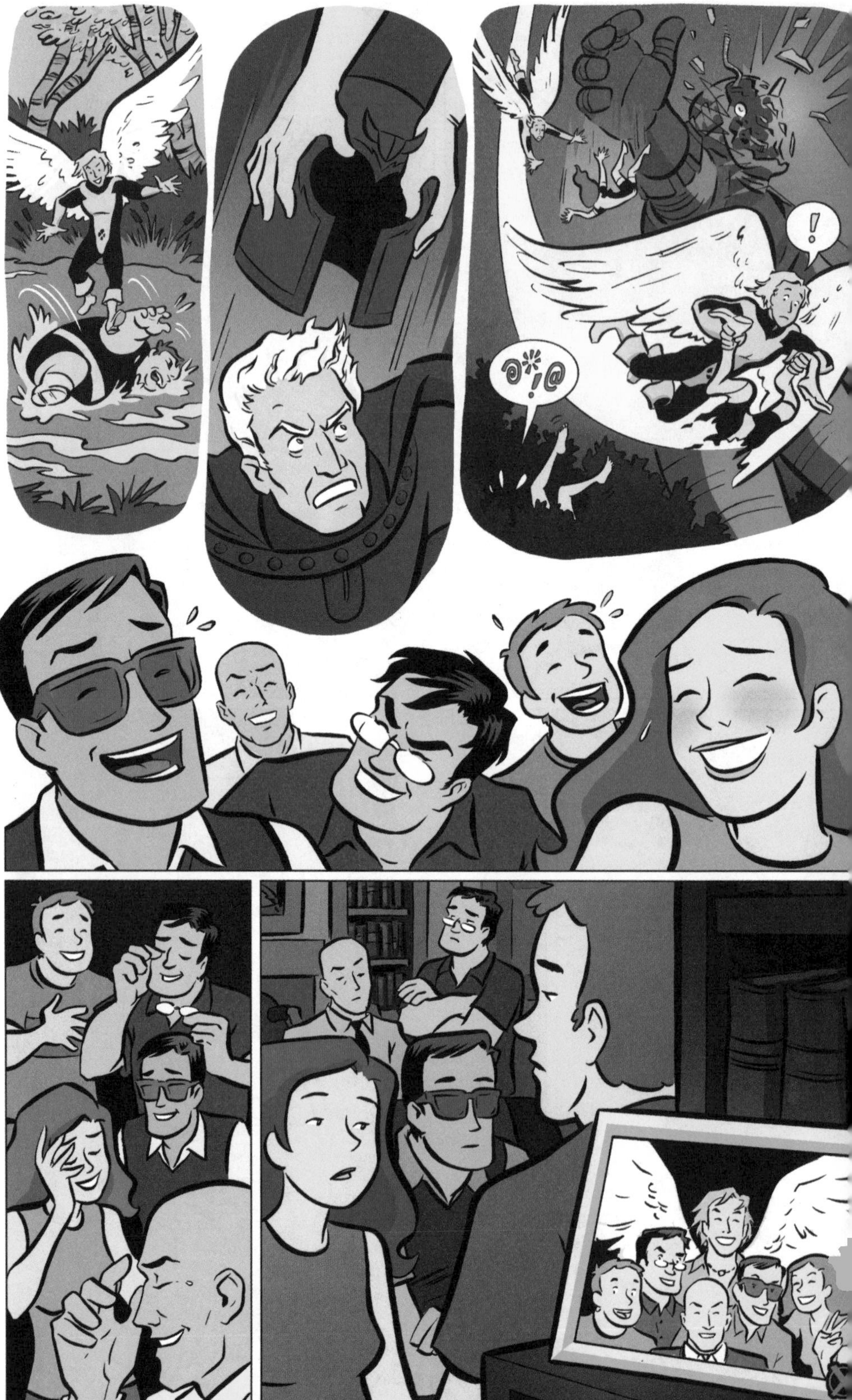
!

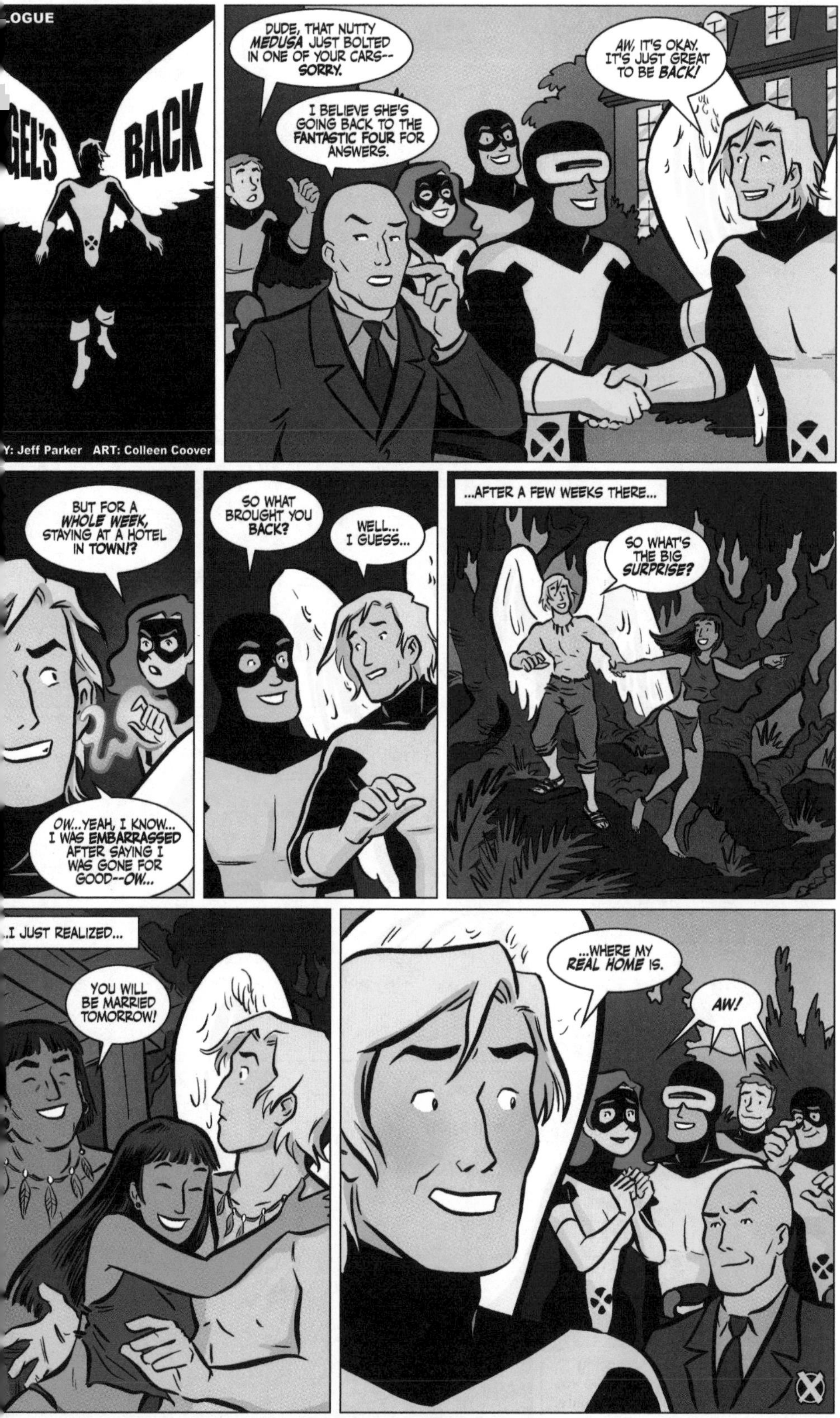

.OGUE
GEL'S BACK
Y: Jeff Parker ART: Colleen Coover
DUDE, THAT NUTTY MEDUSA JUST BOLTED IN ONE OF YOUR CARS-- SORRY.
I BELIEVE SHE'S GOING BACK TO THE FANTASTIC FOUR FOR ANSWERS.
AW, IT'S OKAY. IT'S JUST GREAT TO BE BACK!
BUT FOR A WHOLE WEEK, STAYING AT A HOTEL IN TOWN!?
OW...YEAH, I KNOW... I WAS EMBARRASSED AFTER SAYING I WAS GONE FOR GOOD--OW...
SO WHAT BROUGHT YOU BACK?
WELL... I GUESS...
...AFTER A FEW WEEKS THERE...
SO WHAT'S THE BIG SURPRISE?
..I JUST REALIZED...
YOU WILL BE MARRIED TOMORROW!
...WHERE MY REAL HOME IS.
AW!

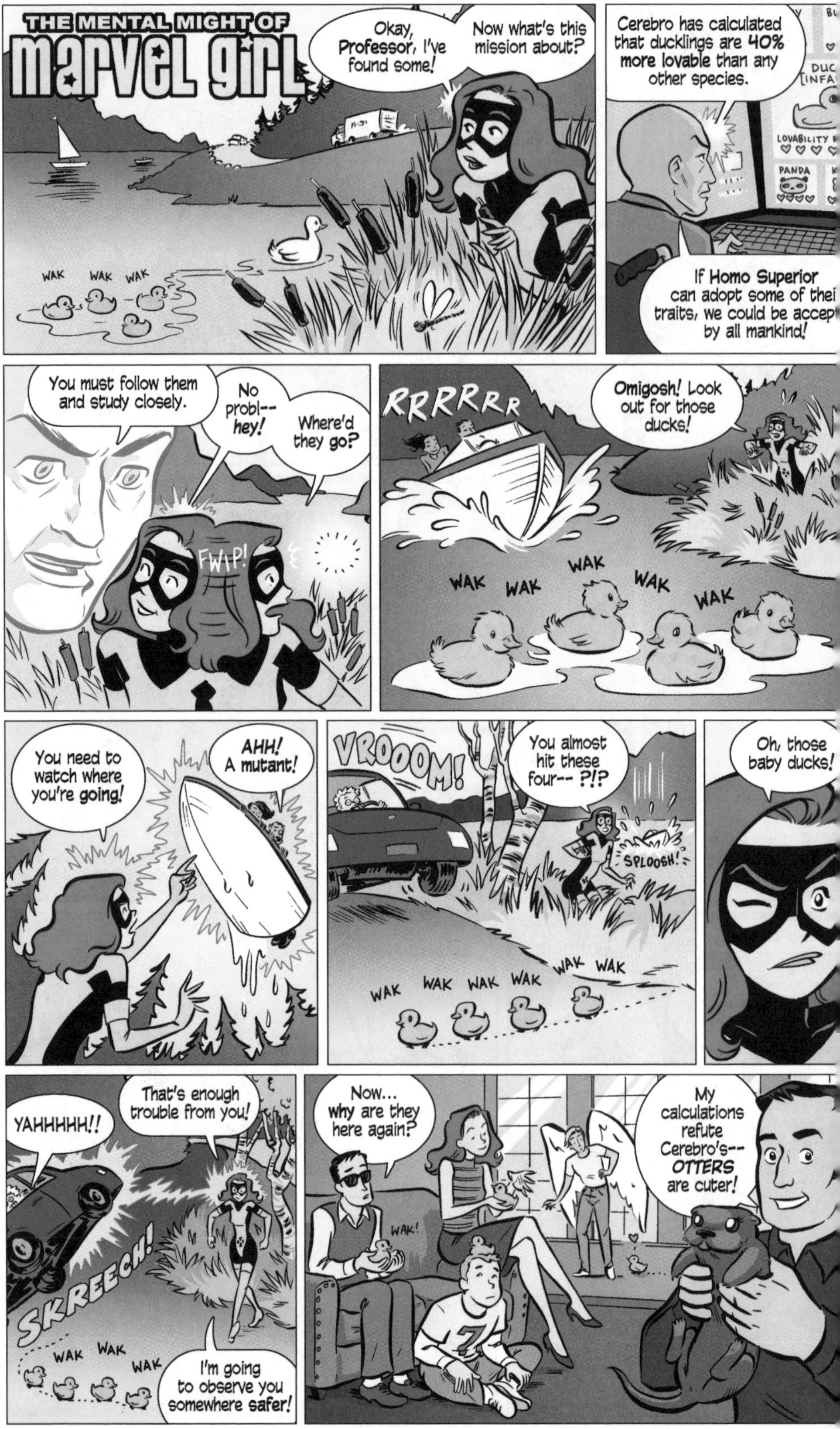
THE MENTAL MIGHT OF
marvel girl
Okay, Professor, I've found some!
Now what's this mission about?
WAK WAK WAK
Cerebro has calculated that ducklings are 40% more lovable than any other species.
LOVABILITY
PANDA
If Homo Superior can adopt some of thei traits, we could be accep by all mankind!
You must follow them and study closely.
No probl-- hey!
Where'd they go?
FWIP!
RRRRRR
Omigosh! Look out for those ducks!
WAK WAK WAK WAK WAK
You need to watch where you're going!
AHH! A mutant!
VROOOM!
You almost hit these four-- ?!?
SPLOOSH!
WAK WAK WAK WAK WAK WAK
Oh, those baby ducks!
YAHHHHH!!
That's enough trouble from you!
SKREECH!
WAK WAK WAK
I'm going to observe you somewhere safer!
Now... why are they here again?
WAK!
My calculations refute Cerebro's-- OTTERS are cuter!

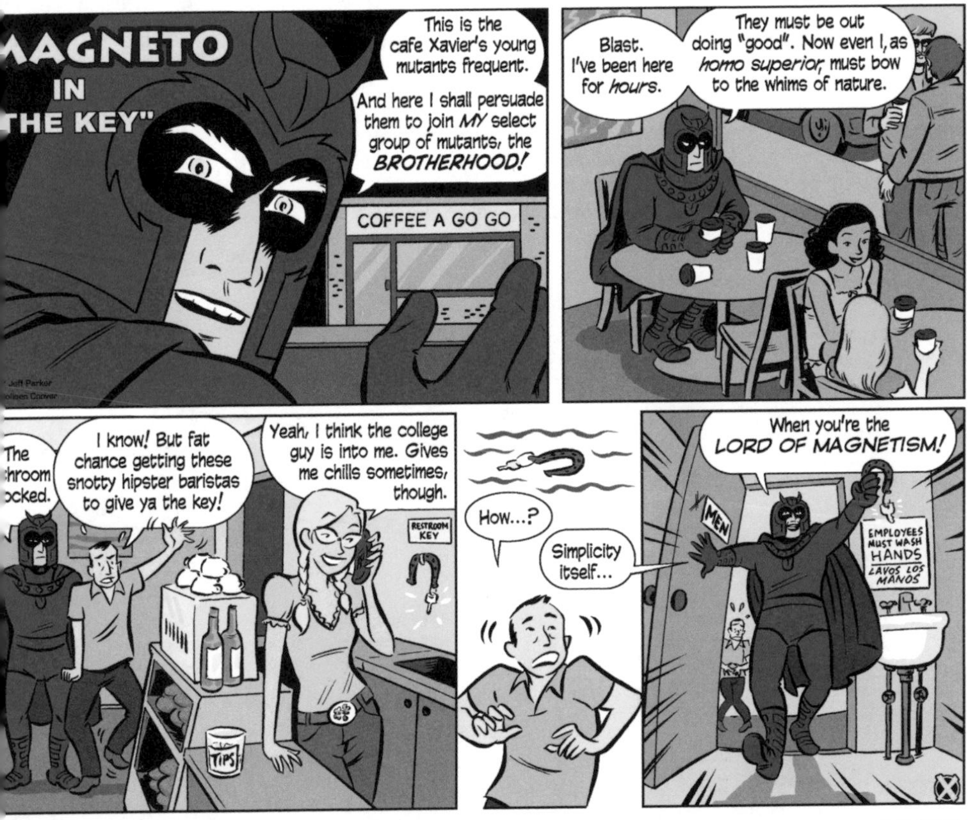
AGNETO
IN
THE KEY"
This is the cafe Xavier's young mutants frequent.
And here I shall persuade them to join MY select group of mutants, the BROTHERHOOD!
COFFEE A GO GO
Jeff Parker
olleen Coover
Blast. I've been here for hours.
They must be out doing "good". Now even I, as homo superior, must bow to the whims of nature.
The hroom ocked.
I know! But fat chance getting these snotty hipster baristas to give ya the key!
Yeah, I think the college guy is into me. Gives me chills sometimes, though.
RESTROOM KEY
TIPS
How...?
Simplicity itself...
When you're the LORD OF MAGNETISM!
MEN
EMPLOYEES MUST WASH HANDS
LAVOS LOS MANOS

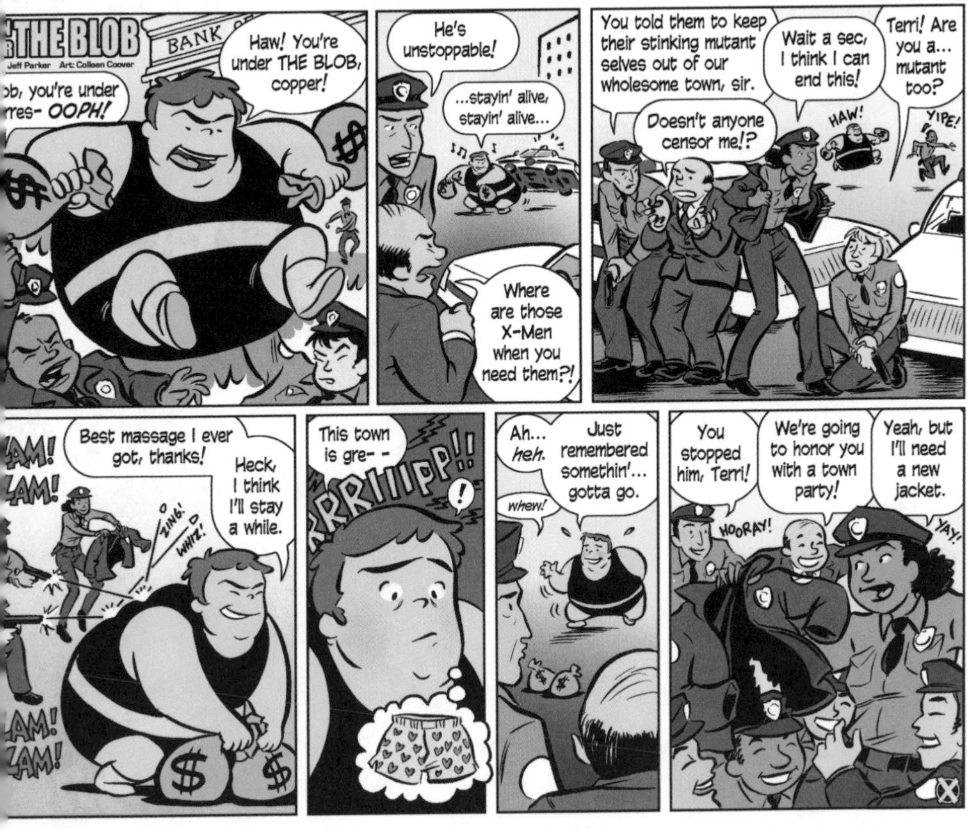
THE BLOB
Jeff Parker Art: Colleen Coover
BANK
ob, you're under rres- OOPH!
Haw! You're under THE BLOB, copper!
He's unstoppable!
...stayin' alive, stayin' alive...
Where are those X-Men when you need them?!
You told them to keep their stinking mutant selves out of our wholesome town, sir.
Doesn't anyone censor me!?
Wait a sec, I think I can end this!
Terri! Are you a... mutant too?
HAW!
YIPE!
AM!
AM!
Best massage I ever got, thanks!
ZING!
WHIZ!
Heck, I think I'll stay a while.
AM!
AM!
This town is gre- -
RRIIIPP!!
!
Ah... heh.
Just remembered somethin'... gotta go.
whew!
You stopped him, Terri!
We're going to honor you with a town party!
Yeah, but I'll need a new jacket.
HOORAY!
YAY!

# CELEBRATING THE WOMEN of MARVEL®

***Marvel is proud to shine the spotlight on our rich cast of female super heroes as well as the women working in comics today. Look to this page in our books for a new interview with one of the top women in comics today.***

**MARVEL:** *First of all, who is your favorite Woman of Marvel?*

**COLLEEN COOVER:** I have a special fondness for Millicent Collins, Millie the Model. She was a pivotal character in one of the first things I did for Marvel with my husband Paul Tobin, but aside from that, I just like the idea of this smart, sassy, non-powered career girl running around having adventures.

**MARVEL:** *Over the years, the women of Marvel have changed and grown, becoming some of the strongest characters in the world of super heroes. Is there a defining moment for you regarding any of our super heroines?*

**CC:** Like a lot of other people who were teenagers in the '80s, Kitty Pryde was my personal hero. My first X-Men comic was Uncanny X-Men #141, the first issue of Days Of Future Past. Kitty's story just resonated with me. She was my age, she was awkward, she had a big crush on this dude-- I immediately got a subscription and followed the X-Men faithfully for several years.

**MARVEL:** *Girl Comics debuted as part of the part of the Women of Marvel celebration. What can you tell us about your contribution?*

**CC:** I'm writing and drawing a two-page introduction for each issue, which provides a mission statement for the anthology from the mouths of dozens of Marvel heroines. For the second issue I'm drawing a story written by Kathryn Immonen that stars Shamrock!

**MARVEL:** *This is a huge anthology involving some incredibly talented women. What's your experience been like working with them? Which story from another creator are you looking forward to most?*

**CC:** One of the real treats I've had with the Shamrock story is getting to work with Kathryn for the first time. And that story is being colored by Elizabeth Breitweiser, which is exciting because I love her work on Agents Of Atlas, and because I'll get to see my art colored by someone else for the first time! I'm really looking forward to Lucy Knisley's Doc Ock story; the preview looks so funny and sweet.

**MARVEL:** *You're known for being an "indie" creator, often writing and drawing your own work. Do you find your approach to working on Marvel characters a different one than when working with your own creations?*

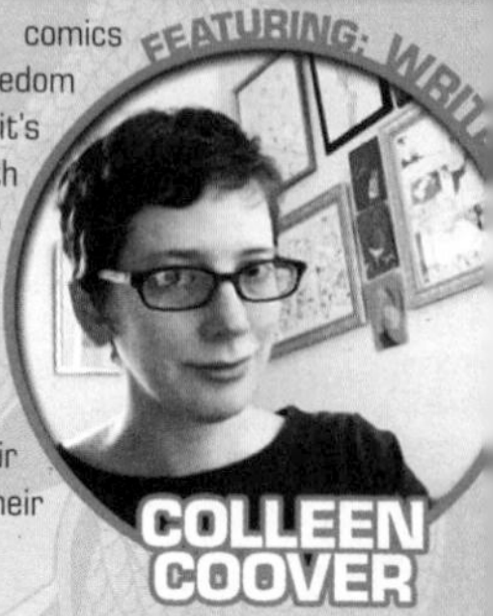

FEATURING: WRIT
COLLEEN COOVER


**CC:** While working on comics I own offers complete freedom to do whatever I want, it's always fun to play with the characters I grew up reading. And even when I work with newer Marvel characters, once I get to know them it's just as satisfying to explore their motivations and tell their stories.

**MARVEL:** *Finally, what would you say to those female fans creators who still think there is a "glass ceiling" or that comi is strictly a boy's club? Any advice for breaking in?*

**CC:** Well, I know too many women making comics to think th ceiling hasn't been pretty well shattered. The best way to bre into super hero comics, and in my opinion the ONLY way that h any real chance of success, is to make comics of your own. Y have to show that you are compelled to make comics—that i in your blood—and you have to show that you have the discipli to do it well and on time. No one is going to hand anyone any gender a job in comics based on nothing more than th enthusiasm.

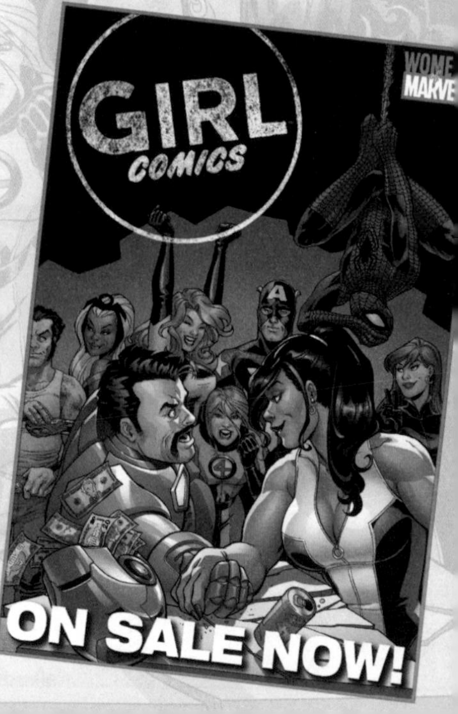

WOME
MARVE
GIRL COMICS
ON SALE NOW!